WRITING IN THE FATHER'S HOUSE
The Emergence of the Feminine in the Quebec Literary Tradition

Those who follow current trends in Canadian literature are aware that many of its most exciting and challenging new forms are coming from women writers of Quebec. Patricia Smart studies the historical roots of this development in her study of gender differences in Quebec literature. She offers a feminist perspective on 100 years of Quebec writing by both women and men, and argues that it is the women who historically have modified or subverted the traditions. This new work is her own translation of her study that won the 1988 Governor General's Award for Non-Fiction, *Ecrire dans la maison du père: l'émergence du féminin dans la tradition littéraire du Québec.*

Smart begins with a feminist reading of Laure Conan's *Angéline de Montbrun*, the only major novel written by a women in nineteenth-century Quebec, and moves on to close readings of other classic works, from the novel of the land to post-modern and feminist works of the present era.

The Quebec literary tradition is not only 'his story' of the national dilemma. There is another telling, Smart concludes, in a different voice, from a different perspective, by women writers and by female characters in works by men. Smart proposes a radically new interpretation of Quebec literature, one that includes that voice, that other perspective. For when they are listened to on their own terms, and not according to criteria based on men's writing practices, the voices of women writers and characters point to a way out of the female tradition of alienation and violence and to the possibility of a habitable future.

PATRICIA SMART is Professor of French and Canadian Studies at Carleton University. She is the author of *Hubert Aquin, agent double: la dialectique de l'art et du pays dans 'Prochain Episode' et 'Trou de mémoire.'*

Patricia Smart

WRITING IN THE FATHER'S HOUSE

The Emergence of
the Feminine in the Quebec
Literary Tradition

UNIVERSITY OF TORONTO PRESS

Toronto Buffalo London

ISBN 0-8020-2732-6 (cloth)
ISBN 0-8020-6771-9 (paper)

Printed on acid-free paper

Canadian Cataloguing in Publication Data

Smart, Patricia, 1940–
Writing in the father's house :
the emergence of the feminine in the Quebec literary tradition

Translation of: Ecrire dans la maison du père : l'émergence du féminin dans la
tradition littéraire du Québec. Includes bibliographical references and index.
ISBN 0-8020-2732-6 (bound)
ISBN 0-8020-6771-9 (pbk.)

1. Canadian literature (French) – Quebec (Province) – History and criticism.*
2. Canadian literature (French) – 20th century – History and criticism.*
3. Women authors, Canadian – Quebec (Province).   4. Sex differences
(Psychology) in literature.   I. Title.

PS8073.4.S513 1991   C840'.9'0054   C90-095789-1   PQ3917.Q4S513 1991

This translation of Patricia Smart's
Ecrire dans la maison du père:
l'émergence du féminin dans la
tradition littéraire du Québec
(Montreal: Editions Québec/Amérique 1988)
was made possible by a grant from the Canada Council.
It has been published with the help of a grant
from the Canadian Federation for the Humanities,
using funds provided by the Social Sciences and
Humanities Research Council of Canada.

FOR JOHN

Contents

Preface

Do women write differently than men? If so, is it possible to characterize that difference without falling into the old dualisms by which literary criticism has relegated what used to be called 'the feminine sensibility' in writing to the private realm, denying its links with – and its possible oppositions to – the ideologies and practices of the dominant culture? In the area of Quebec literature, even a superficial glance at the major works of the canon suggests that when women write the tradition shifts considerably, that change is introduced into the solid 'edifice' made up of cultural representations. Although these changes have not gone unnoticed by literary critics, they have never been seen as more than individual anomalies: that is, no one has ever suggested that it might be possible to generalize about them on the basis of gender. For example, it is a cliché of nineteenth-century literary history to acknowledge that Laure Conan's *Angéline de Montbrun* is the first 'psychological novel' in Quebec literature, as well as the first to break with the convention of third-person narration. And no critic would seriously challenge the accepted notion that Germaine Guèvremont's novels mark the end of the 'classic' period of the novel of the land, demonstrating as they do that the rural world represented for almost a hundred years in that tradition as enduring and 'unchangeable' has reached the final stages of its dissolution. Published in the same year (1945) as Guèvremont's *The Outlander*, Gabrielle Roy's *The Tin Flute* was rightly hailed by critics as the first literary work to acknowledge that Quebec had become an urban society. And finally, Anne Hébert's poetry has traditionally been seen as the *symbolic* break with the old order in Quebec, that long period of psychological alienation and exile mirrored in the tormented poetry of her cousin, Saint-Denys Garneau.

By neglecting to see these 'ruptures' and 'deviances' of women's writing as anything more than individual cases, literary criticism has been able to assimilate them and to ignore their *difference* within a literary tradition it has continued to define according to the criteria of men's writing. Critics since the Quiet Revolution period have automatically assumed, for example, that the tragedy, the wandering, the blackness, and the frustrated mysticism that recur in Quebec men's writing from the poetry of Emile Nelligan to the present are the reflection of a *national* search for identity, condemned to unending circularity or paralysis by the ambivalence of Quebec's situation within Canada. But what if this alienation were also a gender-based phenomenon? And what if, existing alongside 'his story,' there were an '*other*' story, offering a different perspective not only on the national dilemma, but on reality in a more general sense? Reading Quebec literary texts with a consciousness of gender difference, one becomes aware not only of new dimensions in the thematics of nation or country, but of the opening of the tradition onto the possibility of an inhabitable future.

The main link between the chapters that follow will be the question of representation, in the broad sense referred to above; that is, each chapter will examine the relationship between the literary text, its cultural context, and the gender of the writer. Together, the chapters trace the intertwined relationship of the two overarching narratives – 'his story' and 'her story' – made up of all the individual texts: narratives played out against the backdrop of a national history threatened by the possibility of extinction from its very beginnings, and influenced by a nationalist ideology all the more rigid and powerful because it was created to protect this fragile collective identity. As well, as we move from chapter to chapter, the preoccupation with the process of representation will lead to a questioning of the presuppositions inherent in 'realism,' that literary convention so central to the tradition of novel writing that the word is used almost interchangeably with the term 'the traditional novel.'

Finally, while this reading of most of the classic texts of Quebec literature insists on their relationship with the national context, it also attempts to go beyond that dimension in order to make visible and audible what I consider to be their primary 'message' when taken as a whole: that of the urgency of the coming-into-discourse (and into reality) of a true *dialogue* between women and men, those 'sisters' and 'brothers' inhabiting the same 'house' of language and culture, and made enemies by the Law of the Father, which dictates the rules of the house. As Luce Irigaray asks, 'Why does he refuse, over and over again, a contra-diction, a narrative based on the other sex?'[1] Indeed, when placed side by side and read from a point of view that emphasizes sexual difference, these Quebec literary texts appear as an aborted dialogue, stages in a history that is both Québécois and universal, and whose conclusion remains as yet in doubt. An apocalypse of the 'end of history' if one shares the perspective of a Victor-Lévy Beaulieu, a painful and precarious transition if one listens rather to Hubert Aquin or France Théoret – but in all these texts one senses the presence of a cultural crisis, one that will not be resolved without the recognition of women and their status as subjects within history.

Abbreviations

AM	*Angéline de Montbrun*
BM	*Bloody Mary*
CP	*Complete Poems of Saint-Denys Garneau*
G	*Grandfathers*
HT	*Hamlet's Twin*
JRE	*Jean Rivard économiste*
MC	*Maria Chapdelaine*
MR	*Master of the River*
Néc. put.	*Nécessairement putain*
NP	*Nous parlerons comme on écrit*
O	*The Outlander*
P	*Poems by Anne Hébert*
S	*Les Songes en équilibre*
SS	*The Swallower Swallowed*
SW	*In the Shadow of the Wind*
TA	*Thirty Acres*
TF	*The Tin Flute*
VO	*Une Voix pour Odile*
WM	*The Woman and the Miser*

Author's note on the English translation

This book is very much about families, and the work of translating it into English so soon after I had completed the French version could not have been done without the help of several members of my own family. I am grateful in particular to my sister, Judy Hamelin, for her excellent first draft of the translation of chapters 3 and 5. As well, I thank my daughter, Mary Ann Smart, for our ongoing discussions on music, literature, and feminist criticism; my niece, Christine Hamelin, for bibliographical assistance; my son, Michael Smart, and my brother-in-law, Marcel Hamelin, for computer and typing help; and my husband, John Smart, for his constant and imperturbable support. The Faculty of Graduate Studies at Carleton University provided me with two superb research assistants. Dominique Garnett corrected some of my initial attempts at translating my own prose into English and spent many hours locating the published English equivalents of passages quoted from Quebec literary works. Angela McAffer did much of the work on the index.

As many feminist writers have pointed out, our cultural and individual selves are intimately bound up with the language in which we write, and the experience of writing and translating this book has brought home to me some of the paradoxes of working in both of our two cultures. Although I had done most of my writing over the years in French, as befits a critic of Quebec literature, it was in English that the title and the original vision of this book first came to me. For reasons I didn't fully understand at the time, writing in

French seemed to have become an arid and overly theoretical exercise, cut off from the excitement I felt in reading women's writing of the past and present. In the spring of 1985 I spent a few painful weeks labouring over an article (in French) on Laure Conan's *Angéline de Montbrun*. As I worked, I became increasingly conscious that I was writing for a small number of 'specialists' – almost all of whom, I began to realize, were male, middle-aged Québécois university professors! For distraction from my growing sense of frustration, I was reading everything I could get my hands on about Laure Conan's life; and as I read I began to see that what I really wanted to do was to tell other women about this courageous and solitary nineteenth-century foremother. And English, it seemed to me, was the language that would allow me to do that in a down-to-earth way, for a non-specialized audience who, I hoped, could be made to share my enthusiasm. It was at that point that the project of the book took shape, and for several months I wrote furiously in English – until I gradually realized that the detailed textual analyses I was doing required an audience familiar with those texts. So I began again, in French, and wrote the book in that language, but always with the idea that eventually it would appear in English as well. With the publication of this translation, the project has finally come full circle.

The above explanation of the (ambivalently Canadian?) genesis of this book may help to explain a very occasional irregularity in my practice of citing translations of literary works, for which I take full responsibility. While my own analyses of the works are based on their original French versions, it was clear that my English-speaking readers might well want to refer to the works in English translation, and I have therefore provided page references to those translations. On a relatively small number of occasions, I have however found it necessary to change a word or a phrase to make the translation more faithful to the original French.

Writing in the Father's House

The denial of subjectivity to women is without a doubt the
foundation underlying every irreducible constitution of an object:
whether in representation, discourse, or desire ...
   But what if the 'object' started to speak?
   Luce Irigaray, *Speculum of the Other Woman*

To what extent is there such a thing as 'feminine' writing? To the
extent that women, for historical and biological reasons, experience
reality differently than men. Experience a different reality from men,
and express it. To the extent that women do not belong to the
dominating group but to the group that has been dominated for
centuries; to the extent that they have been objects, objects of
secondary status, often of men who are themselves objects, and so
by their social situation have always been attached to the 'second
culture'; to the extent that they no longer want to make fruitless
efforts to become part of the madness of established systems. To the
extent that, in their writing and in their lives, they aim for autonomy.
That is where they will meet men who are also aiming for autonomy.
   Christa Wolf, *Cassandra*

Introduction:
Traces of a murder

Through its direct or disguised rites of initiation, masculine culture forces
men to renounce their origin, the mother tongue in which they were
first formed, and thus it begins with a murder that it never ceases to
repeat. Feminine culture avoids this trauma: it develops and consolidates
the origins at the same time as it moves beyond them, maintaining a
constant link between maturity and childhood. Thus it begins neither
with a murder or a suicide, nor with a shameful obliteration of memory.
    Françoise Collin, 'There is no female cogito'

It may be that every book is born of an image that haunts its author,
calling him or her to unravel the hidden meanings it contains. In my
case, that original image was scandalous, even obscene: it was the
image of a corpse buried under the foundations of a building, a
corpse that – resisting the violence that had been done to it – refused
to remain silent. Appropriately enough, I first came across it in a
detective-type novel, Hubert Aquin's *Blackout*, where the narrator –
obsessed by the memory of Joan Ruskin, the woman he has murdered, not only identifies her corpse as 'the unverifiable focus of a
story whose only function is to disintegrate around her mortal
remains,' but describes his own book as 'an accumulation of vanities
that are only the multiple masks of the atrocious truth that a simple
shift in point of view allows us to see as a murder.'[1] In a novel by
a woman published only two years after Aquin's – Anne Hébert's
Kamouraska – the perspective on this same reality of a murder shifts

to that of the victim herself, a woman 'buried alive' for centuries by a society built on fear of her power. The image of the 'black woman' that appears on the final page of *Kamouraska* (significantly, at the precise moment when Elisabeth d'Aulnières is returning to her role of 'model wife') contains an enormous but repressed power, suggestive of all the feminine energy held in thrall by patriarchal culture, and on the verge of exploding:

Off in a parched field, under the rocks, they've dug up a woman, all black but still alive, buried there long ago, in some far-off, savage time. Strangely preserved. Then they've gone and let her loose on the town. And all the people have locked themselves in. So deathly afraid of this woman. Everyone thinks that she must have an utterly awesome lust for life, buried alive so long. A hunger growing and growing inside the earth for centuries on end! Unlike any other that's ever been known. Whenever she runs through the town, begging and weeping, they sound the alarm. Nothing before her but doors shut tight, and the empty, unpaved streets. Nothing to do now but let herself die. Alone and hungry.[2]

The shift from the male to the female perspective here is significant, in the literal sense of 'productive of new meaning.' Everything depends on the angle of vision, as Nicole Brossard was to write a few years later of her own voyage towards feminism: 'I am talking here about a certain angle of vision. To get there, I had to shift my position in such a way that the opaque body of the patriarchy would no longer obstruct my vision ... This displacement gives rise to all the others.'[3] For me, as for Brossard, feminism was the decisive change in point of view, one that led me little by little to remove the mask of 'universal reader' conferred on me by culture and to begin to read as a woman. And as I began to look at the familiar texts of Quebec literature from that new perspective, what I saw first was a melancholy cohort of murdered women, sisters of Joan Ruskin and Elisabeth d'Aulnières across the generations, and resisters like them. All the dead mothers of the novel of the land – Angéline de Montbrun's mother, Laura Chapdelaine, Menaud's wife, Alphonsine Moisan, Mathilde Beauchemin, and many others – came together in this first stage of my reading like a group of sister-victims, their silenced voices erupting into the Quebec cultural text

through the delirious cry uttered by the perfect wife, Donalda Poudrier, at the moment of her death: 'I'm thirsty! I'm burning! ... I've
been killed ... Mother! Mother!'[4]

This female voice – always echoing the maternal origin – traverses
the writing of men and of women, but differently. In men's writing
it is almost always hidden deep down in the unconscious level of
the text, but from those depths it speaks, often contradicting the
apparent intention of the author – merging with the voice of nature,
imprinting itself in the gestures of the idealized or scorned (but
always silent) female characters in the text, expressing itself through
all the 'otherness' that male writers seem to feel the need to dominate
in order to assure themselves of their identity within writing. In
women's writing, where it is listened to as the voice of 'sameness,'
and not of an 'other' that must be reduced to silence, the voice of
the feminine-maternal element is more audible, and more *subversive*
in the way it works within the text. To take another example from
Anne Hébert's writing, the image of the 'little dead girl' lying on
the doorstep of the troubled house where the poetic experience is
unfolding continues to disturb the occupant of the house until her
poetry 'explodes' from within, allowing expression to the repressed
elements of experience:

> The life we lead, so minuscule and still,
> Lets not one languid motion
> Pass through the other side of this limpid mirror
> Where this sister that is ours
> Bathes blue in the moonlight
> While her heady odour swells and rises.[5]

The change in perspective that is feminist consciousness begins
almost inevitably with a feeling of anger, indignation, or horror at
the discovery of this founding murder on which the edifice of
Western culture is built. Echoing Aquin's detective-novel image,
Louky Bersianik writes that 'the history of humanity that has been
given to us as *true* is a huge science fiction novel full of fabulous
monsters and extraterrestrial beauties: and also a giant detective
novel, full of anonymous murders, where *all the bodies have been
removed from the scene*, so that we no longer believe in the *reality* of

these murders.'[6] We've always known, though, that the literary critic has something of the detective in her; and as her initial anger is replaced by the curiosity of the investigator – in fact of the whole network of investigators made up of present-day feminist critics, writers, and readers – it is the entire system of traditional representation that begins to disclose its relationship with the structures of patriarchal culture, revealing how the culture restricts and imprisons men as well as women. In this sense writing is an activity that takes place in the Father's House; and the house is evidently a metaphor for culture and its ideological, artistic, and linguistic structures of representation, shown by feminism with increasing precision and clarity in recent years to be the projection of male subjectivity and male authority. The writings of Luce Irigaray and Hélène Cixous were among the first to demonstrate that this house is built on the foundation of a reified other, a woman-object constructed to serve as a reflection and a support for masculine subjectivity. According to Cixous, 'If one questions literary history, it is always the same story. It all goes back to man, to his torment, his desire to be (at) the origin. To the Father ... The philosophical is constructed on the basis of woman's subjection. And this subordination of the feminine to the masculine order appears to be the condition of the machine's functioning.'[7]

In fact we are so used to the immensity and the otherness of the feminine-maternal in literature that we hardly notice its presence. It is the abyss into which the poet Emile Nelligan falls after his brief voyage on the sea of language, the bottomless ocean that closes around his successor, Saint-Denys Garneau, and swallows up his words, and the emptiness that underlies the complicated language structures of Hubert Aquin and Réjean Ducharme, two other successors or 'grandsons' of Nelligan. When she is not fantasized as immense and threatening in literature, woman is immobilized and reduced to silence in the restrictive feminine roles of the traditional novel; and that imprisonment is both the mirror image and the result of the terrifying maternal immensity she seems to represent for her sons. But in each of these two manifestations – immense or imprisoned – the woman-object has been the immutable foundation that guarantees the solidity of the house.

It is not surprising that men and women write differently, differently positioned as they are within this same house of language and culture. To become an author – as the etymology of the word suggests – means to accede to *authority*; and in a tradition where authority is reserved for the fathers, the seizing of authority within literary space will necessarily be different for women and for men.[8] To use French critic Claudine Hermann's term, women are truly 'thieves of language,'[9] and their writing is *by definition* a subversive act within the Father's House. With a different relationship to the Law of the Father and to the maternal origin from that of their literary brothers, women who write – whether or not they choose to be so – are a presence that disturbs the order of the Father's House.

A subversive texture

But how can we read the differences between men's and women's writing without falling into the stereotypes that have always been used to imprison women? There is textual evidence, for example, to indicate that women have a tendency to write autobiographically, or in fragmented structures like letters or diaries, rather than feeling at ease behind the distancing eye of an omniscient narrator; that the body and the material realm 'speak' differently in their writing; and that their texts contain a less hierarchical, more emotional concept of *reason* than one finds in men's writing. But the question of gender specificity in writing raises as many problems for the feminist critic, who fears imprisoning woman in yet another category or 'essence' dictated by the old binary hierarchy, as for critics of a more 'universal' tendency, who can always cite an exception or two to deny the possibility of sexual difference in writing. Like the feminist writing that inspires it, feminist criticism is in constant evolution and can only be defined by its movement and its openness. For example, the French and Québécoises theorists of *écriture féminine* or the 'writing of difference' (Hélène Cixous, Luce Irigaray, Madeleine Gagnon, Nicole Brossard, and others), who transformed our field of perception by daring to affirm with pride and pleasure what it could mean to write as a woman, have already moved on to new ways of articulating their feminist preoccupations, as if sensing the danger that the characteristics of the 'feminine' they were valorizing would be frozen into an imprisoning strait-jacket into which women would hitherto be expected to fit. The only trait that is truly characteristic of the feminine, writes Belgian feminist Françoise Collin, is the *absence* of a territory and the impossibility of distinguishing between what we 'are' and what culture has made of us:

Thus what women claim as specific to them often resembles what men have imposed on them, the 'feminine' seems not very different from traditional 'femininity.' For example, is it free choice or constraint that explains women's supposed indifference to power, their fluid writing, their non-violence, their preference for certain material elements, their polymorphous sensuality – all those dimensions recently rehabilitated by a certain strain of feminism? It is doubtless unnecessary to decide, as the negative shades so easily into the positive, and vice versa. The danger would be to limit the affirmation of women to a simple mirror image of the old values and images.[10]

After twenty years of feminist thought, however, after the critique of phallocentrism in discourse and in the symbolic order that has taken place in French and Québécois thought, and the numerous close readings of women's texts that have been produced within the Anglo-American–Canadian tradition, feminist criticism has by now acquired the tools that will allow it to read *differently*, and in their historical and social context, the major texts that make up a literary tradition. Such a situated and comparative reading of the texts of women and of men should make it possible to reach some generalizations about what characterizes sexual difference in writing, while at the same time respecting the differences that exist *among* women and *among* men. By combining a critique of representation with an attention to the individual voice of the male or female writer speaking through the common structures of representation privileged by culture, it should be possible to reach new insights about the canon of texts that make up a national literature. Film critic and semiotician Teresa De Lauretis suggests the political possibilities opened up by this type of feminist criticism in a passage locating the specificity of feminist theory

not in femininity as a privileged nearness to nature, the body, or the unconscious, an essence which inheres in women but to which males too now lay a claim; not in a female tradition simply understood as private, marginal and yet intact, outside of history but fully there to be discovered or recovered; not, finally, in the chinks and cracks of masculinity, the fissures of male identity or the repressed of phallic discourse; but rather in that political, theoretical, self-analyzing practice by which the relations of the subject in social reality can be rearticulated from the historical experience of women.[11]

As one attempts to define the various dimensions of this difference between men's and women's writing, one becomes aware of the recurrence of a dialogue – or a dialectical tension – between two 'poles' in the text that could be called 'texture' and 'the Law.' Men's writing has a tendency to privilege linearity, logic, and a concept of identity that is closed, distanced from what it perceives as 'other,' and reassured by the presence of borders: in other words, it exists in a relationship of proximity (of 'sameness') to the Law. In women's writing, it is rather *texture* that dominates – the density of what resists closure within the sign, the gestures, rhythms, and silences that underlie language and that speak in the gaps between the words. Leaving the Quebec corpus for a moment, one thinks immediately of the fluid and ever-shifting quality of Virginia Woolf's writing, or the down-to-earth sensuality of a typical sentence by Colette. Elusive by definition, in that it is precisely that which resists codification, feminine texture escapes a critical reading that focuses only on meaning in the text. On the contrary, it often begins to reveal its presence only when one pays attention to aspects of the text that don't seem to signify anything: the exchange of 'so many trivial feminine matters'[12] made possible by the epistolary form in Laure Conan's *Angéline de Montbrun*, for example, or the deviations of the plot of Germaine Guèvremont's *Marie-Didace* from the traditional patterns of narrative. Texture may in fact be the literary manifestation of the way women have traditionally talked among themselves – the tendency to 'gossip' or 'chat' (that is, to find pleasure in the exchange of words without necessarily caring whether they are leading towards a defined goal) that Quebec critic Suzanne Lamy praises in one of her most lyrical texts on women's writing.[13] In writing, texture corresponds to Eros; not so much *opposed* to Logos as circulating around it, subverting the Law by bringing it back and opening it up to the life-giving possibilities of pleasure. A seduction of the Father by the daughter? One that in men's texts tends to appear in reverse form, as a reduction of the daughter to silence by the authority of the Father? We shall see that in the novel this eminently *textual* struggle between texture and the Law has repercussions within the narrative structure and informs the relationships between the male and the female characters.

Realism and the real

With its emphasis on linguistics, psychoanalysis, and the mechanisms of the literary text, French literary theory of the past thirty years has made an invaluable contribution to our understanding of the way ideological codes traverse language and are present in its very texture – so that the writer, by the very act of writing, finds him or herself not only positioned in relation to those codes but obliged to *take* a position in relation to them. To take a very simple example, women and men writing in French cannot write so much as a sentence without confronting the law that the feminine is coded with a mute 'e,' a silent ending that can be removed without any effect on the syntax of the sentence.[14] The feminine in grammar is a spare part, an accessory, a silent embellishment to structure and meaning. The same cannot be said of the masculine form, which cannot be removed without destroying the sentence. It is clear that within language there is no symmetry – rather, there is an asymmetry – between masculine and feminine. And it is of course in this house of language that the literary adventure takes place.

Less obvious, but related to the question of language, is the asymmetry between the masculine and the feminine in literary form. Entering into literary language, every male and female writer encounters the unwritten laws that regulate the codes of representation and narrativity; and, like those of language, these laws privilege masculine subjectivity and exclude female subjectivity. Already in *The Pleasure of the Text*, Roland Barthes detected the presence of the male identity formation (the Oedipus complex) at the very heart of narrative: 'Death of the Father would deprive literature of many of its pleasures. If there is no longer a Father, why tell stories? Doesn't every narrative lead back to Oedipus? Isn't storytelling always a way of searching for one's origins, speaking one's conflicts with the Law, entering into the dialectic of tenderness and hatred?'[15]

As Barthes points out, this structure is far from innocent, for it depends on a violence perpetrated by the male subject against that otherness which is at once language, the maternal body, and nature:

No object is in a constant relationship with pleasure ... For the writer, however, this object exists: it is not language, it is the *mother tongue*. The writer is someone who plays with his mother's body ... in order to glorify it, to embellish it, or in order to dismember it, to take it to the limit of what can be known about the body: I would go so far as to take bliss in a *disfiguration* of language, and opinion will strenuously object, since it opposes 'disfiguring nature.'[16]

What our culture has always called the 'traditional novel' (realism) is in fact a literary manifestation of the Father's House: a solid construction of language through which, we have been told, the writer 'captures' reality and 'transcends' the temporal realm through the eternal forms of art. Within this structure, the writer consolidates his power by robing himself in the authority of an omniscient narrator, who dominates the multiplicity of the real and reduces it by means of his gaze to the smooth fabric of a unified vision. Since Derrida we have been aware of the correspondence between this vision and that of the Cartesian subject, which splits itself off from the object it wishes to possess and reduces it to an image in the mind's eye. However, it has not been noted often enough or explicitly enough to what extent both these attitudes to the real are examples of *masculine* epistemology. As we move from chapter to chapter, we will see how not only the positioning of the narrator and the roles assigned to the characters in realist representation but also the 'pact' by which the text-object is exchanged between two subjects (the author and the reader) correspond to the modalities of domination and rivalry between two male subjects.

If women writers have tended to fragment novel form through the use of letters, diaries, and autobiography, it could be that this is not (as has so often been claimed) because they are unsure of themselves, or lack the authority and experience to write like men,

but rather because their writing presents another way of re-present-
ing, listening to, and touching the texture of the real. Between the
'realism' glorified by patriarchal culture and the 'real' as it appears in
women's writing there is a world of difference, and it is a world that
needs to be explored.

Speaking of the possibility – and the necessity – of a relationship
to reality other than that of domination, women's writing proposes
a new epistemology, a different synonym for the verb 'to know'
than 'to possess,' which patriarchal culture has always associated
with the act of knowing. Wouldn't it be more interesting, their texts
seem to ask, to interpret 'to know' in the sense evoked by its French
equivalent, 'connaître?' For 'co-naître' is 'to be born together': that
is, to be in relationship with; to write in such a way that otherness,
the real, and the temporal realm speak through the disorganized
texture of the text; to open oneself up to the reader in an invitation
to exchange and sharing.[17]

Quebec: A hidden patriarchy

If language and literary forms are gendered and asymmetrical, what
of ideology? What meanings are attached to the symbolic father and
mother figures that every writer meets up with and internalizes in a
configuration particular to his or her own culture? In Quebec, the
ideology of national survival that presided over literature from its
beginnings depended entirely for its coherence on the adherence of
women to their traditional reproductive role – for according to
clerical and lay leaders it was only through the 'revenge of the cradle'
that French Canada could hope to regain its former power within
North America. Traditional Quebec has often been called a 'matriarchy,' and the mythical mother evoked by Jean Le Moyne corresponds
to the magnified image of the mother that inhabits the collective
unconscious:

the French Canadian mother stands, dressed in calico, on her linoleum
floor in front of the stove with a large pot on it; an infant on her left hip
and a large spoon in her right hand, a bunch of kids hanging around her
knees and another one in the crib by the wood box ... It makes little
difference that this image scarcely corresponds to today's reality; it is

insistent just the same, it is familiar to us all and constitutes a valid frame of reference. What we are really dealing with is a myth.[18]

In reality, however, this solitary and powerful mother figure was an ideological construct created by a male-centred hierarchy based in the Catholic church and modelled on pre-revolutionary France, where power descended in a direct line from God the Father to the king of France to the father of the family and thence to the oldest son – the wife and the other children being relegated to the status of 'others.'[19] One has only to read the speeches, sermons, articles, and editorials devoted to the role of woman and the dangers of feminism in early-twentieth-century Quebec to get a sense of the extent to which this idealization of the mother was a male creation. In a series of articles opposing women's suffrage (not achieved until 1940 in Quebec, twenty-two years after Canadian women had won the right to vote in federal elections), Henri Bourassa notes perceptively that the traditional mother role is the foundation of French-Canadian society, and that if feminism, an Anglo-Saxon import, is allowed even the slightest foot in the door, the whole system will collapse into anarchy:

And let us not delude ourselves: the social fabric of the province of Quebec can only maintain itself ... through the total conservation, indeed the restoration, of the Catholic family, which is the source and the foundation of our social life. If that vital organ is cut into, the whole body will rapidly be destroyed ... When that happens, we will be in danger of becoming dangerous revolutionaries ... for we lack that instinct for political cohesion and material conservatism that has kept Anglo-Saxon society together for so long, and that would protect us against our own excesses and preserve us from decadence.[20]

With Thomas Aquinas and St Paul to rely on, it was easy for clerical leaders like Mgr Louis-Adolphe Paquet to demonstrate that 'man, by virtue of his constitution and through the properties of his intelligence and his reason, is usually more qualified than woman to rule within the family,'[21] and that 'it is not those women who have rubbed up against Greek and Hebrew who will repair the damage done to the family.'[22] 'The Poem of the Mother,' written by a man and published in 1924 in *La Revue moderne* (the forerunner of *Chatelaine* magazine), shows how this ideology was communicated to women in the popular press. Its idealization of the mother is linked to the idea that her self-realization will be achieved not only through the child, but through the *male* child. Further, this ability to 'create a future man' is presented as her version of man's creativity through art:

> No poet, no matter how great, even Homer
> Has ever made ...
> A poem as beautiful as the mother's:
> The child, pure masterpiece of love.
> Her life and her fleeting beauty she gives
> To the sons who will resemble her ...
> To make a child walk and talk – to create a man!
> What can man do that is greater? ...
> So that in her son, her glory and her poem
> The mother with happiness later
> Finding herself entirely in him
> Says: He is my voice, he is my gaze![23]

If such ideas contributed to trapping women in the maternal role and discouraged them from daring to write, they also help to explain the kind of mother, totally dependent on her son for identity, who appears later on in Quebec literature[24] as the monstrous mother against whom the son must struggle in order to exorcise his own demons. It is against this background that the violence against women in the novels of contemporary male writers must be read.

The patriarchal triangle: Escaping from Oedipus and Electra

What then is the structure underlying this asymmetry between the masculine and the feminine and assuring its perpetuation from generation to generation? For the lasting power of the Law of the Father must depend on the complicity (or the defeat) of the sons and daughters, on their acceptance of the roles assigned to them in the cultural text. From the writing of Laure Conan to that of Hubert Aquin and France Théoret, we will in fact see the presence of a

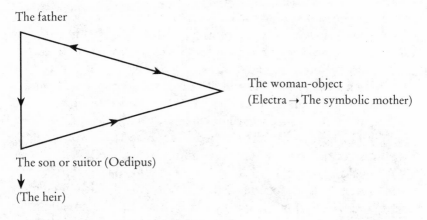

The father

The woman-object
(Electra → The symbolic mother)

The son or suitor (Oedipus)

(The heir)

Figure 1 The patriarchal triangle

common structure: a triangle that I call 'patriarchal' or 'Oedipal,' and that constitutes the basic structure of the Father's House.

With the figures of the father, the son or suitor, and the woman-object constituting its three points, this triangle corresponds to the familial and cultural configuration inherited by each writer, and represents the basic structure the woman writer must explode in order to inscribe her own subjectivity within literary language. Appearing in its 'purest' form in the novels of the land written by men, it is also the starting point of Laure Conan's *Angéline de Montbrun* and the hidden structure towards which the suspense of Hubert Aquin's metafictional detective novel, *Hamlet's Twin*, unfolds. The triangle has specifically Québécois resonances (for example, the transmission of the national heritage depends on it), but behind them one detects a more universal structure – that of the exchange of a woman between two men identified by Lévi-Strauss as the mark of the passage of a group from the state of 'nature' to that of 'culture.'[25] This centuries-old structure, which transmits the name of the Father and the social division between the sexes from generation to generation, is experienced on the level of the individual psyche in the form of the 'Oedipus complex.'[26] In narrative terms, what this means is that 'his story' (the narrative of male development) is dependent on possession of the woman-object – and therefore on the continuing impossibility of allowing 'her story' to come into being. The structure of the Father's House is subverted by every woman who writes, however – by the very fact that women create literary structures in which female *subjects* exist in relation to other female *subjects*. Rereading the works of women writers of past generations, one discovers that the political project of feminism – women beginning to recognize each other as sisters, and daughters rediscovering their mothers by freeing them from the 'statue' of the symbolic mother[27] – has already been begun in their works, with textual results that we are only beginning to decipher.

'Oedipus' and 'Electra' will appear in the following chapters, then, as the universal myths encouraging the son and the daughter, the brother and the sister in the Father's House, to play a complicit role in the perpetuation of a pre-scripted narrative. In their Québécois version, we shall see that these myths give birth to a *tragic* male tradition (that of the 'impotent son,' which can be traced from nineteenth-century poets Octave Crémazie and Emile Nelligan to the present day), and to a *subversive* female tradition. For, as the ambivalent writing of Laure Conan clearly shows, the Electra position is not an option for the woman who writes. In a house where the Father is all-powerful, the position of Oedipus/the son is frustrating, but at least it *is* a position – a corner in the house where he can sit and ruminate on his pain and alienation. For the daughter, on the contrary, there is no place in the house except that of the silent and immobile object that holds the whole structure in place. To write, for her, is to emerge from silence, to break with Electra ... and to explode the patriarchal triangle from within.

His story / her story

To read Quebec literature from a perspective that emphasizes sexual difference is thus to pay particular attention to the way the voice of each writer, female or male, finds expression within the Father's House of the Québécois symbol system. Works of art are not ideological messages, but explorations of contradiction; and what I have tried to make clear in this reading of many of the classics of Quebec literature is how what may be the major contradiction of Quebec history – its attitude to the feminine – emerges in the literary texts, often making them deviate from their prescribed course and become symptoms of a double impasse: that of 'his story' and of 'her story.'

The form I have chosen is as asymmetrical as that of the Father's House, but here the asymmetry works in favour of women. While proposing an overall comparison of men's and women's writing, I emphasize that of women, devoting entire chapters to each of three women writers (Laure Conan, Germaine Guèvremont, and Gabrielle Roy) whose works have been admitted to the canon of Quebec literary works, but according to criteria that have silenced the subversive women's voice they contain. If there was a 'patron saint' who presided over the writing of this book, it was Laure Conan, whose magnificent and solitary *Angéline de Montbrun* contains in an archetypal vision the entire dynamic of the Father's House: not only what is intolerable about women's situation within it (Angéline), but also the danger of complicity and silence it contains for men (Angéline's suitor, Maurice Darville). The first and longest chapter examines the ambivalence towards her own sex that traverses Conan's life and work, and proposes a close textual reading of her *Angéline de Montbrun*, one that detects the presence in the novel of a series of 'voices of resistance,' which struggle against the all-powerful word of the father before being reduced to silence. Chapters 2 and 3 look at the novel of the land, a genre that is both masculine and paternalist in its realist form and disincarnated vision (chapter 2) until the transformations brought about by Germaine Guèvremont's two novels (chapter 3). Chapter 4 moves the exploration of sexual difference ahead a step further by contrasting the work of a male and a female poet linked not only by ties of family and social class, but also by the key images and symbols of their work: Saint-Denys Garneau and Anne Hébert. Chapter 5 confronts the paradoxical fact that the masterpiece of social realism in Quebec literature – Gabrielle Roy's *The Tin Flute* – is the work of a woman, and shows how Roy, by assuming a position of authority in the Father's House of realist representation, succeeds not only in transforming realism, but in making explicit the political message of women's writing. In chapter 6 I return to the image of the corpse under the foundation of the house, analysing the violence done to women in the contemporary Quebec novel as a symptom of the impasse of 'his story.' It is the impasse of a whole culture and of its representations, lucidly analysed 'in the masculine' and 'in the feminine' in novels by two writers who are as consciously Québécois as they are modern: Hubert Aquin and France Théoret. Chapter 7 proposes a feminist analysis of Aquin's final novel, *Hamlet's Twin*, which explores the impasse of representation and of patriarchal culture through a detective-novel plot centred on the ritual murder of a woman. Finally, chapter 8 traces the painful emergence of a woman's voice from within the 'patriarchal rock' of language and representations in France Théoret's writing, and shows how Théoret deconstructs all the dualisms on which the house of patriarchal culture is built, reclaiming for women not only the forms and aims of realism but also the figure of Electra.

By the asymmetry of the chapters, and by the at times meandering approach I have adopted to the works, this book perhaps reflects its subject. Like the woman writers who have inspired me, I have preferred to listen to the texts and to follow the direction they have led me in rather than to impose on them the limiting 'grid' of a single critical approach. Thus, while the question of the 'patriarchal triangle' comes up in each chapter and forms one of the main leitmotivs of the book, I have chosen to let each work speak according to what seems to me to be its own internal coherence rather than to analyse it solely in terms of this recurring structure. Other threads as well run through all the chapters and emerge as areas in which the differences between men's and women's writing stand out in relief: a tendency to privilege themes and structures related to *vision* (the Father's gaze?) in men's writing, and to *voice* (the trace of the maternal presence and of the body?) in women's writing; a different relationship to nature (especially to the 'maternal' element of water) in men's and women's works. Finally, for me – an English Canadian with a long-standing love of Quebec culture – one of the most fascinating dimensions of this study has been to discover in the course of my readings a different relationship to country and to the 'national question' on the part of women and of men. For there is no doubt that it is the voice of the much-maligned country that male writers believe they are obeying when they cling to a 'dream of enduring forever' as old as men's identity – a dream erected like a fortress against all it perceives as 'other,' including and especially woman. Used to being relegated themselves to the status of 'other,' women seem on the contrary capable of imagining a country in movement and with ever-expanding borders, a house open to diversity and offering solidarity to all those – female or male – who are struggling for justice within it.

CHAPTER ONE

Angéline de Montbrun *or* *the fall into writing*

It was a thousand pities that a woman who could write like that, whose mind was tuned to nature and reflection, should have been forced to anger and bitterness.
Virginia Woolf, *A Room of One's Own*

I don't understand this powerful weight that ties me to the earth.
Laure Conan, *Angéline de Montbrun*

To write as woman: Breaking with Electra

The first volume of Laure Conan's collected works contains a remarkable painting, an impressionist landscape done by the author, the only surviving work by her except for a self-portrait contained in the same volume. In it, Conan depicts a young girl standing somewhat forlornly in a field of flowers against a backdrop of pine trees and grazing animals and brought into focus by two large trees in the centre of the painting. In the foreground, separated from the girl by a fence covering the whole width of the painting, stands a male figure: a nineteenth-century *seigneur*? a lawyer? a priest reading his breviary? The contours of the figures are blurred, but what is striking in the painting is the separation of the male and female figures into two distinct spaces: she stands outside the enclosed space, with her gaze fixed on him, while he is inside and oblivious to her presence. In the caption accompanying the reproduction critic

Laure Conan, 'Paysage de Neuville'
Reproduced by permission of Roger Lemoine

Roger Lemoine explains that, like Conan's novels, it is a symbolic representation of an unhappy love affair with an older man that left her with a broken heart: 'In the landscape – the only surviving one by her – Laure Conan has depicted a young girl, placed between two trees, fixing her attention on an older man from whom she is separated by an almost unreachable fence. Thus she was attempting to show, as she did in her written work, the impossibility of reaching the beloved one.'[1]

Presented by a man, the painting and the written work of Laure Conan thus appear as a transparent reflection of the author's life; and that life, itself presented through the filter of a male gaze, is reduced to the long disappointment of the life of an 'old maid' rejected by her fiancé.[2] It is as if, since it is inconceivable that any other event in her life could matter as much as this rejection by a man, the entire constellation of dominating fathers and submissive daughters that traverses Conan's work can then be reduced to a simple compensation or nostalgic memory of this moment in her life.

But if we shift our perspective somewhat, the painting takes on new meaning. Certainly the young girl is outside an enclosed space inhabited by an authoritative male figure, and certainly she seems to want to be *inside* that space and not in her own – which is an undefined space clearly associated with nature and the animal domain. As well as being excluded from a desired centre, the young woman also seems *imprisoned*, in spite of the vastness of the space she is assigned to, because of the two trees which enclose her in a reduced pictorial space. Ironically, even though the young woman's gaze is directed towards a centre situated elsewhere, in the space occupied by the man, for the spectator it is she who constitutes the focal point of the painting. Could it be that Laure Conan has depicted her own ambivalence towards her sex and her culture? Looked at from a modern feminist perspective, the painting does in fact evoke the situation of a woman writer without a 'context' for her writing, one who finds herself condemned by biology to remaining on the 'margin' of culture. Or alternatively, she has the option of identifying with Electra: that is, of trying to abstract herself from her female condition in order to find a place for herself in the space reserved for man. If we let our imaginations play a bit, we can see that had

Conan's milieu provided the slightest encouragement for her, she would have written *from* the margin, defining it as her own space and the space of potential wholeness.

However, even for modern women, strengthened by a growing list of 'foremothers' and a community of other women sharing the exploration of their uncharted literary space, the access to that space is difficult and fraught with risks and detours. Women's writing, says Irma Garcia, is always a 'painful birth, for it is truly a beginning that is taking place, the moment when language detaches itself from the body in order to become writing, at the price of risk and suffering ...'[3] For Laure Conan, a woman who wrote without female models or fellow writers at a time when conservative and clerical nationalism had consolidated their grip on the literary institution, how much more painful this 'birth' must have been! And how ambivalent her feelings towards the status of 'virile'[4] writer that was quickly granted her thanks to the protection of her powerful mentor, Abbé Henri-Raymond Casgrain.

The role played by Casgrain in Laure Conan's life clearly seems to have been that of the male mentor one discovers in the lives of so many women artists. Writing (or painting or composing) in a milieu where their own perceptions are undervalued, it is not surprising that so many women have felt the need for a symbolic father to give them confidence, to believe in the value of their work. While it is true that we owe the works of a number of women artists to the encouragement of such mentors, one cannot but wonder to what extent their influence must have created ambiguities, silences, and self-censorship in those works. In Conan's case, the abandonment of purely psychological analysis and the move towards nationalist themes after her first novel, *Angéline de Montbrun*,[5] cannot be unrelated to the reservations about her novel expressed in Casgrain's preface to it: 'The gravest problem with her present manner is that she gives her book too European a mien ... One is sorry not to meet more truly Canadian passages, such as Angéline's pilgrimage to Garneau's tomb. Our literature can be seriously original only by identifying itself with our country and its inhabitants, only by painting our customs, our history, our features: it is its only reason for existing.'[6]

Indeed it is hard to imagine how this woman, whose correspondence with Casgrain reveals a veritable terror related to the idea of being published, and who consented to publication only because of his insistence, could *not* have felt an identification with Electra. Writing to her mentor after reading a first version of the preface he was drafting for the publication of *Angéline* in book form, she reveals a typically feminine fear of *transgression* linked to the idea of writing: 'You have understood that I had to be strongly reassured. In spite of your kind words, I feel the need to justify myself for having tried to write. I must say that it is entirely, or almost entirely, due to circumstances. My will, I assure you, has little to do with it. Only necessity has given me this extreme courage of seeing myself in print.'[7]

In reaction to revelations about her personal life made by Casgrain in the preface, she insists again on the fact that being exposed in this way before the public eye is a 'torture' for her: 'Since you were kind enough to ask for my impressions, allow me to request that you cut all that out. I assure you that that would be more distressing than I can tell you. Please don't inflict that torture on me. I am already shamed enough by having myself printed. Perhaps, sir, you will not understand this feeling – men are made for publicity.'[8]

This feeling of 'shame' and of the illegitimacy of her literary venture are surely signs of the ambivalence felt by a woman who has dared to break with Electra's silence and make her own voice heard within the Father's House of a literary institution defined according to male criteria. Writing in a relationship of proximity to the body and to the reality of their experience, women seem particularly vulnerable when they write, as if by inscribing their vital traces on the page they are exposing themselves to the gaze of a judge, a censor, or a seducer. Such 'feminine modesty' in relation to the idea of *exhibiting oneself* on the printed page may explain why Félicité Angers hides behind a pseudonym when she writes, and why she chooses the name of 'Laure' – the silent and beautiful Petrarchan muse whose patronage could not help but guarantee male approval. Indeed, Conan confided to a female friend near the end of her life that, were the choice of a pseudonym given to her again, she would choose a man's name: Jean de Sol.[9] Here again we find ambivalence, for the word 'sol' could mean 'soil,' reflecting her love of her native land and the French-Canadian rural ideal; or it could suggest the idea of 'sun,' indicating Conan's desire to identify with a virile centre of warmth and value. Such *double entendres* are typical of her life and work, and are at the heart of her enigmatic *Angéline de Montbrun*: the first novel written by a woman in Quebec, and an archetypal work presenting the struggle of the female imagination imprisoned in the Father's House.

Angéline de Montbrun: A bomb in the Father's House

By deciding to publish her *Angéline* in spite of her hesitations, Laure Conan placed within the patriarchal structures of literature and society a time-bomb whose explosive effects are only beginning to be felt.[10] The fragmentary form of the novel, with its reliance on the traditionally feminine literary forms of letters and diary, represents a striking departure from the omniscient third-person narration of the novels of the period, and communicates in a veiled way an equally subversive content.

Briefly put, the novel recounts the story of a powerful and beloved father, Charles de Montbrun, and his beautiful daughter, Angéline, whose Edenic existence is shattered by the intrusion into their world of a suitor, Maurice Darville, who claims the daughter's hand. In a bizarre and brief middle section of the three-part novel, the father is killed on his return from a hunting trip when his gun entangles itself in the branches of a tree, and shortly thereafter his inconsolable daughter falls on the pavement and disfigures her face irreparably. In the third section, written in diary form, Angéline is alone, having rejected her suitor when she sees that his love has turned to pity for her disfigurement. Her writing is an attempt to recover from her grief and insert herself into the rhythm of time and nature, but the memory of her father is too powerful to transcend. The diary gradually turns into a praise of renunciation and a despairing acceptance of the church's teaching that happiness on earth is not only impossible but sinful.

In spite of – or because of – its fairy-tale surface, there is a power and a mythical depth in this novel that have made it one of the most analysed novels in French-Canadian literature. But the history of its critical response is itself an example of the way the cultural institutions of patriarchal society can empty women's writing of its subversive content.[11] Whether praising it as 'edifying' or expressing shock at its 'scandalous' nature, critics have unfailingly noted the presence of the 'Electra complex' in the ambiguous relationship between Angéline and her father. But the overall effect of their analyses is to paint Angéline as a submissive and often distasteful victim, while the image of the powerful and beloved father figure remains intact.[12]

If, on the contrary, one listens for what might be specifically female in the novel, one detects the path followed by a woman's voice seeking to emerge into writing and to insert itself in time and reality; as if, by the very act of putting pen to paper, Laure Conan's imagination had conjured up the various mirrors of traditional femininity and male power through which she must navigate in order to reach her own literary space. Strikingly modern in its hesitation, the text seems to defer indefinitely the act of marriage (and later the commitment to religious faith) towards which the whole surface level of the plot is constructed to lead – as if the act of writing itself were leading the author and her heroine towards a space incompatible with those roles. Full of contradictions, the novel seems to circle around what it wants to say, as if that something were forbidden, even unspeakable. With almost every sentence of rebellion followed by a disclaimer voiced in the edifying rhetoric of the time, the novel is far from the linearity and logic of traditional narrative form. But looked at as a woman's writing, it reveals an astonishing coherence; its structure constituted by a series of voices of resistance replacing one another as they are destroyed by the dominant ideology, until at last – after the death of the father and the loss of the stereotypical beauty of the heroine – a female 'I' emerges from the destruction wrought in the literary edifice.

Critics have often noted the presence of the myth of Paradise and the Fall in *Angéline de Montbrun*, but have tended to read the third part of the novel as a nostalgic yearning for the 'pretemporal' world of the paternal estate at Valriant, from which Angéline/Electra is expelled through an inexplicable 'fault' to which she refers in her diary. Such a reading is true on the surface level, but it explains neither the ambiguities nor the violence of the novel. Reading *Angéline* as a novel of feminine resistance and rebellion, we see that the paradise of the first part of the novel is the world of patriarchal power from which women must emerge in order to accede to their own subjectivity, and that Angéline's 'fall' is a fall into writing.

VALRIANT — OR THE FATHER'S STRATEGIES FOR CONTROL

The paternal mansion at Valriant (Laughing Valley) is explicitly described in the first section of the novel as an 'earthly paradise' (AM5); more specifically, it evokes the 'paradise' of nineteenth-century French-Canadian culture, where father and daughter are united in a harmony reflected in the tamed and artificial nature of their surroundings. In contrast to Conan's painting, where she presents herself as outside the enclosure of culture and male power, here she begins her story within that enclosure, before the emergence of the female voice – as if the entry into literary language had made her more sensitive to the relationship between the creative psyche and social power. United to a father presented as the source of all light and warmth, Angéline does not have the right to speak: she is the woman-object who will be exchanged between the father and the suitor.

Structurally, this opening corresponds perfectly to the laws of the traditional novel, and more specifically to the French-Canadian novel of the land. We will see in the following chapter how the exchange of a woman between two men in those novels constitutes not only the event permitting the perpetuation of the paternal heritage, and therefore of the narrative's linearity, but also a metaphor of the exchange between author and reader in patriarchal culture. In *Angéline de Montbrun*, the condition that would have made possible a linear plot and a 'traditional' form for the novel would have been an *action* growing out of the exchange of Angéline between father and suitor. What happens, on the contrary, is that the object of the exchange – Angéline – begins to speak, and under the impact of this voice emerging from silence the whole structure of representation explodes.

Charles and Angéline: The perfect patriarchal couple

Charles de Montbrun is the archetype (and perhaps the unconscious parody) of all the French-Canadian patriarchal values of Conan's era. Powerful, rich, and generous, a model of 'Christian charity,' he is a former military man turned gentleman farmer, who carefully puts on gloves to protect his hands before going to work in the fields (AM55) – in somewhat the same way as the ideological leaders

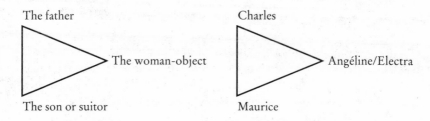

Figure 2 Novels by men   Figure 3 *Angéline* (1)

of the period espoused the 'agriculturalist' dream on behalf of the French-Canadian people! A benevolent patriarch, he combines all the qualities valued by his society, and it is easy to see why rebellion against him would be unthinkable. Maurice's sister, Mina, who like all the female characters in the novel is susceptible to Charles's charm, says of him: 'That man has an adorable tactfulness, delicacy. There is something of the peasant, of the artist, and particularly of the military man in his nature, but there is also something of the subtlety of a diplomat and the tenderness of a woman. All that makes for a rather rare entity' (AM25).

Charles's advice to Maurice once he has finally accepted him as a suitor for Angéline's hand is as good an exposition of the values preached from the pulpits of the period as can be found in the pages of Quebec literature. Not only must Maurice unite within himself the values of nation and faith with those of hard work, but he must avoid the corruption of political life: 'party spirit has replaced national spirit ... [and] patriotism, that noble flower, is hardly found in politics, that soiled arena' (AM31). Far more important than 'knowledge, genius, glory, and everything the world admires' is 'the splendour of a pure heart' (AM29), and the only way to maintain this purity and to serve the country is to cultivate the 'sacred soil' (AM31). Further, if Maurice is to be a proper husband to Angéline, he must learn to exercise his authority over her and remain impassive in the face of her need for 'tenderness': 'It will pain you, Maurice, not to show to your beloved wife all the foolish tenderness which, by misunderstanding her dignity and yours, would lead you both to inevitable sorrow' (AM32).

If Angéline has any difficulty with such a concept of marriage, there are few indications of it in the first section of the novel, where in fact she is almost entirely silent (writing only two letters in a total of thirty-one). Always shown in the company of her father, she is the 'shining beauty' (AM25) who takes her light entirely from the 'sun' of his presence. Maurice's reaction on seeing her for the first time at Valriant is that she has lost the pallor of the previous winter and seems 'gilded by a ray of sunshine' (AM4). Watching from his window early the following morning, he sees Angéline, 'radiant as the rising sun' (AM6), join her father in the garden and be embraced by him with a proprietary gesture ('He seemed to be saying: "Let anyone try to take this my treasure away from me!" ' [AM6]). Later, in the famous Arcadian scene in which Angéline feeds the swan that critics have seen as an image of her father, she is once again shown as bathed in the light of the sun. Like Charles, the swan in the artificial pond he has built admires its reflection narcissistically in the water, and Angéline ecstatically admires him admiring himself – just as the young girl in Conan's painting watches the male who is oblivious to her presence:

The bird seemed to take great pleasure in being the centre of attraction. He would look at himself in the water, dive, then proudly follow the flowery shore of the miniature lake where the setting sun was reflected.

'Isn't he beautiful, isn't he beautiful!' Angéline said with warmth ... The burning rays of the sun were filtering through the trees and surrounding her as if by a fiery cone. (AM21)

As the perfect patriarchal daughter, Angéline is also the perfect feminine counterpart to her father's French-Canadian and Catholic version of authority. In accordance with his wishes, she dresses in the blue and white of the Virgin Mary, and like the Virgin Mary she occupies a position of power in the universe of Valriant that is dependent on her submissiveness, silence, and denial of her body. As her name suggests, she is an angelic presence in her father's firmament; as Maurice observes, 'She lives in him somewhat as the saints are said to live in God' (AM6).

Like almost every other female protagonist in the traditional Quebec novel, Angéline is a daughter without a mother. Explaining to Maurice why he has difficulty in consenting to the idea of marriage for Angéline, Charles explains that he has been both a father and a mother to her 'since the sad day when, returning home after my wife's funeral, I took in my arms my poor little orphan who was tearfully asking for her mother. As you know, I did not assign to anyone else the task of educating her ... ,' he adds. 'I wanted her to be the daughter of my soul as well as of my blood, and who can say to what extent this double parenthood has bound us one to the other?' (AM26–7).

It is this 'double parenthood' that makes Charles the perfect image of patriarchal power in Quebec, where (unlike countries where men have had access to real economic and political power) male authority has veiled itself in the feminine robes of the curé and the sentimental imagery of traditional Catholicism. Both father and mother to Angéline, Charles has become not only the object of her love, but her only model. Like Athena, she seems to have sprung full-grown from her father's head; and the twin portraits of her parents hanging in the salon accentuate both her distance from her mother, 'a pretty brunette whom she resembles not at all' (AM4), and her resemblance to her father. The only other reference to her mother in the first section of the novel is the evocation of the wedding day of this model wife who, abandoned by a husband who chooses to spend his wedding day working in the fields, decides to take the role of farmer's wife seriously and prepares a hot meal that she carries to the field for her 'lord and master' (AM13). Mina, whose ironic point of view represents one of the voices of resistance in the novel, warns her brother that 'this beginning of married life pleases Angéline, and that should make you think' (AM14).

Where can rebellion come from in such a perfect universe? Certainly not from Angéline, who has been trained in masochistic submission to her father's reprimands from early childhood: 'Angéline ... has a good character,' says Charles; 'when I scold her, she always kisses me' (AM8). With remarkable precision, Laure Conan has unveiled the face of Electra behind the mask of the obedient daughter in the Father's House. When Maurice asks her if she enjoyed studying when she was a child, she replies – 'looking towards her father coquettishly' – 'Not always ... But I feared him so much!' (AM15). Without passing through marriage or motherhood, Angéline has already acceded to the position of 'queen of the household,' to which young girls of her culture were taught to aspire. In a letter to Mina, she describes the details of running the household in images of royalty and servitude that clearly indicate her place in the hierarchy of power: 'Every sceptre is heavy ... and yet ... I am thinking of conquering my realm again'; 'Old Monique forgets that her regency is at an end, and will not let go the reins of power'; 'I will end up like the powerless kings'; 'my right to command'; 'I would rather be his servant than the daughter of the most prominent man in the country' (AM34–5). Referring to her difficulties in assuming a position of authority with the servants, she remarks that she could be more assertive, but 'I run the risk of becoming angry, and my father says that one shouldn't yell' (AM34).

In spite of the ambiguity in the relationship between father and daughter, it is not hard to see why generations of readers and critics regarded Laure Conan's novel as a rather syrupy defence of established values. To the extent that one restricts one's reading of the first section of the novel to the point of view of Charles and Angéline, the novel is indeed – to paraphrase Abbé Casgrain – as edifying as a visit to a church 'perfumed with incense.' It is here that the use of the epistolary form with its fragmented point of view reveals its subversive potential, especially in a social context where the possibility that a unified point of view would emerge in opposition to the dominant ideology was unthinkable.

Voices of resistance: Maurice and Mina

Unlike the traditional or 'realist' novel, where an omniscient narrator controls all the action as the plot unfolds, the epistolary form permits the emergence of a texture of writing that escapes linearity and of a pleasure consisting in the simple fact of exchange between two human beings. Of all literary forms, this is possibly the most perfect illustration of Bakhtin's 'dialogic' imaginary space,[13] as well as being the transposition onto the literary level of women's legendary love of 'chatting.' The epistolary form privileges voice over gaze and to some extent allows the characters to escape from the roles assigned to them in the realist narrative. Not every detail in a letter has to be *significant*; on the contrary, the writer often lets him or herself speak of such precisely *in*significant things as the texture of the present moment, a passing mood, whatever in the routine of daily life gives particular pleasure.

In addition, Laure Conan uses this literary form to make her narrative deviate subtly from its path towards a *different* female perspective, diametrically opposed to that of the submissive Angéline. Of the thirty-one letters that make up the novel's epistolary section, only two are written by Charles and two by Angéline. Of the remaining twenty-seven, nine are written by Maurice, one is to Mina from her friend Emma S., and the remaining seventeen letters are by Mina. Together Maurice and Mina – who, like all contestatory figures in French-Canadian literature, come from the city – represent a challenge to the rural and patriarchal ideal of Valriant. When one compares their functions in the novel, however, it is clear that Maurice – like Nelligan and all the sons in the novel-of-the-land tradition – is easily defeated or co-opted; while Mina, the character who has no real structural role in the novel's plot, emerges as if from the author's unconscious and articulates an alternative vision – that of a woman aspiring to autonomy.

Both Maurice and Mina's letters are written in an almost coded language in which their criticisms of the world of Valriant are immediately masked or contradicted by their assurances of what a 'charming' world it is – not a surprising language given the censorship and self-censorship under which Conan was writing. But their letters make clear that there is something decidedly sinister about the charm of Valriant, which exerts its seduction on both of them. Shortly after his arrival there Maurice writes to Mina that he is losing his sense of himself in this pre-temporal world that seems to tempt him to silence: 'I feel myself so different from what I usually am ... Mina, I want to hush up all the noises around this mossy nest, and love here in peace' (AM10).

One could explain these lines as simple romanticism if it were not for the fact that his sister experiences a similar loss of will-power as she gets close to Valriant. While packing her suitcase for a short visit to the Montbrun estate, she finds to her surprise that she is preparing for a long stay: 'I had resolved to arrive among you with a simple valise, as suits a noble soul on a trip. But one rarely knows what one wants and never what one might need: I ended up by packing all my fineries. Truly, I don't understand it, and I catch myself dreaming

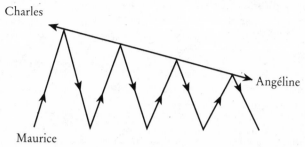

Figure 4 Maurice's desire

before my bulging luggage and my empty drawers' (AM38). On her arrival at Valriant she confides in a letter to her friend Emma that she usually hates gardens, but 'this one gives the impression of a paradise. Frankly, I would like to spend my life in this spot' (AM42).

Maurice: Or how the son is defeated

Through Maurice's experience at Valriant, Laure Conan shows how the desire of the son/suitor is forbidden and how he is reduced to silence by the complicity between the father and the woman-object. Associated with a constellation of themes related to voice, music, desire, and art, Maurice represents the first manifestation in the text of an erotic presence that in women's writing provides an alternative to the Law of the Father.

Conan's characters are often literally speechless, paralysed by silence, but through the singing voice can make their presence felt and seduce their interlocutors, as if the body were insisting on speaking in spite of repression and censorship.[14] Maurice is as intimidated by Angéline's beauty as he is by her father's authority, but he seduces her by the 'penetrating sweetness' of his singing, plunging her into a state of emotion that the perceptive Mina recognizes as desire: 'having never read any novel, she is not self-conscious at the tears which your sweet singing makes her shed' (AM7). It is significant that it is Charles, the figure representing paternal censorship, who advises Maurice to abandon music in favour of more 'serious' occupations (AM30).

Each time Maurice tries to express his desire for Angéline, an obstacle or a displacement intervenes in the narrative, reducing him to silence. Strangely, Charles and Angéline seem leagued against him, and their scornful laughter reduces him again and again to a state of abject humiliation. Charles's tactic is to use his position of authority, gazing at the young man with the look of a disapproving father, while for her part Angéline taunts him with the flagrant nature of her relationship with her father:

I remained half annoyed, half confused. Could he have guessed? Then why make fun of me? (AM11)

I must risk the big question, but I think he puts me out on purpose. (AM15)

I called upon all the courage I have, and as I opened my mouth to bring up the subject directly, Angéline appeared at the window where we were sitting. She put one of her pretty hands over her father's eyes; with the other she brushed my face with a bunch of lilacs damp with dew.
'Shocking,' M. de Montbrun said. 'See how Maurice blushes at your country manners.'
'But,' Angéline said with the clear laugh that you know, 'perhaps M. Darville blushes on his own account.' (AM16)

Combined, these strategies reduce Maurice from the state of a desiring adult male to that of an impotent and silent son – being punished, it would seem, for his desire. Described on several occasions as an artist, he offers an image of the male writers of his culture, defeated by the sinister workings of the patriarchal triangle. The power relations operative in the triangle are seen in the following passage, where the three characters are looking at a portrait of Charles:

'I had it painted for you, daughter,' M. de Montbrun said; and to me he said: 'Don't you think she will have no excuse if she ever forgets me?'
My dear, I made an answer that was so horribly ambiguous and awkward that Angéline burst out laughing, and although she has such white teeth, I don't like to see her laugh when it is at my expense.
You will hardly believe how humiliated I am at the awkwardness of my

speech when I am with her, an awkwardness that is never there any other time.

She asked me to sing, and I was delighted. Believe me, little sister, man didn't speak in the earthly paradise. No, in the days of innocence, of love and of happiness, man didn't speak, *he sang*.* (AM5)

Charles is the only character who speaks directly in this scene: behind their charm his words contain a veiled threat to Angéline, who will 'have no excuse' if ever she should forget him. Maurice is rendered tongue-tied by this statement, and stammers out such a clumsy reply that Angéline laughs at him, thus cementing her alliance with Charles against him. To extricate him from his embarrassment she then asks him to sing, as if the diversion provided by a *pre-scripted* text were less threatening to the security of the universe she occupies with her father than Maurice's own words (just so were artists of the period encouraged to censor their own words in the interest of ideological conformity). Maurice is 'delighted' to perform on cue, and to be accepted in the house even at the price of his own silence.

In fact to call Maurice a 'resister' is to flatter him, for the life of a silent son in paradise is not without compensations, and Maurice accepts without any hesitation his initiation into the hierarchy of paternal power once it becomes clear that Charles's mantle will eventually fall to him. The conditions of marriage imposed by Charles are however somewhat bizarre: not only must Maurice wait two years, until Angéline is twenty (for, says Charles, 'she is a child, and I very much want her to remain a child as long as possible' [AM22], but he must also agree to 'marry' Charles, since according to him Angéline will never agree to being separated from her father: 'Think about it, my dear friend, and see if you have any objection to *marrying me*' (AM26). Like the male novelists who were Conan's contemporaries, Maurice is only too happy to repress his desire and to join as a son in what he himself calls Angéline's 'worship' of the father: 'And why, please, would I not be a true son to you? I confess humbly that I have caught myself occasionally being jealous of you;

* The italics are Conan's, here and in the other quotations in this chapter.

the thought has even crossed my mind that she loves you too much. But now I only ask to join in her worship of you' (AM28).

Mina: Or the paths of woman's resistance

But authentic writing refuses to play according to the rules of the established order, and as soon as Maurice has been reduced to silence Conan's novel produces another resister – his sister, Mina. As Angéline's positive double, Mina is the woman-subject who will make the story deviate towards a truth other than that of the Father's House: a texture of women's writing made up of pleasure, finesse, and humour.

Writing in a society hostile to their perceptions, women have often divided the female psyche into two parts in their writing, thus expressing the contradictions and the eternal wandering or exile of female literary space. For critic Irma Garcia, the frequency in women's writing of 'two female characters who curiously seem to complete each other, and even at times to blend into each other ... [who], far from being in opposition, act as a support to each other' corresponds to the search for a female identity that is 'always elusive, constantly thwarted or off-centre.'[15] Mina, whose most striking characteristic is her love of the earth, is Angéline's double in all respects: not the idealized image of woman created by men, but an autonomous woman who lives in the city, enjoys going to balls and banquets, goes to the port of Quebec on occasion to welcome a fleet of sailors from France, and who has acquired some reputation for the number of male admirers (including a Protestant minister) she has left in her wake. Her letters are by far the wittiest in the novel, full of amusing anecdotes such as the one she tells her friend Emma about the fussy widow who reproached her for distracting so many young men from their studies: 'Yes, my dear, I am a great criminal and have caused rivers of tears to flow. Some are known to have had their hearts reduced to ashes. I have caused young men to neglect their studies and to waste away sadly' (AM49).

While Angéline is a 'country girl,' Mina is from the city and is often accused of being 'worldly.' Angéline is compared to the Virgin Mary, Mina to Eve: 'What teasing you indulge in to make me admit everything! Wretched daughter of Eve!' (AM10). In their attitudes to French politics, Angéline and her father are royalists (that is, they believe like the clerical élite of their time that the French Revolution should never have taken place), while Mina and her brother are republicans. Behind the two women's friendship there are subtle conflicts as well. In writing to invite Mina to Valriant, Angéline tells her she wants to 'reform' her: 'It will be such a pleasure to *make you unworldly*... I want to reform you completely' (AM34–5). As for Mina, she confides to her friend Emma that the too-perfect Angéline makes her uncomfortable: 'No dust has ever touched that radiant flower, and consequently I always feel restrained in her presence; with you, I can be freer' (AM45). And later on: 'Angéline often arouses in me a pity which I can't explain. I find her too beautiful, too charming, too happy, too beloved' (AM48).

Unlike Angéline, Mina has a 'philosophy of life' that can be seen as a female counterpart to Charles's views. Rather than espousing the hierarchy of authority over tenderness as he does, she argues for a blend of reason and emotion that breaks with the dualism of patriarchal values; this will perhaps not be so cogently argued again in Quebec writing until the advent of modern feminism.[16] Like modern feminists, Mina argues for a knowledge based in experience ('I have observed the joys of reason closely') and states that, separated from emotion, reason is 'a frightful common sense which is horribly rigid, detestably narrow, which I never meet without feeling like doing something foolish' (AM37–8). 'The power to feel is not something that frightens women,' she says, and 'true common sense' is far from 'that so-called wisdom which admits only the dull and the lukewarm, and whose dry cold hand would extinguish everything that shines, everything that burns' (AM38). After this passionate speech by Mina, as in all the instances where Conan has allowed her characters to challenge the established order, there is immediate self-censorship: 'My little flower of the fields,' Mina goes on, 'you are so lucky not to have seen much of the world! If I had it to do over again, I would choose not to see it at all, to keep my candour and my ignorance' (AM38).

If Mina reveals herself to be susceptible to Charles de Montbrun's seductive charms, it is because as a woman seeking to live fully she has been unable to find a man worthy of her. The frequency in Laure Conan's writings of female characters who reject marriage and choose instead to live alone and in celibacy should be looked at in light of Mina's comments on the men in her milieu:[17] 'Poor men! Everywhere the same!' (AM38), she writes to Angéline. What a dream it would be to find a man one wouldn't have to 'educate'!

I think, as did Madame de Staël, that a woman who dies without having loved has not lived, and, on the other hand, I always felt that I could love only a man who was worthy of being loved.

It is true that many pleasant 'little nobodies' tried to persuade me that it was all up to me to make them perfect, or almost. But I think it is a sad thing for a wife to have to educate her husband. (AM64)

Mina knows very well that certain gossips find her too independent to make a good wife, and she laughs about it: 'It seems that the Mlles V— keep on saying that I am basically impertinent, that I will treat my husband as a slave. Poor man! Don't you pity him?' (AM64).

Elsewhere, she refers to men as women's 'oppressors,' and jokes about women's patience with them: 'Women, instead of slandering their oppressors, usually try to discover some good qualities in them, which is not always easy' (AM12).

Mina's destruction: Or how he teaches her self-hate

Mina's destruction at Valriant is a moving sequence, which illustrates the impossibility of existing as a female subject within the Father's House, the doubt and self-hatred that invade the female psyche when it finds itself reflected in the mirror of the Father's censoring gaze. As she gradually loses her identity, moving from the status of subject to that of object, Mina – like Angéline before her – begins to inhabit the archetype of Electra.

Bewitched by the triangle of father, virgin daughter, and castrated son, she begins to doubt herself and eventually finds herself in a state of profound internal conflict. When she compares herself to the perfect Angéline, her own relationships with men begin to seem inadequate; when Maurice tells her he has knelt in adoration before Angéline, she writes: 'I know that such beautiful things will never happen to me. It's true that sweet words are readily enough whispered to me, but I don't have "the regal charm which takes reason away," and no one thinks of kneeling before me' (AM24). Once she has arrived at Valriant, she becomes the daughter destroyed by the Father's critical gaze. Convinced by Charles's constant reproaches that she is 'frivolous,' she tries to transform herself into a being worthy of Valriant, but with difficulty, as she sees the hypocrisy of their idealization of poverty ('I always look with respect on the poor house of a settler, and yet –' [AM57]), likes sleeping in in the morning (AM53), and confesses that she sometimes thinks life in heaven will be boring! 'She says that, according to St Francis of Assisi, music will be one of the pleasures of heaven, and that thought appeals to me. At bottom, I think that we all have a secret dread that we might be a little bored in immortality' (AM53).

Mina's struggle with Valriant is in essence a struggle against the values of renunciation preached by the church. Writing to her friend Emma, who has decided to enter the Ursuline order, she argues against religious austerity and the idea that any kind of 'absolute selflessness' (AM46) is possible. Emma has sent her a passage on self-love from the cynical seventeenth-century moralist Fénelon ('If it were not for self-esteem, you would no more desire to see your friends attached to you than to the king of China'); and her response is that this king of China 'sticks in [her] craw': 'What! is that what you want? There will come a time when it will matter little to you whether I share a thought, a memory with you!' (AM46).

It is precisely on friendship and sharing (particularly among women) that Mina's value system is based. Warning Emma against the danger of letting the life-flow between them harden and die, she evokes the flowing movement of a feminine, maternal water, threatened and contained by the rigidity of imposed values:

I fear that religious austerity will interfere with our friendship. There are so many trivial feminine matters that one must speak about; friendship without confidence is like a flower without scent. Then, sometimes, it takes so little to change friendship into indifference. It seems to me, at certain moments, that the heart is like the northern seas, which, when the summer is over, turn to ice at the least shock. Let us be careful. (AM47–8)

Like Charles's stern warning that Angéline must never forget him, and Maurice's recurrent dream that he will 'die a Jesuit' (AM43), this passage is a premonition of the traumatic events ('turn to ice at the least shock') that will take place later in the novel. But it is also a vision of life as process and change, whose vulnerability in the religious climate of the time Mina shows herself fully aware of. Already before the end of her letter she has begun to speak of friendship in the language of Valriant, as *an illusion ... which evaporates as the years go by and as one's interests change*' (AM48).

At Valriant, friendship is an illusion, reason dominates emotion, and the flowing current of the river is trapped in the confines of an artificial pond. In the cold light of Charles de Montbrun's sun, women's values have little chance of survival. Like her creator in the cultural milieu of her era, Mina finds herself deprived at Valriant of a context that would allow her own values to flower, and gradually – like Maurice – she begins to succumb to the seduction of the patriarchal ideal, incarnated in Charles de Montbrun. But unlike Maurice she is a woman, and there is no place for her in this hierarchical universe. As her stay at Valriant lengthens she falls more and more in love with Charles and begins to internalize his negative gaze. 'Does he think me incapable of a lofty sentiment?' she writes to Emma. 'I will prove to him that I'm not as frivolous as he thinks' (AM44). Incapable of renouncing her love of the earth and her sense of herself, she falls into a growing state of self-hatred and depression: 'To love is to get out of oneself. I admit that I cannot stand myself anymore' (AM41).

As she experiences this process of dissolution under the disapproving eye of the Father, Mina confusedly begins to sense the need for a maternal voice and body to give her back her sense of self. Like Angéline she is an '*orpheline de mère*' (her mother is dead), and the 'maternal' element of the sea, whose rhythmic movement seems to offer a caress as gentle and tactile as 'velvet,' provides some consolation against the state of suicidal depression that is enveloping her:

From my window, I have a glorious view of the river. Truly it is the sea. I don't tire of looking at it. I love the sea. The music of the waves throws a velvet cloak of melancholy over the sadness of my thoughts, because, I admit, I am sad, and I would gladly say as some queen of old: 'Fie on life!' Yet I have no real reason for my sorrow, but as you know, one stops loving oneself when one is not loved. There it is! I can see the day coming when I will hate myself. (AM45)

As her crisis intensifies, Mina is haunted by a recurring dream in which all the tenacity and pain of her resistance against the Father's values are crystallized. In it she is returning from a ball during the 'wee small hours' of the morning and, as the bells of the nearby Ursuline convent toll 'the nun's rising' (AM51), she sees a vision of the famous widow Mme de Repentigny, a member of New France's 'high society,' looking at her with a gaze of 'deep sympathy' (AM52) and directing her by a gesture towards the gate of the convent. Mina is paralysed: 'I could not move: a terrible force was fastening me to the earth' (AM46, 52). Noticing her resistance, Mme de Repentigny rests her 'luminous' forehead on her hands joined in prayer, and 'then I felt I was being torn away, but what pain I felt in my whole being!' (AM52). Still struggling on awakening against the implications of this dream, Mina writes: 'May God permit me to retain the healthy enjoyment of life!' (AM52).

In the final stage of dissolution of her self, Mina has adopted the language of Valriant: 'I am visibly turning to austerity ... In spite of everything, at times one feels that sacrifice is worth more than any joy' (AM58–9). Her friend Emma's letters as well have hardened into a vision of the futility of earthly love: 'It is the cold, the barren and the dull which make the bottom of the sea, and it is not love that makes the foundation of life' (AM61). Mina's last words to Emma are a striking repetition of the hierarchical imagery Angéline had used to speak of her own relationship with her father: 'I would rather obey him than give orders to others. That's the way it is – and I'm grateful to him for wanting to tear me away from those puerile and futile matters that men usually appear nobly to surrender to us' (AM64).

By her own admission, Mina has come to scorn the female values that formerly made up the centre of her universe, losing her own centre of gravity to become an insignificant planet gravitating around the sun of Charles. In her last letter to Maurice, who is now studying in France, all traces of struggle have disappeared, and Mina has become the inoffensive mystic who a few generations later will be

a familiar figure to readers of Quebec women's poetry. Winter has
come to Valriant, and in spite of her friends' earlier predictions that
she would die of boredom there, Mina spends hours walking along
the shore, ecstatically contemplating 'something tempestuous,
something delightful': 'These terrible east winds enchant me. I enter
with delight into the month of storms, and if I had my way I would
often go down to the shore; but the proud aristocrat who reigns
here does not allow it' (AM71). Ironically, for Charles she has become
a weak person. While formerly he would ask her opinion using the
term coined by Louis XIV for his formidable mistress, Mme de
Maintenon ('What does "your solidity" think?' [AM9]), now 'He
says I'm like an unoccupied water nymph: he disdainfully calls me
his trembling one, his delicate one. (Angéline has never had a cold
in her life)' (AM71). Mina claims to be content; but then, those who
aren't admitted to the banquet often make do with the crumbs.

THE FALL FROM PARADISE

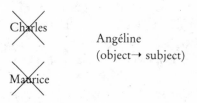

Figure 5 Angéline – from object to subject

In the second section of the novel, all the repressed violence of the
preceding pages explodes in a bizarre sequence that moves author
and reader in less than three pages from a state of eternal bliss
('nothing, absolutely nothing, was lacking to the young, charming,
deeply enamoured couple' [AM72]) to the solitary space of writing
('This noble young woman, who in her sorrow had drawn apart from
others, with the proud timidity of delicate souls, used to write
occasionally' [AM74]).

Angéline's fall from Paradise is caused by two irreparable events:
the death of her father and the loss of her beauty. As if the author
wanted to insure that this part of her novel at least could not be

recuperated by the dominant ideology, she presents it through the authoritative voice of an omniscient narrator and in the unchangeable time of the past definite tense. But even here, where Conan's writing is close to more 'male' forms of representation, there are signs that it is a woman who is writing and a *female* narrator who is telling the story.

Both unprepared for and 'unrealistic' according to traditional novel standards, these events correspond to a rebellion of nature against the sterile culture of Valriant and a plunge into time, reality, and female literary space for Angéline. Significantly they also allow her to refuse the traditional female roles of marriage and motherhood.

Returning from a hunting trip, Charles inexplicably entangles his gun in the branches of a tree and in less than a sentence the patriarch is dead: 'His rifle became tangled in the branches of a tree; a shot fired and he was mortally wounded' (AM72). The economy of narration here makes all the more striking the symbolic contrast between the patriarchal hunting trip and gun, on the one hand, and the tree on the other, as an image of nature's revenge. A little further ahead in the Quebec literary landscape there will be other symbols of a dominated nature taking its revenge: the forest in *Maria Chapdelaine*, the river in *Master of the River*, the land in *Thirty Acres*, the fire in *The Woman and the Miser*. Unlike the biblical account, where the tree is the symbol of knowledge of the earth and Eve is the *active* transgressor of the Law of the Father, here the tree itself seems to intervene and force the passive Angéline to metamorphosis. We shall see in the following chapter how this pattern is replicated in the novel of the land, where nature plays the role of a powerful ally of the all-too-submissive female characters.

Making the link with the Genesis myth even more explicit, Angéline in her weakened state literally falls, injuring her face so badly on the pavement that an operation is necessary, from which she emerges disfigured. Many of the psychoanalytical analyses of the novel have pointed out that this unrealistic event seems to correspond to some blocked impulse in the author's psyche; and certainly the description of the weakness leading to Angéline's fall is close to being psychoanalytical in its language: 'In this girl of mysteriously deep sensibility, pain seemed to act as a poison' (AM73). Pain also acts as a catalyst for liberation, however, since it frees Angéline from her stereotypical beauty and leads her towards writing.

From the loss of beauty it is indeed a short step to the solitude of the writer, and that step will be made possible by the fiancé's reaction. That Maurice's love does not survive Angéline's loss of beauty is not entirely surprising, given that in the first section of the novel she revealed little of substance beneath her too-perfect surface. For the narrator, however (and it is here that we begin to suspect the presence of a *gendered* narrator), Maurice's inconstancy is all too typical of his sex: 'In the love of a man, even when it seems as deep as the ocean, there are lacunae, unexpected dry spots. And when his fiancée had lost the enchanting charm of her beauty, Maurice Darville's heart cooled' (AM74). Too proud to accept the pity he offers as a substitute, Angéline returns Maurice's ring to him and withdraws to the now empty house at Valriant. Mina has also abandoned her, having entered the Ursuline order soon after Charles's death, and for Angéline the loss of her friend is a 'cruel separation' (AM73). This bridging section ends with a presentation of Angéline's diary, which makes up the third and final section of the novel – and to which all the preceding violence was perhaps only the necessary prelude: 'These intimate pages may interest those who have loved and suffered' (AM74).

THE DIARY OF ANGÉLINE: A WOMAN'S WRITING

Even the title of the third section of the novel – '*Feuilles détachées,*' or 'Torn-out leaves' – suggests the fragmentary nature of the literary space into which Angéline has fallen. A space of exile and spiritual wandering, it is surprisingly modern, unlike anything that has preceded it in the nineteenth-century French-Canadian novel, and a remarkable example of female literary space. Having blown apart the patriarchal triangle that conferred an 'identity' (that of the woman-object) on her heroine, Conan is here writing in a voice that seems close to autobiography: the author's 'face' and the character's 'mask' blending in the voice of this heroine whose face is henceforth hidden by a black veil. Angéline writes to communicate with an absent other who bears the successive names of father, fiancé, female friend, mother, and God – and who could also be called 'reader,' or, better still, 'female reader.' Her openness to this other is at once a sign of her vulnerability and an invitation to an intimate exchange, one that refuses to hide behind the masks and roles of realism.

As she writes, Angéline surveys the space of her own deepest self and discovers her links not only with others but with time, the rhythms of nature, and the female body. With the patriarchal triangle exploded and the heroine on the verge of her own subjectivity, we can begin to sense the presence of a new literary structure attempting to emerge, one that *almost* emerges, one that *could have* emerged if the cultural context had been different – a 'hypothetical' structure of women's writing towards which one might expect each of the literary texts by women written after *Angéline de Montbrun* to bring us a step closer. Unlike the patriarchal triangle with its one-way arrows indicating the desire for *possession* of the object, the movement in the diagram representing women's writing is more like a circulating field of energy – one that aims not at freezing the 'other' into a fixed object-position, but rather envelops or embraces it in an unending spiral movement. What the diagram attempts to approximate is the *texture* of female friendship and of women's writing: the openness and pleasure of the women's friendships that literally erupt into the text and subvert its closed linearity.

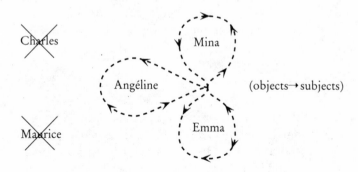

Figure 6 Women's writing

Writing for the Other

Unlike her male contemporaries, whose identity and adherence to ideological doxa seem to have been threatened neither by any sort of mysticism related to religious belief nor by the disorientation brought about by the experience of authentic writing, Laure Conan seems to have experienced in a dramatic way the loss of self that accompanies the entry into uncharted literary space. As Angéline begins to write she is alone before the blank page, away from the sustaining gaze of father and fiancé that had conferred an existence on her; and the alternately advancing and retreating movement of the entries in her diary chronicles the difficult attempt to begin to exist as a female subject. From its opening lines on, her diary is a mirror of her solitude: 'I have a kind of bleeding inside, suffocating and inescapable,' she writes in words unlike any others in the novel of her time. 'And there is no-one to whom I can speak the words that might console ... I must get used to the most terrible of solitudes, the solitude of the heart' (AM75). That this solitude is however a chosen one and that she senses its necessity is several times reiterated in the text, both in her refusal to see Maurice and in her reaction to the well-meaning friends and servants who surround her with their pity. 'How can this isolation that I desired, and that I still desire, be borne?' she writes. Several passages of the diary are addressed to the absent loved ones she conjures up in her imagination, but always she falls back into the silence of her space of exile: 'So many desolate appeals, so many passionate entreaties, and yet always inexorable silence, the silence of death' (AM109). 'My poor soul finds itself alone in a terrifying void' (AM154).

The search for a female Other

Like many patriarchal daughters cast into their own space, Angéline feels the need for a female presence, a strong mother or sister figure to act as model and confidante. 'How I would love to see Mina!' (AM129) she writes: but Mina is separated from her by the walls of the cloister and, on the one occasion when Angéline leaves Valriant to visit the Ursuline convent where her father is buried, Mina is bedridden and unable to see her. After the departure of an aunt who has irritated her with her tireless care, Angéline reflects that she needs the intimacy of 'a strong soul. Who will help me climb the difficult path? Solitude is good for those who are calm, for those who are strong' (AM78). Like her creator, she will find this maternal figure in the person of a nun who will become her spiritual adviser, and the description of her visit to an unnamed monastery on the shores of the Yamaska River is clearly modelled on Laure Conan's relation with Sr Catherine-Aurélie Caouette: 'My own mother would not have been any more tender. I could feel it, and leaning against the grille that stood between us, I burst into tears' (AM162). Unlike this spiritual mother, whose role will be to help reconcile Angéline to the values of renunciation, her own mother appears in the diary in a significantly different way than in the first section of the novel. As she herself struggles to affirm the values of life and earthly happiness against the sacrificial values of her milieu, Angéline remembers a 'young and vibrant' mother whose only fear on her deathbed was that she had been too happy in life:

Her love, her happiness weighed on her as a remorse.
'I have been too happy,' she wept, 'and heaven is not for the likes of me.' (AM137)

The call of the earth

Heaven is not for those who have been 'too happy'; and the earth, the body, all the material realm that is associated with the feminine is a temptation and a 'seduction' to be avoided on one's path to spirituality. It is not surprising that it should be a woman writer who articulates the clearest resistance to this devastating dualism, which splits heaven from earth and makes spirituality dependent on renunciation. Like Mina before her, Angéline through her love of the earth becomes a resister, incapable of the detachment demanded by her religion. In fact the roles of Angéline and Mina are reversed in this section of the novel, so that it is now Angéline who is horrified by the religious vocation of her friend, as previously Mina had been by Emma's way of life. Detachment, she reflects, is 'the death of nature, and in face of that death, like any other, everything in us rebels' (AM141).

Forced to choose between heaven and earth, Angéline again and again chooses the earth, putting off her commitment to faith in words that must have scandalized Abbé Casgrain: 'Ask Jesus Christ that he grant that I love him before I die' (AM86), she begs Mina; and elsewhere she writes 'I no longer know how to pray ... O Lord Jesus ... it is not you I desire; it is not for your love that I thirst' (AM121). When she does succeed in praying, it is in the words of a rebel daughter rooted in the earth: 'My God, I must learn to forget how beautiful the earth is! ... I try in vain to look towards heaven' (AM120). In a scene striking in its parallelism with a scene from *Maria Chapdelaine* thirty years later, Angéline emerges as a more stubborn resister than her famous literary daughter. Counselled by the *curé* to abandon her mourning for her dead lover, François Paradis, and assume her duties as a French-Canadian daughter, Maria accepts his words without question: 'In any case, since those were the priest's words ... '[18] But in an almost identical scene, Angéline rebels so violently against the idea that her father's death is a manifestation of 'God's will' that she faints: 'My whole being rebelled against that will and with what force! what violence!' (AM81). On awakening, she hears the words of the *curé*: 'My daughter, look towards heaven,' but her response is one of refusal: 'And turning towards the earth I wept' (AM82). A final reference to the heaven-earth duality shows how Angéline has come to regard her instinct for earthly values as a deformity or an illness: 'I wish I could think about heaven. But I cannot. I'm like that sick woman spoken of in the Gospel, who was all bent over and unable to look upwards' (AM153).

This inability to accept the teachings of her religion seems to provide a far more convincing explanation for Angéline's guilt and inner division than the 'incest theme' that has been so dear to the Freudian critics. Angéline's tragedy, like that of her creator, is that she lacks a 'context' – other voices in her milieu that could sustain her in her instinctive perception of the alienation inherent in the religious values of her time: 'Eternity, that shoreless sea, that bottomless abyss in which we will all be engulfed!' she writes. 'If I could only get that thought thoroughly into my mind' (AM100). Her female bond with the earth seems at times stronger than her will, stronger than her self, as if nature were acting through her and pushing her towards transgression. Called to heaven by culture, she is attached to earth as if by a 'powerful weight': 'I don't understand this powerful weight that ties me to the earth ... Mina, heaven is very high, very far away, and I'm just a poor creature'* (AM100–1).

Powerful too, however, is the weight of culture and ideology, the entire patriarchal past that speaks to Angéline through the memory of her father and its associated guilt. 'If I could forget him I would be full of contempt for myself' (AM69) she writes; and the strange choice of the verb 'pouvoir' (could) rather than the use of a simple imperfect (*'si je l'oubliais'*) is indicative of her ambivalence. Charles's first words in the novel ('Isn't it true that she will be without excuse if she ever forgets me?') are surely a factor in the paralysis and guilt against which Angéline struggles in her diary. By the very act of writing she has lost her innocence, distanced herself from him and from the 'heavenly father' who would keep her in silence; by writing herself into language as a woman and a subject, she has torn apart the whole ancient hierarchy of values based on women's submission: 'I loved my father with an ardent tenderness, and yet I would have left him without any regret for my heavenly father,' she writes to Mina. '... Now the Christian woman, blinded by her faults, no longer understands what a child's innocence understood. Mina, I have seen near at hand the abyss of despair. Neither God nor my father is pleased with me, and that thought adds still more to my sadness' (AM101).

Writing in the Father's House

Isolated within her father's house as she writes, Angéline provides an image of all women writers seeking to define their own uncharted space within patriarchal culture and language. And given the role

---

* Note: The original French here is the word *'créature,'* which, in addition to its connotation of 'creature' or 'human being,' was also commonly used in popular speech during Conan's period as a condescending but apparently affectionate way of referring to women.

assigned to women in assuring the survival of French-Canadian culture, the patriarchal house is a particularly privileged symbol of Quebec women's literary space.

For Angéline, the house in which she writes is repeatedly described as a place of 'eternal mourning': 'When I came back here, when I crossed the threshold which his body had so recently passed through, I knew that mourning had taken root here for ever' (AM142). Her eventual defeat by the forces of rigidity and death seems indissociable from her inability to leave her father's house, and, like Mina, the reader is tempted to urge her to flee Valriant: 'Dear friend, you suggest I travel now that my health permits it. I think about it sometimes, but really I cannot bring myself to leave this place. My heart has its roots here' (AM127). It is here, despite the intolerable weight of the past casting a shadow over her present, that she feels she must confront the drama of her self: 'Oh! the sadness of these walls. At times they seem to be oozing melancholy and coldness. And yet I love this house where I have been so happy – this dear house where sorrow has entered forever!' (AM125). Like her pet canary beating its wings against the windows of the house, Angéline remains trapped within it and writes without any real hope of metamorphosis, exhausting herself in a constant battle against her own instincts: 'My canary is bored; he beats his wings against the window panes. Poor little one! having wings and not being able to use them! Who does not know that frustration?' (AM110).

The sea and the moon: Female presences

Outside the window, however, nature is a constant reminder of time, process, and the possibility of regeneration. Waking in the morning in sadness, Angéline hears the song of the birds 'delightfully' calling her to hope (AM77), and from her open window the smell of the salt air invites her to walk on the shore and breathe the 'harsh and bracing perfume of the beach' (AM79). While in the first section of the novel she had been a silent reflector of the paternal sun, here she discovers her closeness to the maternal elements of the sea and the moon.

The sea in particular is associated by her with the human psyche and with her own drama. Angéline loves the sea, and it is constantly speaking to her as a maternal presence, urging her to metamorphosis: 'The voice of the sea rises above all the others' (AM125). Associated with time and change, it is however an ambivalent symbol, calling her to a 'dangerous' birth, forbidden by the accepted ideas of her time. Before her, Emma had felt this same sense of a 'shimmering, marvellous' presence in the depths of the ocean, and, giving in to the ideas prevalent in her society, had concluded that it was a deceptive beauty (AM61). Mina as well had felt caressed by the 'music of the waves,' which threw 'a velvet cloak of melancholy' over her pain (AM45). For Angéline, the sea hides in its depths some disquieting truth, a dangerous fluid circulating in the depths of the psyche and threatening to overwhelm her: 'To upset the sea a storm is needed, but to trouble a heart to the very bottom, what does it take? Alas, a trifle, a shadow ... What is the cause of this? Is it not with emotion as with those strong and dangerous currents which circulate everywhere, and the nature of which remains a deep mystery?' (AM113–14).

If the sea is a natural mother calling Angéline to explore those depths, her spiritual or cultural mother, the Virgin Mary ('the Star of the Ocean'), is a rampart against them. Like many women who have broken with patriarchal values or been destroyed by them, Angéline experiences periods of incapacitating depression that fill her with fear and self-contempt: 'I am ashamed of myself ... I am thoroughly incapable of any work, of any application whatsoever ... Oh father! what would you think of me? ... I am afraid of myself' (AM120–1). On one such occasion, while a storm rages on the ocean outside, she takes shelter in the church and prays to the Virgin Mary to save her from the abyss: 'Yesterday there was a raging wind, a terrifying storm. – Kneeling in the church ... I listened to the sound of the sea, which was still less agitated than my heart. In the deepest recesses of my soul, strange wild sorrows were answering the roars of the waves ... Oh Mary! stretch out your gentle hand to those whom the abyss wants to swallow. O Virgin! O Mother! have pity!' (AM121).

Taken together, the passages referring to the sea form a constellation of images linking *mer* (sea), *mère* (mother), and *amertume* (bitterness); liquidity, birth, sadness, nostalgia for the maternal origin. However, despite the fear of the 'abyss' expressed in the above passage, Angéline does not allow herself to dissolve in the watery depths – as Conan's famous contemporary and literary 'brother' Emile Nelligan was to do a decade or so later, in the final line of his best-known poem: 'Alas, he has drowned in the abyss of his dreams.'[19] On the contrary, she inhabits and appropriates for herself the space of sadness to which she seems condemned, commenting on a woman who has showered pity on her in the following words: 'Poor woman! She strikes me as the type of woman who expects to sweeten the bitterness of the sea with a drop of water at the end of her finger' (AM114). The birth to which the sea has called her is finally an impossible one, and the images of sterility that gradually triumph over those of growth in the text are a sign of her weakening resistance: 'Nothing on earth has ever grown out of ashes ... the extinguished edges of a volcano are forever sterile. No flower or moss will ever be seen there' (AM114). The following passage, where Angéline reflects that the sea always closes over its treasures, leaving only bits of debris on the rocks to speak of their former existence, offers a striking objective correlative for Laure Conan's own coded and censored writing in this novel: 'The sea keeps its wealth, the heart keeps its treasures. It cannot speak of life, it cannot speak of love, and all the efforts of passion are similar to those of the storm which draws from the abyss only scattered debris, those delicate bits of seaweed one sees on the sand and the rocks, mixed with a little foam' (AM143).

Like the sea, the maternal moon is an ambivalent symbol, awakening by its soft light a sense of earthly joy, but throwing Angéline into a troubled state by its forbidden message of life:

Delightful evening ... if any earthly joy could still stir my heart, I would want it to be on a night like this, in this beautiful garden where the peaceful light of the moon rests ...

But this kind of meditation is not good for me. My youth is reawakened, passionate, and keen. Nature is always for us only a reflection, an echo of our inner life, and this soft transparency of beautiful nights ... these murmurs that rise everywhere, only disturb me. (AM147)

By the end of the novel, when she has finally ceased to struggle against the ideology of abnegation and self-sacrifice, Angéline will abandon the moon along with her belief in human love: 'the memories of love bring no consolation – no more than the rays of the moon bring us warmth' (AM161).

The fall into the body

As well as awakening her to the rhythm of nature, Angéline's fall into literary space also plunges her into the forbidden realm of the body. With her loss of beauty comes the dismaying realization that this body she inhabits is a prison from which there is no escape. Women's beauty may be condemned as a vanity and a 'seduction,' but without it, she learns, they are nothing in the eyes of society: 'In spite of my fortune, a beggarwoman would refuse to trade places with me,' she realizes (AM84). Again and again she returns to the humiliating truth that Maurice's love has been replaced by pity: 'Was my beauty the only thing he loved in me, then?' (AM112).

The introduction of a secondary character afflicted with a 'horrible ugliness' (AM90) – the spinster Véronique Désileux – underlines the fact that Angéline has fallen into a universe inhabited by scornful fathers who, while themselves pretending to spirituality, communicate to their daughters that approval depends on their physical beauty. Learning of Mlle Désileux's death, Angéline recalls that as a child she would be taken by her father to visit this poor woman and forced to overcome her repulsion and kiss her. Speaking 'most casually,' the benevolent patriarch would oblige his daughter to 'perform her duty': ' "You see," he would say, "she knows that she is frightful, and we must try to make her forget that terrible truth" ' (AM81). Such a hypocritical insistence on physical appearance has of course the effect of increasing Mlle Désileux's own self-contempt and her devotion to Charles. In a letter written to Angéline shortly before her death, she calls herself a 'poor disgraced woman' totally dependent on Charles's benevolence and relates that after his death 'I wanted to do like the faithful dog who crawls to his master's grave and dies there' (AM92). 'I have lived without friendship, without love,' she adds. 'Even my father could not conceal the aversion I aroused in him' (AM93).

A woman capable of describing herself as a 'faithful dog,' a woman unable to love herself and tempted to die when her beloved 'master' disappears, a woman guilt-ridden because of some unnamed 'disgrace' related to her appearance: such is the world in which Angéline must now attempt to find her way. Her own sense of the positive value of the body is suggested by the images she uses to evoke Mina's entry into convent life, all of which suggest an unnatural death. The pain she feels on receiving from Maurice a lock of his sister's formerly magnificent hair seems much more than a simple preoccupation with appearance; but it is not until sixty years later, in Anne Hébert's first volume of poetry,[20] that the association between women's hair and the erotic will reveal its liberating potential: 'Poor little Mina ... Dear sister, I cannot look without emotion at those beautiful brown curls which you used to set so well. Who could have told us that some day that superb hair would fall under the monastic scissors?' (AM100). Mina's new role is evoked in images of constraint and death: the day of her entry into the cloister, she appears 'pale as a corpse' (AM131), the sound of the cloister door closing behind her is 'sinister,' and the words of the nuns around her are 'incomprehensible' to Angéline (AM131). 'So now you are consecrated to God, obliged to love our Lord with the love of a virgin and a wife' (AM100), she writes to her friend. Religious life, she concludes, is like the death of a child, 'a tearing away from nature, but, in the eyes of faith, full of ineffable consolations' (AM130).

Angéline's defeat

If these consolations elude Angéline, it is because she confusedly senses that the peace she seeks is a death in life: 'Pray that I will find peace, that supreme good possessed by those whose hearts are dead' (AM102). What critics have seen as Angéline's 'masochism'[21] is also her inability to accept this death and to leave the troubled depths of the psyche alone; she herself is horrified by the fascination they exert on her and blames herself for her inability to sublimate: 'Foolish woman! I pray for peace and I seek trouble. I am like a wounded person who feels a bitter pleasure in aggravating her wounds, in seeing blood flow from them' (AM103). 'This behaviour is not wise, I know; yet who does not love the storm more than the flat calm – that terrible calm which destroys, which annihilates the proudest bravery?' (AM120).

Like the voices of Maurice and Mina, Angéline's own voice will finally be defeated – but only through the intervention in the narrative of a male voice that provides a precise image of the dominant ideology of the period. A letter from Father S., a missionary priest working with the Chippeway Indians of northern Quebec and a protégé of Charles de Montbrun, constitutes a *deus ex machina* ending that offers another striking parallel with *Maria Chapdelaine*. Even more explicitly than the voices that call Maria to obedience at the end of Hémon's novel, that of Father S. represents the imposition of French-Canadian Catholic culture on all that its instinct for domination sees as 'other' and therefore inferior: the native peoples, nature, the body, and women.

After describing his baptism of a dying young Indian woman who, he assures Angéline, has become his 'protectress in heaven' (AM156), Father S. urges her to abandon the 'cold joys of the flesh' and the 'poor happiness of this earth' (AM156): 'If [God] destroyed your happiness, it is that happiness was not good for you' (AM157). Significantly, he holds up before her the model of the female martyrs of Christianity, who knew that 'to be a Christian was to know how to suffer': 'How many young girls there were among the martyrs! Can you imagine them crying over earthly happiness and the sweetness of life?' (AM158). An image of Father S.'s imposition of cultural values on nature is the medal of Mary Immaculate he sends to Angéline, telling her that he often attaches such medals to the trees of the forest, 'to scent the solitude' (AM159).

As the next entry in Angéline's diary indicates, this medal indeed has a strange power – not only over the forces of nature but over the related ones of writing. She begins by noting that she has not written in her journal for several days, and adds that she has begun to wear the medal, substituting it for the locket containing portraits of her father and Maurice that she had worn and that she has now thrown in the fire along with Maurice's letters: 'Is it the impetus given by a strong hand? – there is within me a strange power which pushes me towards renunciation, towards sacrifice' (AM159).

The novel approaches its conclusion with a final visit to the realm of nature, a walk in the Valriant woods, now devastated by approaching winter: 'The sun was gilding the bare fields, and crickets were singing in the dry grass; yet autumn has done its work well, and one can feel sadness everywhere' (AM163). In the cycle of nature's death there is however a peace from which Angéline feels excluded: 'But what a profound serenity is part of it all. And why, in my deathly calm, should I not also have serenity?' (AM163). Recalling a passage from St Francis de Sales, she reflects on 'that farewell that we must eventually say to everything,' and concludes with a denial of all the values her writing had struggled to affirm: 'Since we must die, it is the happy ones we must pity' (AM163).

In this final renunciation Angéline has rejoined her mother, defeated like her by the forces of death. The only remaining farewell to be made is to the ever-faithful Maurice, and the exchange of letters between the two lovers with which the novel ends echoes by its wording the struggle of life over the values of death that has been the main theme of the novel. This time, however, Maurice's voice carries the resistance theme and affirms the values of life and process. Begging Angéline to abandon her suffering and marry him, he points out that, according to those close to her, even her disfigured face has begun to heal: 'the traces of the cruel event fade daily ... Everybody says it; can you ignore it?' (AM165).

Angéline's reply – a refusal of happiness and the values of life, but also a refusal of marriage, of men, and of her father's wishes – is as ambiguous as the entire novel. Her own explanation for this refusal is entirely in conformity with the ideology of self-sacrifice she had formerly struggled against. It is clear that she still loves Maurice ('O my loyal friend, I have nothing, absolutely nothing, to forgive you' [AM166]), but, now firmly committed to the teachings of the church, she argues that 'life is sorrow' and that their happiness, if it had survived, would have been a deviation from the divinely ordained path of suffering: 'Tell me, if the enchantment of our love and happiness had continued, what would have become of us? How could we ever have resigned ourselves to dying?' (AM167).

But Angéline's refusal also offers a coherent ending to her narrative journey and a desolate image of the woman writer's situation. It is finally religion that has triumphed over this woman's writing – the Word of the Father, thanks to which she has finally come to believe that Christ himself has been the hidden presence behind the events in her own story, the author and the omniscient narrator controlling a plot in which her own sense of freedom was no more than an illusion. Defeated, she has no further role to play, other than that of the daughter who 'repeats' the paternal word:

I see and feel that He asks of me complete renunciation, that I must be His alone.

Maurice, it is He who has directed everything, it is his will that is keeping us apart. This is the word my father spoke to me at the hour of his anguish, and I am repeating it to you. (AM167)

At the same time, it is possible that the final image of Angéline as a daughter in mourning and as an 'eternal fiancée' was the only option available to a woman writer desiring to conserve a subject status for her female character. By eliminating from the plot both the father and the fiancé for whom Angéline was an object of exchange, Laure Conan has allowed her heroine a sad kind of independence. Maurice is certainly conscious of this fact, for he tells Angéline in his final letter that he and Charles should have *ordered* her to marry: 'My goodness, why didn't I think of having him order you, at the last, not to delay our wedding? Unfortunately, neither he nor I thought about it; but do you believe that he approves your resolution?' (AM165).

Maurice is right: women are 'slippery customers' once you forget the orders. For it is precisely in this *deferral* of the exchange of Angéline that female literary space has found room to unfold. In a strange passage in the novel's first section, Mina describes how she and Angéline envy the women of New France whose lovers and husbands were killed in battle or scalped by Indians, for not only had these women thereby achieved autonomy, but the men they mourned were strong men, deserving of love: 'There is no doubt that that was a great era for Canadian women. It is true that once in a while they heard that their beloved ones had been scalped, but what did that matter? The men of that time were worth crying over' (AM18).

Dressed in the black of her 'eternal mourning' and with her devastated face covered by a veil, Angéline has joined these women and achieved a position other than the one of wife and mother prescribed by her culture. If only by its refusal of this role, Conan's novel is subversive; but what violence to self has been necessary, and what a twisted version of autonomy has emerged from the fragmented narrative! Women writers after Conan will inherit this negative legacy, and paradoxically Angéline in her defeat has in a sense become for them a monstrous mother who has betrayed them in the name of God and country.

But it is before that defeat that the literary space of *Angéline de Montbrun* exists for the reader, and it is in the voices of resistance that constitute the novel's structure that we find the positive heritage left by Laure Conan to the women writers who follow her. True to the coded nature of the entire novel, Angéline's last letter to Maurice contains a final image of resistance submerged within its edifying rhetoric – that of a ravaged nature that persists against all that would destroy it: 'To be disillusioned is not to be detached. You know, my friend, the denuded tree still clings to the earth' (AM167).

In any case, it is clear to the reader that she will continue to write.

'Yes, Monseigneur ... but ...'

Laure Conan also continued to write, in spite of the co-opting of her novel by the dominant ideology – or could it be that it was *thanks* to the official consecration of her novel that she was able to continue writing? The ambivalence of her work, beneath its irreproachable surface, is so total that it is impossible to know. Up until the words spoken on her deathbed, however, Conan continued to articulate a voice of female resistance to the very values that on the surface level her works uphold and propagate.

Taken as a whole, Conan's writing seems to exhaust itself in a lifelong, guilty hesitation between submission and revolt, its entire structure corresponding to a space where male and female values are engaged in an uneven struggle, with the triumph of the male assured by its control over the concepts of religion and nation. In different ways, it tells the same story over and over again: that of the daughter reduced to silence by the voice of the father-censor. In *Si les Canadiennes le voulaient* (If Canadian women really wanted to),[22] a patriotic play addressed to women that appeared only two years after *Angéline de Montbrun*, the author's spokesperson is a male character who exhorts women to abandon their futile preoccupations and undertake the task of building a strong Catholic nation, impervious to English domination. The message corresponds perfectly with that propagated by the clerical and political leaders of the period, and it was one Conan herself seems to have tried to follow in her life as well as in her work. In *Aux Canadiennes* (To Canadian women), an anti-alcoholism tract published in 1913, she subscribes entirely to the doctrine of 'separate spheres' that gave women a prestige linked to their 'feminine' influence on morals while at the same time reserving real power and authority for men: 'What you can do? Mesdames ... but you can do everything ... Even though you lack authority, you have charm and you have sovereign and irresistible influence, and your duties are the foundation of social life as well as of human life.'[23]

However, two recent studies of Conan's work suggest that the conflicts underlying the writing of this 'well-behaved daughter' are ideological in nature, and that they are the veiled expression of the author's resistance to established values. According to René Dionne, Conan's female characters, unlike their male counterparts, never attain the resignation society demands of them. In *A l'oeuvre et à l'épreuve* (At work and through hardships, 1891), Gisèle Méland never succeeds in following her adored Charles Garnier on the path to sacrifice and abnegation, for 'her will is as weak as her flesh: sacrifice brings her not joy but pain, [and] she feels that joy is equally important to her.'[24] In *La Vaine Foi* (Faith in vain, 1919), Marcelle Rochefeuille resists committing herself to religious faith because she needs – and these are Conan's words – 'freedom, life, enjoyment and pleasure.'[25]

According to Dionne, the conflict between the values of heaven and earth is finally resolved for Conan through her commitment to the national struggle, 'a noble cause which was tangible and close to her.'[26] And there is in fact little doubt that from the final pages of *Angéline de Montbrun* on, patriotism offers a glimmer of potential meaning in the drab landscape of religious faith: an important struggle into which this woman who appears to have been made for commitment threw herself with passion. But a study of Conan's work by Maïr Verthuy demonstrates convincingly that her heroines manifest a great deal of ambivalence about their society, and especially about a nationalism that in many ways was built on women's backs:

the heroines of these works are autonomous and useful to society only when they live apart from men ... Celibacy is a choice they make not only in relation to the occupant, but to their own compatriots. The challenge for them is not to preserve the integrity of their country in the face of the enemy, but to preserve their own integrity in the face of a country that refuses their values ... These novels are novels of waiting.[27]

The resistance that traverses all of Laure Conan's life and work appears in perhaps its most heartrending form in *L'Obscure Souffrance* (A hidden suffering, 1919), a short novel published when the author was seventy-four years old. As if obsessed with a wound that refuses to heal, the plot of the novel gravitates around the same tension as that of *Angéline de Montbrun*: the unresolved struggle of a young girl against the influence of a father who is opposed to her own self-realization. Called by filial duty to sacrifice her own life in the care of an alcoholic father, the young Faustine (whose name evokes a rebellion that is at once unlimited, sacrilegious, and destined to defeat) is torn between the voice of the fathers, who summon her to sacrifice, and a woman's voice, which urges her on the contrary to live according to her own instincts. Suffocating under paternal rule, she leaves the countryside where she was born and travels to Montreal, where an aunt invites her to stay until she has had time to resolve the problems that are troubling her. On the point of accepting, she makes the mistake of going to confession, and is counselled by the priest to return to her father's house and to accept her duty in a spirit of resignation. So much for the attempt to live happily! Like all Conan's other heroines, Faustine finally gives in to the voice of patriarchal authority, but the contradictions she experiences indicate that age has done nothing to appease her creator's inner struggle between her own instinct for happiness and the teachings of her church:

I expect nothing of the future. But youth can only be partially suppressed, and a dormant and intense sensibility has strange moments of awakening.

The need that all beings feel to make another attempt at happiness still lives in my soul like a hope. I feel in myself an immense power for happiness ... But ... I know that this happiness would not be enough for me, that I would get tired of it, that I would always have within me an abyss of eagerness.[28]

It is this insatiability, this struggle for incarnation against enormous odds, that makes Laure Conan a model of resistance for her literary daughters. The last words of hers that we possess capture in a dramatic way her typically female tenacity. Her friend Renée Des Ormes recounts that on her deathbed, in response to a priest who asked her to pray for her country and her compatriots on her arrival in heaven, Conan said: '*Yes, Monseigneur... but as a woman who remembers having lived on this earth.*'[29]

CHAPTER TWO

Alphonsine Moisan's subversion:
The voice of the repressed feminine
in the novel of the land

It may have taken centuries for man to be able to interpret the sense of his work, of his works: to construct for himself, unendingly, substitutes for his prenatal dwelling place. From the depths of the earth to the heights of the firmament? Taking from the feminine, again and again, the tissue or the texture of space. In exchange – and it is no real exchange – he buys her a house, even imprisons her in it, imposes limits on her that are the counterpart of the unlimited site where he places her in spite of herself. He envelops her within walls even as he envelops himself and his possessions in her flesh ...

But, to the extent that she remains alive, she is constantly undoing his work, distinguishing herself from both the envelope and the possession, incessantly creating a space of interval, play, movement and freedom that disturbs his perspective, his world and his limits.

Luce Irigaray, *Ethique de la différence sexuelle*

What a fine girl, Séraphin was thinking, unable to take his eyes off her. And son of a bitch! What buttocks too, what buttocks! Young Omer Lemont won't be bored with that around.

Claude-Henri Grignon, *The Woman and the Miser*

In the first scene of Ringuet's *Thirty Acres*,[1] the protagonist, Euchariste Moisan, and his future father-in-law are sitting on the porch of the latter's house. Before them lies the splendour of the Laurentian landscape in autumn; their exchange of words circles around its

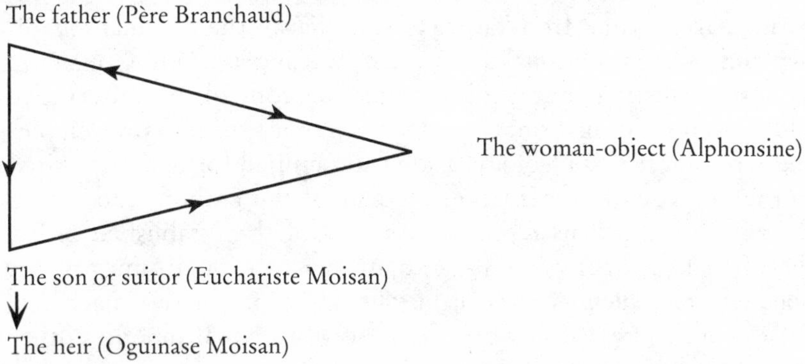

The father (Père Branchaud)

The woman-object (Alphonsine)

The son or suitor (Euchariste Moisan)

The heir (Oguinase Moisan)

Figure 7 Novels of the land by men: *Thirty Acres*

object without ever stating it directly. What is being concluded between the two men is the exchange of a woman, Alphonsine Branchaud, whose status as the older man's daughter will be changed to that of the younger man's wife. Significantly, the subject of Alphonsine is never brought into the two men's conversation: there is indeed no need for her name to be spoken in order that this pact be concluded. As for the Laurentian landscape, that 'brilliant symphony' (TA17) of colours with which the author punctuates the silence between the two men, it also will be the object of exchange in a pact that will never be made explicit in the text: that which links author and reader in a shared complicity.

In the novel of the land we are in the territory of the 'traditional novel.' Unlike Laure Conan, who must depart from this form in order to allow her female character to accede to the status of subject, the novelists of the land are more like Angéline's suitor, Maurice Darville, who agree to 'play the game' according to the Father's rules in exchange for initiation by virtue of their maleness into the 'rightful' possession of woman and of the world. While in Conan's novel the object, Angéline, begins to speak and in so doing explodes the forms of traditional narrative, here it is the *exchange* of the woman-object that makes possible the development of the male protagonist's identity and the linear unfolding of his narrative journey.

Like their protagonists, the male novelists of the land have a heritage to transmit from father to son: that of the dominant ideology and of the traditional novel form. Writing as Laure Conan did in a paternalistic culture firmly under the control of conservative and Catholic nationalism, they create a literary form that resembles and reproduces this ideology: a solid and unified form ideally suited to the purpose of perpetuating the Law of the Father. And cast in the role of 'guardians of the house' and of the established order, their female characters conform to an ancient male dream: passive, obedient, and silent, beasts of burden and reproductive machines, these women created in words have no real textual function other than that of reflecting the male ego. One cannot but wonder what it is these male novelists are attempting to exclude or keep at bay by erecting such solid walls around the territory of the imagination. Is it solely 'the strangers [who] have surrounded us,'[2] as Quebec literary criticism has traditionally argued? Or could it be, as the passage from Luce Irigaray cited at the beginning of this chapter suggests, that these carefully built structures also hide a fear of the feminine?

As far as the act of writing is concerned, one of the disadvantages of being a Maurice Darville, or an obedient son in the Father's House of the Quebec literary tradition, is that one finds oneself confronted by an *already written* text. Rather than facing a blank page on which he can inscribe his own story, the novelist of the land confronts a world that, like the landscape in the opening scene of *Thirty Acres*, resembles an 'ancient missal' (TA17): a sacred text to which he can only add his approval. And it is perhaps this lack of freedom that explains the 'rage to possess' that increases from novel to novel, and that finds specific expression within texts in an ever tighter control exercised over female characters as the genre develops from its nineteenth-century beginnings up until its apogee in the period preceding the Second World War. From Maria Chapdelaine, who stands on the doorstep of the house dreaming of the happiness that awaits her, to Menaud's daughter, Marie, confined within the interior of the house and renouncing a happiness that would be 'bought at the price [of] her father's disapproval,'[3] to the corpse of Donalda Poudrier, the 'perfect wife,' the history of the novel of the land is that of a struggle between the orthodox novelist and a text riddled with fissures and contradictions, through which emerges (though often unheard by the novelists themselves) the voice of the repressed feminine.

Possessing woman / possessing the world

It is perhaps useful to state explicitly at this point what the reader will certainly have deduced: except for Germaine Guèvremont, whose two novels bring the classic period of the novel of the land to a close by *opening* it, paradoxically, to 'otherness,' all the novelists of the land admitted to the Quebec literary canon are men. All these male writers use 'traditional' novel form: that is, a story recounted by an omniscient narrator (that figure critics have often compared to 'God the Father') who sees all and who manipulates all the plot's twists and turns. An essential characteristic of this form is the *illusion* of truth on which it is based: like the pact between Euchariste and Père Branchaud, the pact between the traditional novelist and his reader owes its power and its solidity to the fact that it is never made explicit. The fictional lie exists, and we agree to believe in it in order to allow a greater 'truth' to emerge; we are reassured by the certainty that, by the 'magic' of art, the chaos of reality will be transformed into order and what is transitory will appear as eternal truth. There is indeed an astonishing resemblance between this 'traditional' view of art and patriarchal ideology: in both, all that is perceived as 'other' by the eye of an invisible observer is fused into a larger unity by its transformation into a reflection of and support for male identity. Within the novel of the land the control of ideology over art is all the more striking and effective because of the interwoven spheres of authority presiding over the genre: that of a Catholicism which privileges eternity over time and fears above all else the female body, and of a 'dream of enduring forever' identified with the survival of the culture. As Louis Hémon had sensed, the particular dilemma of traditional French-Canadian culture was that a refusal of all change and a state of voluntary paralysis was deemed necessary for its survival: 'In the land of Quebec nothing must die and nothing must change' (MC161). The interdiction of change applies particularly to woman, whose role has been clearly defined and prescribed for all time.

If there is fragmentation in the 'solid house' of these novels, it is more subtly masked than in Laure Conan's novel, which exploded the smooth and closed surface of traditional novel form. In the men's novels, the process of fragmentation (almost certainly an unconscious act on the part of the novelists) corresponds to a key element in the Western epistemological tradition – that effected by the gaze of the male observer, which immobilizes the object of knowledge and divides it into ever smaller pieces in order to guarantee its possession. And strangely, it seems – at least at first glance – that in these novels the resistance of the external world (nature) to this act of possession is more active than that of the female characters, who are confined by the conventions of the genre within the strait-jacket of a rigidly defined role that appears to exclude all possibility of autonomous movement. We shall see, however, that it is precisely by her links with the 'inferior' realm to which she has been relegated (that of the body, of time, and of reproduction) that the female character exerts a subversive action on the novelistic universe.

A detailed comparison of two passages from *Thirty Acres* reveals not only how this appropriation of woman corresponds to that of the 'external world'; but also how textual subversion on the part of the female character can occur.

In the first passage, significantly situated in the opening scene where the exchange of Alphonsine constitutes the unspoken focus of the text, the mechanisms by which the traditional novel assumes possession of the world are used with exemplary mastery. Having situated his two characters on the porch where their conversation takes place, the narrator abandons them momentarily in order to present the reader with a panoramic view of the landscape before them. Despite its length, this passage in which the novelist takes possession of the world through the eye of an anonymous and invisible observer deserves to be quoted in full, for it reflects as if in a mirror the struggle between words and reality that constitutes the substance of the traditional novel:

In front of them and around them stretched the meadows; the shimmering spread of the flatlands, painted with the bright colours of October. The first morning frosts had illuminated the patchwork surface of the fields with the colour of saffron or old gold, making them look like an ancient missal whose pages would soon be turned by winter. Here and there the eye was drawn to copses where the black of already naked willows was interwoven with the brighter hue of still green beeches. Still further away, in the distance where the soil curled over like the rim of a cup, was a long strip of forest, a symphony of colours in which the bass notes constituted by the invincible green of the evergreens blended with the high note of the scarlet flat-leaved maples that in Quebec we call simply '*plènes*.' In the foreground, not far away, the tiled effect of the fields clashed with the russet-coloured thicket of small alders, through which could be seen the metallic shimmering of the river.

The whole spectacle was bathed in a pearly mist which caused the blue of the sky to fade and divided the landscape into strangely clearcut sections; the nearby fields; then the clumps of trees bathed with light only to the height of their trunks. From there the gaze leaped over the gap of a large space filled with milky light only to be blocked by the hermetic horizon formed by the vaporous and shimmering violet of the woods, blending into the dullness of an autumn sky. The whole scene resembled the painted sets of a cyclorama.

But neither of the two men saw the face of the land, that excessively made-up old woman's face on which the imprint of winter could already be detected. For their arms, not their eyes, linked them to the Great Mother ... (TA17)*

In the second passage, situated shortly after the conclusion of the 'pact' between Euchariste and Père Branchaud, we see Alphonsine through the eyes of her future husband:

He could see her in his mind's eye just as she was a little while before when he held her close to him on the Branchaud's veranda just before leaving, and more particularly as he saw her with the avidness of his desire: her breasts firm and generous, her mouth rather heavy, her wide hips swaying with a motion like the rocking of a cradle. A warm feeling of contentment washed over him, and its waves struck his temples repeatedly. He was going

* Note: The translation of *Thirty Acres* is based on an abridged version of the original novel, from which much of the above passage is missing. For the reader's convenience, I have however provided the corresponding page number in the English edition.

to reap far more than his imagination had sown. His heart had already felt a surge of warmth when the words assuring his possession of the desirable body of this beautiful young girl had passed between him and Branchaud. (TA28)

Reading the first of the two passages, one is immediately struck by the mastery of its execution, the solidity of this 'symphony' of colours that the author brings into existence for the reader by filtering it through the gaze of his invisible observer. The text proposes the analogy with 'the painted sets of a cyclorama'; but for the modern reader it is rather an analogy with film technique that comes to mind. In precisely the manner of a cinematic 'travelling' shot, the narrator's gaze fragments the landscape ('In front of them and around them ...,' 'Here and there ...,' 'Still further away, in the distance ...,' 'In the foreground ...') in order to reconstitute it in a new totality constructed of words. While the world that is described owes its existence to the power of this gaze, there seems nonetheless to be a dimension of *struggle* between the gaze and the world it is attempting to 'capture' (the eye is 'drawn' here and there by the landscape), and even a certain *resistance* on the part of the observed reality: 'From there the gaze leaped over the gap of a large space ... only to be blocked by the hermetic horizon ...'

In the description of Alphonsine, on the other hand, the 'object' seems less resistant to the observer's gaze. Not only is woman reduced to the status of a 'body' without face or identity existing in the 'mind's eye' of the man who contemplates her, but this body is also fragmented by the gaze into pieces easily digested by the 'greedy' subject: 'breasts,' a 'mouth,' 'wide hips.' Perceived as a body that awakens desire, a reproductive body (her hips sway with 'a motion like the rocking of a cradle'), and a body whose possession is *already assured* by the word of the father, Alphonsine enjoys none of the idealization bestowed on nature. For example, the description of her contains no suggestion of mystery or of the infinite, as the evocation of the landscape does. On the contrary, in each of the two passages the identification between woman and nature serves to diminish woman and to exalt nature: in the first, the comparison of the 'face of the land' with an 'excessively made-up old woman's face' in effect destroys the luminosity of the landscape and reveals its link to the corruption of time; in the second, the comparison between Alphonsine and the land ('He was going to reap far more than his imagination had ever sown') simply reinforces her status as an object.

Where in this strait-jacket imprisoning the female character is the possibility of subversion to be found? Precisely in the constellation of associations or images in which the author confines her. In the above passage, Alphonsine's subversion makes its appearance in the text through the desire she awakens in the forbidden realm of the body; through the introduction of another forbidden element – 'movement' – which enters the text with the oscillation of her hips; and finally through the rhythm and the power of the sea with which she is indirectly associated (the 'waves' of contentment that 'washed over [Euchariste] ... and ... struck his temples repeatedly'). 'Struck' precisely in the site of the 'mind's eye' from which he exercises his domination over woman, Euchariste here offers an image of all the protagonists (and creators) of the novel of the land. In the solidly built walls of the Father's House, female characters introduce a fissure through which will gradually seep all the values relegated to the rejected 'feminine' realm: those of the body, of desire, of time, and of change. Eventually, this inundation will be powerful enough to bring the house down.

Displacing the angle of vision: The point of a feminist reading

To attempt to grasp the meaning of the novel of the land through an examination of its female characters may well seem a dubious venture. Women, after all, occupy only a tiny corner in the vast territory of these novels, a space traversed by the nomadic *coureurs de bois* and civilized by the tenacious settlers, in which the meaning of a man's life is inseparable from his passion for the land, and the dream of a whole people is crystallized in the incantation from *Maria Chapdelaine* that haunts Félix-Antoine Savard's archetypal hero, Menaud, the master logger: 'To hold fast and endure!' (MR10). There is no doubt that the *obvious* principle of coherence in these novels (and probably the one that corresponds to the conscious intent of the novelists) lies in the reference to the national reality and its associated themes. Reading the novel of the land from this perspective, we have always taken for granted the fact that it is centred on man and then proceeded on the basis of this unexamined gender asymmetry to explore the meanings of the works. Thus the evolution of the novel of the land has always appeared to us as the gradual collapse of a beautiful dream: a *space* made dynamic at its time of origin by the equilibrium between the archetypal *coureurs de bois* and the settlers (seen as the complementary halves of the collective psyche), which gradually disintegrates as the foreign presence increases within Quebec; and a *time* symbolized by the fierce and unrelenting struggle to 'perpetuate the lineage' from father to son, a struggle that is mysteriously interrupted or blocked by the death of the son (*Master of the River*), his desertion of the family farm (*Thirty Acres*), or his weakness (*The Outlander*).[4]

Although simplified in the extreme, this 'pattern of coherence' corresponds to the broad outlines of the novel of the land tradition, a tradition which thus appears not only as *tragic*, but as condemned to tragedy by the very terms of its definition – the opposition between the need to maintain the old ways and the inevitability of change. Within this pattern, the fact that woman plays a passive but essential role is taken for granted. She is man's 'partner,' and her space is that of the house while his is that of the land or surrounding nature. Above all, she is the 'reproducer' who assures the continuation of the lineage.

A closer reading of the texts, however, reveals unresolved questions and disturbing lacunae in this nation-centred interpretation of the novels. Why is it, for example, that in this tradition based on the perpetuation of the lineage from father to son, at least one novel[5] – the most 'classic' of all, *Maria Chapdelaine* – features a female protagonist? What changes, if any, result from this shift in emphasis? Why is Menaud, the hero of Savard's *Master of the River* who is portrayed as a passionate lover of nature, *punished* by the very nature he loves, which takes his son from him and leads him to madness? In just this way François Paradis, Maria Chapdelaine's lover, had been destroyed by nature, and Euchariste Moisan, the hero of *Thirty Acres*, is betrayed by the land he considers his spouse. Even more disturbing is the question of why Menaud's daughter, Marie, falls in love with a 'traitor to the race,' the aptly named le Délié ('the untier'), whose aim is to dismantle the links in the heritage so sacred to her father.

And finally, traditional criticism has provided no explanation of the symbolic and violent fires that ravage the house in *Master of the River, Thirty Acres*, and *The Woman and the Miser*.[6] There appears to be a strange alliance between women and nature in these novels, and even to some extent between women and the 'foreigners' who threaten the continuity of the national heritage – an alliance whose function in the tradition is to subvert the paternal lineage.

A reading of the novel of the land that places woman at the centre rather than at the periphery of the reader's perception suggests the presence of another level of coherence in these novels, one that, without contradicting the 'nation-centred' interpretation or denying its validity, perhaps represents its repressed truth. In a recent feminist and structuralist reading of the novel of the land,[7] Janine Boynard-Frot demonstrates convincingly that these novels reproduce not the image of the society of their period, but that of the dominant patriarchal ideology. Boynard-Frot's exhaustive study of the female characters in novels of the land from 1860 to 1960 leads her to conclude that 'there is in fact no example of an active female subject in any of these novels.'[8] According to her interpretation, woman literally does not exist in the novel of the land; and the female character is simply 'an apparent subject whose status is analogous to that of an object.'[9]

But if Boynard-Frot's methodology allows her to make the all-important connection between these novels and patriarchal ideology, it does not permit an analysis of their equally important relation with historical reality. For, with the possible exception of Antoine Gérin-Lajoie, the author of the completely orthodox *Jean Rivard*,[10] the novelists of the land are artists and not simply purveyors of an ideology. If their novels remain alive and still speak to the modern reader, it is to the extent that they transcend their 'message' and reveal the contradictions of their era, one of the most glaring of which was without a doubt the relationship to women and to the feminine.

'To possess! To expand!'

An examination of the 'dream of enduring forever' that inspires all the protagonists of the novel of the land reveals its striking resemblance to the dream of possession that underlies the esthetic of these novels. Although it was undoubtedly justified on the collective level by the need for national survival, this dream has disquieting characteristics on the level of the individual psyche, perhaps for the precise reason that spatial expansion is not an option for its adherents. For in order to 'possess' and 'expand' (MR63) when one is dominated from outside one's own borders, it would seem that there is need of an 'other,' an echo or a reflection who will reply as nature does to Menaud: 'I am yours! I am yours!' (MR63). In Savard's novel it is clear that the male itinerary is a continuation of the Law of the Fathers ('Such was the command of the race' [MR63]), and that *her* response (that of woman and nature) is equally pre-scripted within the national text. For 'by the right of the dead whose sacred relic [she is]' (MR63), she belongs to him.

As presented in the famous lyrical ending of Louis Hémon's *Maria Chapdelaine*, the dream of enduring forever exhibits none of the rage or impotence that characterize its later manifestations. And yet it is clear even in Hémon's formulation that at the origin of this project, which provides the energy for French-Canadian survival in North America, is the dream of possession by a male subject of a 'virgin' nature that awaits his imprint before it can begin to exist in his consciousness. Although the voice of 'the land of Quebec' is presented as feminine ('now the song of a woman, now the exhortation of a priest' [MC159]), the language it speaks is that of a male lineage, that of the French 'fathers': 'Three hundred years ago we came, and we have remained ... We traced the boundaries of a new continent, from Gaspé to Montreal, from St. Jean d'Iberville to Ungava' (MC160). Paradoxically, in spite of its relative youth and energy, this dream of identity founded on the conquest of nature by culture is already obsessed with the fear of death: 'In the land of Quebec nothing must die and nothing must change' (MC161). While this fear overlaps with the fear of the arrival of foreign conquerors ('Strangers have surrounded us' [MC160]), it is nonetheless a symptom of the rigidity of an identity constructed through the mastery of all it designates as 'other.'

Reformulated by Félix-Antoine Savard twenty-five years later, the dream of enduring forever reveals itself more clearly as the expression of the dualistic world-view propagated by the clerical élite of the period. In spite of the presentation of Menaud as a passionate lover of nature, his 'pact' with nature is less an exchange than a desperate exercise in mastery. It would indeed be difficult to find a more striking illustration of the process described by Luce Irigaray, in which man, although terrified by the feminine-maternal 'otherness' that has given him birth, envelops himself in it and takes sustenance from it, all the while inserting it into a hierarchy over which he presides as lord and master. In this hierarchy where 'nature' has placed him, Menaud perceives himself as not only sovereign over the animal and plant realms, but surrounded and enveloped by them as if by the caress of a mother:

It gave him the pure and unsullied mountain air, the water of its springs, the wood for his house, the bark for his roof, and for his hearth the fire which in evening, *for his eyes' delight*, danced wildly like youth itself along the logs, while *its warmth caressed his face, wrapping him* in its golden radiance ... It gave him the fish of its lakes too, the game of its thickets; revealed to him the secrets of the silent cloisters, the high pastures where the mountain caribou graze; lent him the *science* of wing, fang, talon, of noises ... (MR44, italics mine)

It is through his *head*, through the 'science' gleaned from nature and turned back against 'her' in an act of domination, that man exercises his mastery over the world. To be 'eternal,' for him, is to erect the structure of his own identity over and against an object that he must immobilize or kill in order to assure himself of its possession. 'All of his old body given over to an unrelenting thought' (MR124), Menaud 'reflects on things,' lives in his head, and scorns the 'flesh' embodied in the love story of his daughter, Marie.[11] Far from the 'Lowlands' of the village, the house, and of woman, he soars in the ether of the 'Highlands,' seeing the mountain he adores as an 'image of the *eternal*, the *motionless* blue between the double field and the ephemeral' (MR99, italics mine). Is this the reason why the old 'master-logger,' whose joy and energy have always depended on his mastery of the river, feels mysteriously guilty when the river 'takes his son back' from him? The connection between this guilt and some violence directed against the feminine realm (that of women and nature) is in fact made explicit in the text: 'And the unhappy man reproached himself for drawing his son into a world of violence, leading him far from his mother's counsel, and even, in the midst of danger, egging on that ardent, high-strung nature, always asking ... ' (MR48).

Perceiving the world as an empty space awaiting the trace of man, the novelists of the land invent protagonists who also 'write' themselves into existence and into male identity by means of the traces they inscribe on the natural world. By the frantic beating of his snowshoes on the mountain snow, Menaud marks nature with his sign and the sign of the 'fathers,' signifying his 'will to conquer' (MR101) and writing 'on the new pages of winter ... as in the beautiful book [*Maria Chapdelaine*]' (MR115). In front of the marks left by hunters in the snow he stops, 'happy to knock twice ... to announce his presence as master to the unquiet land' (MR123). In the world of the settlers, the same rite of inscription takes place through the spring sowing ritual: 'the grain that had been blessed was taken out very early so the father, chaplain of furrow and harvest, could make the holy mixture with the seed' (MR51).

But the ambivalence of the male subject's relationship with this land he perceives as feminine disturbs the coherence of the national text. What Menaud is seeking in his wild trek across the frozen mountain is a confrontation with the enemy, the male rival who challenges his possession of the land and the cultural heritage. And yet the object both he and his rival lust after, the beloved country, is already fantasized as 'corrupted' or 'profaned' (MR84) (like a woman's body?), even before the foreigner's arrival. As well, Menaud perceives his duty to the 'fathers' to be 'not to bastardize the race' (MR59) – that is, not to permit a situation in which the name and identity of the sons would develop within a feminine context, freed from the control of the fathers. It is not surprising that Menaud's tragedy – symbolized by his fall into a snowy chasm similar to the 'dark pit' of nature (MR45) that had swallowed up his son – suggests the revenge of the feminine-maternal against his attempt at domination. Nor is it surprising that his tragedy takes the form of a loss of reason, a descent into madness that pulls him back wounded to earth, 'like a great black bird being dragged by the wings' (MR132). Justly famous as a 'warning' (MR134) of impending national disaster, Menaud's madness is also a warning of a deeper disaster in the cultural unconscious, one illustrated as well in the dramas of Séraphin Poudrier and Euchariste Moisan.

Reading *The Woman and the Miser*, in which the dream of enduring forever assumes the shape of a monstrous obsession – the avarice of Quebec's archetypal miser, Séraphin Poudrier – one is tempted to give its author credit for a subversive, even a feminist, aim. But to to so would be a delusion, for Claude-Henri Grignon's preface to the first edition of his novel informs us that for him, 'Donalda's edifying death' provides an image of 'the death of the Christian woman ... which always fills me with a seizure of supernatural grandeur.'[12] The author confides to us that he experiences a similar state of 'seizure' (the original French word '*saisissement*' suggests both a state of elevation and a freezing into stasis or ecstasy) at the sight of the Laurentian landscape. The description he gives of this experience – an excellent example of the 'angelism' of the male subject in his relation to the external world – is explicit about the link between landscape and female body:

Once you reach the plateau, you are not far from heaven. From this earthly and spiritual height, no matter which side one looks on, an intense poetry emanates from the surrounding countryside. The broken lines of the hills merge with the mystery of ravines and valleys where lakes and rivers with a soul of crystal sleep. I know of no sight more delightful or more dazzling for the eye. It is a spectacle that provokes a sensation of 'eternal being,' a feeling of perfect joy, comparable to the seizure one experiences at the sudden sight of a woman's body in all the purity of its lines.[13]

In addition to an emphasis on height, clarity, and eternity reminiscent of Savard, this passage also recalls the techniques of representation used in Ringuet's description of the landscape and of woman's body: the privileging of the visual over the other senses, and the fragmentation used by the observer in his attempt to capture the mystery of a landscape with feminine or maternal contours ('the broken lines of the hills merge with the mystery of ravines and valleys'). Pushed to their logical conclusion, as Grignon's novel will show, these technologies of possession produce the avarice of a Séraphin Poudrier.

To a large extent, the fascination exercised by the character of

Séraphin is due to what is familiar or easily recognizable in him. Indeed, as his angelic name suggests, one would only have to substitute the concept of 'God' for that of money in his scale of values in order to recognize it as an image of the ideal of sainthood long preached by the Catholic church. Although obsessed by 'the flesh,' Séraphin renounces it in favour of a greater good – money – which for him is the equivalent of 'life, heaven, God. Everything' (WM36). The symbolic relationship between money, the ultimately 'possessable' object, and the feminine-maternal in this novel has already been analysed in Sr Sainte-Marie-Eleuthère's study of the mother in the French-Canadian novel[14] and in Gérard Bessette's Freudian analysis;[15] and in fact, the author himself insists throughout the novel on the parallel between the sin of avarice and that of lust. Looking at his cousin Bertine's 'bouncing rump,' her 'firm and thick calves visible below too short a skirt,' and 'particularly ... her bosom, the most beautiful in the world, which burst out of her bodice' (WM31–2), Séraphin is 'shaken by desire' (WM32): 'Lust, the old lust that he had been fighting off for twenty years, was regaining the upper hand. In the end it might crush him in its coil of flesh and delight. He let himself go. He completely forgot that his wife might be dying and that Bertine was there on her account. He was thinking of the means he might employ to possess, perhaps in the hay loft in the barn, this tempting peasant girl' (WM32). Gold is less resistant, less dangerous, and easier to possess than women, and the text insists on the sexual nature of the pleasure it provides Séraphin:

Séraphin could no longer restrain himself. He would dig his bony, cold hand into the sack. Slowly, softly, he would feel around, grope among the oats, and when finally he touched – oh supreme caress – the leather purse or even just the draw strings, his pleasure reached a paroxysm which the most thoroughly satisfied lustful man could never know, and his heart would pound, almost fail. Several times a day he wallowed in this sensuous pleasure. (WM9)

What has been less commented on than this parallel between money and the female body is the conformity of Séraphin's behaviour with a value system that promises implicitly to men (and only to men) that eternity can be found within the enclosure of their own minds: 'Endowed with a prodigious memory, [Séraphin] never wrote down the loans he made ... But his memory never failed him. Never. And, ever calm, he did not have to reflect very long when he turned to his scribbler. His mind had become a machine that recorded his affairs with never an error of even a cent or a date' (WM26).

Like Menaud contemplating his beloved mountain, and like Grignon before the Sainte-Adèle landscape, Séraphin finds in his bag of gold a 'permanent and eternal food' (WM26), an 'unending present ... which offered more pleasure than any courtesan in the world could ever do' (WM71). For Euchariste Moisan, the most typical of the farmer characters in the history of the novel of the land, this need to stop time in order to assure himself of the solidity of his male identity is expressed by similar mechanisms, but in a more 'realistic' vision.

More precisely, it is not Euchariste who best symbolizes the dream of enduring forever in *Thirty Acres*, since that novel's dynamic tensions result from his confrontation with the contradictions inherent in the dream. It is rather his uncle Ephrem, a farmer of the previous generation, who has the good fortune to live and die 'as a true peasant.' One wonders if it is simply a coincidence in the text that this archetypal peasant, who 'had died pressed close to this farm of his that could not consent to a divorce' (TA35), is a bachelor – a man who has lived and died happily in an uninterrupted marriage with the land and has been able to transmit the Moisan lineage to his nephew without ever entering into a relationship with a woman.

For Euchariste, a more novelistic hero, the perpetuation of the lineage requires more conventional means – and more 'dangerous' ones, in terms of the dynamic of the feminine in the novel. For his sense of identity and his consciousness of having acceded to his appropriate place in the hierarchy of existence come to him gradually as he brings Alphonsine into the paternal house: 'Now that he had taken an outsider under his roof, it seemed to Euchariste that he was clothed with a more absolute authority and it gave him, along with a feeling of his own importance, the assurance that he was at last in complete possession of the Moisan heritage' (TA43). But only at the moment when he learns he has planted his seed in his wife's body does he recognize that he has 'become, by the miracle of this begetting, the master of the land where yesterday he was a stranger'

(TA45). Certain that he is henceforth 'eternal,' he can now turn away from his wife and children and devote himself entirely to his marriage to the land. According to the narrator, this is 'the human norm,' the way things are meant to be:

All this conformed to an order established thousands of years ago, when man renounced the freedom of a life devoted to hunting and fishing to accept the yoke of the seasons and subject himself to the yearly rhythm of the earth, his partner. Euchariste had the farm; Alphonsine, the house and the child. Life passed from the earth to the man, from the man to his wife, and from her to the child, who was the temporary end of the chain. (TA50–1)

Transformed into a fetish, the land becomes the female object whose possession will assure Euchariste's identity, the object whose 'rape' by Euchariste's neighbour Phydime Raymond will drive him mad with jealousy and lead to his fateful decision to mortgage his property in a lawsuit: 'Even if I have to give up my land I'm going to stick with this right to the end' (TA169). Euchariste's fall, evoked in an image suggesting a return to the much-abused feminine-maternal domain, is striking in its resemblance to Menaud's tragic end: 'He collapsed among the weeds in a deep ditch that yawned open like a grave. As he fell he gulped at the air, which seemed too heavy to go down into his lungs. And then, as he rolled in the sodden grass with the gentle to-and-fro motion of a child being rocked to sleep, his eyelids burst at last. The rain streamed down his face and so did the bitter flood of his tears' (TA195).

As Menaud had 'caved in' ('s'affaissa') in his fall into the snowy abyss, Euchariste 'collapses' ('s'écroula'), wounded in the site of the gaze that had assured his mastery over the world and over woman. With the collapse of these two heroes, it is not an exaggeration to suggest that the entire solid structure of the novel of the land tumbles into the abyss of the feminine. For, from the *coureurs de bois*'s passion for wide-open spaces to the tenacity of the settlers, the space and time of the dream of enduring forever have obeyed a single Law, the same Law that Louis Hémon had identified as that of the fathers: 'That is why we must remain in the province where our fathers have dwelt, living as they have lived, in order to obey the unwritten command that took shape in their hearts' (MC160). In imposing his identity on the feminine realm beneath him, each of the protagonists has justified himself by referring to that Law: for Menaud, it is 'the law we have been given ... and must pass on' (MR83); for Séraphin, 'a deal's a deal' (WM61, 86); for Euchariste, 'What would be must be' (TA68). Excluded from this legitimacy by birth, the female characters will be more rebellious, at least as far as their impact on the text is concerned.

Woman: How he kills her

Two pages before the end of the first novel published in French Canada, the narrator mentions the wife of the protagonist for the first time, stating in a single sentence both her unimportance to the plot and the fact of her death: 'Amand's wife, whom we have not yet mentioned in the course of this work, since she took no part in the events we have been describing, died soon after Amélie's marriage. Amand therefore found himself alone in the world.'[16]

Although *Le Chercheur de trésors* (The treasurer seeker) is not a novel of the land, the fate it reserves for this anonymous woman, whose death constitutes her sole *signifying* function in her husband's story, will become a recurrent pattern in the novels of the land that follow. Within their narratives, woman is the 'absent presence': the female other who supports the entire edifice of male identity without ever being noticed by him, and the character who has no story – for the existence of 'her story' would be a major structural threat to the permanence and stability of his.

In these novels, it is in man's relationship with nature and not with the female characters that his combat with the terrifying feminine-maternal element is played out. But, not content with replacing woman by a vaster feminine object more in keeping with his dreams of grandeur, man imprisons her as well in a house – and in a role in which he can define her limits. To return to our metaphor of the 'solid house' that corresponds to the shape of these texts, one could say that the authors, like Euchariste Moisan, choose to 'take ... an outsider under [their] roof' in order to 'clothe [themselves] in a more absolute authority' (TA43). But although the role of woman is clearly defined according to the conventions of the *genre*, the authors fail to take into account the strange tendency literary characters have always had of taking on an unpredictable life of their own.

A first clue to the existence of a murder is the striking absence of *mother* characters from these novels, despite the fact that the only accepted role for women in these novels is that of wife and mother.[17] Either the mother is already dead before the plot begins, as in *Master of the River*, in which case she will have assumed the role of 'the dead one,' whose very name seems to have been forgotten,[18] or she dies in the course of the narrative, as do Laura Chapdelaine, Alphonsine Moisan, Donalda Laloge Poudrier, and many others. In the latter case, her death is typically presented as an 'edifying spectacle' – the supreme example of the self-sacrifice demanded of all women, a pretext for arousing the reader's sympathy for the male protagonist, and (one cannot help suspecting) a textual act of revenge against the feminine-maternal.

All these elements are present in a passage from Napoléon Bourassa's *Jacques et Marie*, where the mother is 'sacrificed' by the text in order that the father and children may return to French soil, and where the grief displayed by the male protagonist and narrator seems to find relief in the very act of recounting its exemplary nature:

'My poor mother is dead! ... ' I cried choking with pain, 'and she died in these woods! ... '

'What? It was your mother?' said the story-teller. 'My poor gentleman, I beg you, try to moderate your sorrow, for she is better off than all of us at present, she is a holy martyr who has found her rest in heaven. If only you had seen her last moments! ... It was so beautiful! ... When the whole family was assembled around her pallet, she asked her husband and children to forgive her the pain, sorrow and scandal she might have caused them during her life; then she prayed to God ... to reunite her children around their father some day in a French land; and while we were reciting the rosary with her, she breathed her last.'[19]

Beneath the pious rhetoric of this passage it is possible to detect a latent structure that will recur in a slightly modified form in many of the novels of the land: the obligatory disappearance of the mother in order that the constellation made up of father/children/French land can be preserved; a vague sense of guilt associated with her by the mention of the 'pain' and the 'scandal' that she may have inflicted on her family; the ecstasy of the male observer who recounts her death; and finally the emphasis on the suffering of her bereaved son. Not until *The Woman and the Miser*, however, will this corpse under the foundations of the Father's House be brought to centre stage in the structure of the novel.

When she manages to stay alive, the female character is killed in more subtle ways. As the cornerstone of the patriarchal edifice, she must remain *immobile* within the confines of her role. The only movement permitted her – and it becomes incessant and frenetic – is that of her circular trajectory within the house. From *Jean Rivard* (1862) to *The Woman and the Miser* (1933) and beyond, an unchanging characteristic of the house as described in these novels is the presence of floors that glow as a result of the obsessive rubbing they have received from these 'queens of the hearth.' Never granted the capacity for autonomous thought or words,[20] the female character is able to introduce a crack in the novelistic edifice only by passive gestures: the exhaustion of her directionless movement, the ravages exercised on her body and her face by the passage of time and by numerous childbirths; or, inversely, by the emergence in the text of the voice of desire and the body with which woman is associated by her 'natural' link with the animal realm.

In the two volumes of Antoine Gérin-Lajoie's *Jean Rivard*, where the 'message' of the novel of the land is as yet fairly untouched by the contradictions of the real world, the model of the female character as sanctioned by the ideology of the period is presented with remarkable clarity. Before acceding to the role of wife and mother, woman is precisely *nothing* – just a pretty and somewhat stupid child, waiting to be chosen by a man in order to gain entry into the 'sphere' of maternity and housework that is reserved for her. And yet, because of her 'innate' link with the realm of bodily desire, she already represents a danger for the patriarchal order; and as such she must be dominated by the intellectual superiority of man.

The instructive stages in the process by which Louise Routier becomes the fiancée of Jean Rivard are analysed by Janine Boynard-Frot.[21] Telling his friend Charmenil of the events surrounding the marriage proposal, Rivard describes Louise as an 'excessively timid and awkward being,' who on hearing of his desire to marry her 'became as red as a cherry and stammered that [he] was the one she loved best,' and adds that 'he prefers her this way.' Before the proposal, the only misunderstanding between the two occurs during a party where Louise dances with a young man from the village. Rivard leaves the party to indicate his disapproval, and it is Louise who tries to patch things up between them by heaping blame on herself: 'I'm still only a little girl ... You must have thought I was really silly ... I hope I'll get wiser with age.' Without commenting on the potential for subversion in this feminine taste for the pleasures of the body, Boynard-Frot notes how 'by means of moral constraint, Louise Routier is minimized, forced into a reductive process aimed at excluding female subjectivity, with the result that the marriage is based not on communication between two human beings, but on a power relationship between dominator and dominated.'[22]

In the second volume of the novel, *Jean Rivard économiste*, one sees the change in status conferred on woman by marriage and maternity; indeed, it would be hard to be more explicit than Gérin-Lajoie about the role of woman as the essential but unacknowledged foundation of male identity. Like Alphonsine in the conversation between Euchariste Moisan and his future father-in-law, Louise Rivard constitutes the 'unspoken' element in a list of the attributes that have contributed to her husband's success. After noting Rivard's intelligence, discipline, and organizational abilities, the narrator informs us that 'there is another cause of prosperity which Jean Rivard could have included among his most important *secrets* [the italics are the author's], and which he was doubtless too tactful to mention. This important secret was Louise, Jean Rivard's wife' (JRE340). In the long description of Louise's 'sphere' that follows, the narrator states clearly that the first and most important task of a wife is to look after her husband's well-being: 'Let us say to begin with that Louise contributed a great deal to the courage and happiness of her husband by the affectionate care she lavished on him. She loved him as the Canadian woman knows how to love, with that disinterested, anxious, devoted love that ends only with the end of life' (JRE340). The other duties of the wife are of lesser importance, and indeed are only the different facets of a life devoted to maintaining the hierarchy ruled over by man: Louise's moral and spiritual influence on those around her, her supervision of the running of the household ('all the details relating to meals, clothing and furnishings'), the cleanliness and good taste of her appearance, in order that her husband will find her 'as charming as on her wedding day,' her work in the barnyard and in the garden, so that 'Jean Rivard's table [will be] well-provided from the beginning of the year to the end' (JRE341). Significantly, in this propagandistic novel still relatively untouched by the contradictions of real life, the care of the children 'whose number increased every two years,' and 'the time [Louise] spent in sewing clothes for them' (JRE342) are activities that are seen as secondary to service to the husband. With respect to this model wife, the narrator concedes that 'her part in Jean Rivard's success was not without importance, and she could congratulate herself (which should for that matter be the ambition of all women), for being as useful and accomplished in her sphere as her husband was in his' (JRE342).

Already in Gérin-Lajoie's novel, however, one can detect a crack in the strait-jacket in which woman is imprisoned, an *excess* in the way she carries out her female duties that leads one to suspect the presence of a more sombre reality behind the idealized image. Lacking a goal, the 'little woman' becomes frenetic in her activity, and her concern with order and cleanliness becomes an obsession:

You had to see this clean, active, industrious little woman coming and going, giving orders, putting a piece of furniture back in its place, ceaselessly occupied, always in good humour.

If there was one thing she could be criticized for, it was perhaps an excess of cleanliness. The floors were always so yellow that no one dared walk on them. The little curtains trimming the windows were so white that the men didn't dare smoke in the house for fear of getting them dirty. This cleanliness even extended to the outside of the house; she couldn't bear the sight of a piece of straw on the ground by her door. Her husband teased her sometimes about this, but it was no use. Cleanliness had become second nature to her. (JRE341)

This passage offers a good example of the sort of textual subversion by which the female characters in these novels rebel in the only way a prisoner *can* rebel: by revealing their truth in spite of the constraints of the behaviour required of them. Louise never stops working; she is always 'in good humour'; and for the men in her life as well as for the narrator observing her she is an object of gentle mockery. But the trace she leaves in the text is that of a woman alienated from herself and exhausting herself in the repetitive and mechanical labour of a mindless routine: the ancestor not only of Alphonsine Moisan and Donalda Laloge, but also perhaps of Anne Hébert's Claudine and the numerous other negative mothers of Quebec literature, who have nothing but rigidity and bitterness to bequeath to their children. 'Killed' in the sense that all the qualities that would make her human are denied her, Louise Rivard resists by *signifying* her death in the text.

A woman in the centre of the novelistic world: *Maria Chapdelaine*

A sceptical reader might ask, however, whether it is fair to refer to women's role as a *prison* when dealing with the literary productions of an era in which men's roles as well as women's were clearly defined by social codes. In so doing are we not imposing contemporary values on a traditional culture and therefore falsifying the analysis before it even begins? *Maria Chapdelaine*, in which a female character who is both entirely traditional and fully human occupies the centre of the narrative, provides an answer to this question and shows by contrast to what extent the objectification of women in the other novels of the land is the product of a dualistic world view.

The fact that Louis Hémon was French rather than French Canadian probably goes a long way towards explaining his choice of a female protagonist. For by the very fact that he chooses to *tell the story of a woman*, Hémon places his narrative in a position of fundamental contradiction with the dominant ideology of French Canada. A story implies a beginning, a development in time, choices, and an unpredictable conclusion: in other words, the development of a relatively autonomous subject. For the official ideology, on the contrary, woman has no story: her existence and her value begin and end in the role of wife and mother to which she is destined for all time. Reading *Maria Chapdelaine* in light of this contradiction between Hémon's project and the society he was describing, one becomes aware of the necessity and the coherence of the break in the tissue of the novel constituted by François Paradis's death. Before François's death, Maria is free to dream of a life different from that of her mother (MC29–30). After the break in the text, the plot corresponds to a gradual reduction of her options, leading to her final acceptance of a version of woman's traditional role lacking even the dynamism of that role as lived by her mother in the preceding generation. Something has therefore taken place in the text that has had the simultaneous effect of bringing the novel into conformity with the conventions of the novel of the land and of killing the possibilities open to Maria. Let us look more closely at this invasion of the text by tragedy.

The first section of *Maria Chapdelaine* (the part leading up to François Paradis's death) presents a vision of possibility unique in the history of the novel of the land. By moving his female character from the periphery to the centre of his novelistic universe, Hémon has displaced all the dualisms based on her subjection and created an image of what traditional French-Canadian society could have been (and doubtless *was* to a certain extent, in spite of the dualistic world-view propagated by its leaders) In this first part of the book, placed under the sign of movement (the rapids associated with François Paradis), there is a harmonious balance between man and woman, culture and nature – in that the traditional division of roles and labour does not preclude the possibility of love and respect between the sexes. In spite of her nostalgia for the 'old parishes' she has left behind in following her pioneer husband northward, Laura Chapdelaine finds meaning for her own life in the shared challenge of settling a new territory.[23] As for the men, despite the backbreaking toil of their unending struggle against the surrounding forest, they are shaped by nature to such an extent that seen at rest after the day's work they seem to resemble 'clay-coloured statues' (MC39).

Even though she inhabits a totally traditional female role, Maria has the grandeur of a heroine. In her, the passivity, obedience and silence typical of all the female protagonists in the novel of the land are the outer manifestations of a strength and depth of character and a tenacious desire for happiness that constitute the energy which propels the novel forward. By espousing the subjectivity of a female character to such an extent, Hémon has symbolically opened the Father's House to 'otherness.' During the unfolding of her love for

François and up until his death, Maria typically stands on the door-step of the house, open to the possibilities offered by the outside world, or in front of the open window (in the company of her mother), listening to the joyful sound of the Peribonka River in springtime. Such a harmonious rapprochement between the elements of house and water will not be seen again in the novel of the land until Germaine Guèvremont's works.

Similarly, the frank and healthy eroticism of the famous 'blueberry scene' where François declares his love for Maria offers a striking contrast with the descriptions of the female body in other novels of the land and anticipates the eroticism that will emanate from Guèvremont's Outlander thirty years later. For example, if one compares the following passage from *Maria Chapdelaine* to the passage from *Thirty Acres* in which Euchariste is looking at Alphonsine, one notices – despite a superficial resemblance created by the fragmentation of the female body by the male gaze in both passages – that here the presentation of Maria's body blends imperceptibly into that of her face, and the description of her bodily beauty into that of her character traits, so that François's physical desire is seen as inseparable from the 'marvellous tenderness' he feels for Maria:

François Paradis stole a glance at Maria, then turned his eyes away and tightly clasped his hands. Ah, but she was good to look upon! Thus to sit beside her, to catch these shy glimpses of the strong bosom, the sweet face so modest and so patient, the utter simplicity of attitude and of her rare gestures; a great hunger for her awoke in him, and with a new and marvellous tenderness, for he had lived his life with other men, in hard give-and-take, among the wild forests and on the snow plains. (MC57)

Critical readings attentive to the structure of *Maria Chapdelaine* have tended to present Maria's evolution in the first part of the novel as a gradual move away from the world of her mother (the house) towards that of her father and François (the forest and surrounding nature). Such readings unconsciously reproduce the dualism of a world-view that imprisons both men and women in separate spheres and neglect the fact that Maria's distancing of her mother is the normal pattern of development for a young girl evolving towards maturity. The vision presented by Hémon in this part of the novel is that of a universe that is unified rather than split in two; where the feminine principle – freely emerging and moving towards its full flowering – could join with the masculine principle to form a totality similar to the one evoked in the Christmas night scene: 'Life had always been a simple and straightforward thing for them: severe but inevitable toil, a good understanding between man and wife, obedience alike to the laws of nature and of the Church. Everything was drawn into the same woof; the rites of their religion and the daily routine of existence so woven together that they could not distinguish the devout emotion possessing them from the mute love of each for each' (MC81).

With François Paradis's name as a clue to its meaning, it is not surprising that critics have often seen this first part of the novel as a myth of Paradise; but looked at from the perspective of the emergence of the feminine in patriarchal culture it could more accurately be described as a sort of Utopian world in which the possibility of a full integration of the feminine is imagined. In any case, that harmony will be destroyed and Maria's universe cut in two by an event that has symbolic associations with the arrival of patriarchal culture: François Paradis's death.

François's death has a suggestive resemblance to the fate of the tragic hero of Greek or Shakespearean drama. By deciding against all advice and practical good sense to traverse the forest during a fierce winter storm in order to spend Christmas with Maria, he is guilty of hubris and attracts nature's punishment. Seen from the point of view of the economy of the feminine in the novel, his decision corresponds to the imposition of patriarchal culture and its hierarchy on the natural world. As a white man, he places himself in a position of superiority to the laws of nature and the practical wisdom of the native people: 'When the Indians take that journey it is in company, and with their dogs. François set off alone, on snowshoes' (MC90). He dies as a result, and with his death all the liquid movement associated with him freezes into an image that can be seen as the tragic reversal of the dream of enduring forever: 'Cold and his ministers of death flung themselves upon him as their prey; they have stilled the strong limbs forever, covered his open handsome face with snow, closed the fearless eyes without gentleness or pity, changed his living body into a thing of ice' (MC96).

In her excellent 'Reading of *Maria Chapdelaine*,'[24] Nicole Deschamps sees in this image of François transformed into a block of ice 'a sort of Sleeping Beauty whom Maria will join by her symbolic death.'[25] But Perrault's tale evokes a death that is only temporary, that will last 'a hundred years'; and one can also imagine François as the masculine principle, a princely son of the patriarchy whose awakening will take place only when the feminine has found expression within history.

François's death marks the end of freedom for Maria, whose withdrawal into the symbolic space of the house (henceforth depicted as closed off from the surrounding world of nature), is also a regression in her development, a return to the mother's space next to the stove in the centre of the house. Projected into the absurdity of a divided universe by this death, she is left with a 'choice' between two other suitors that is only an illusion of freedom; the *deus ex machina* ending provided by her mother's death and her resultant decision to remain at home is only a further confirmation of the fact that she now inhabits a universe irremediably opposed to her desire. In that famous ending, the voice of the country has become indistinguishable from the Law of the Fathers; and for women, as for Maria, there is no longer a 'shimmering promise to walk toward' (MC125) – only the eternally repetitive cycle of a role transmitted from mothers to daughters manifestly less and less capable of resistance. While at the outset of the novel she had been a female heroine symbolizing women's potential, in her defeat Maria offers a striking image of the destiny of the women of her race: 'Maria moved not; with hands folded in her lap, patient of spirit and without bitterness, yet dreaming a little wistfully of the far-off wonders her eyes would never behold' (MC161).

Menaud's Marie: An unequal struggle

Defeated in *Maria Chapdelaine*, woman starts to 'move' again in *Master of the River*, and again she must be 'put in her place.' When one looks at the structural dynamics of the novel, it becomes clear that in order for Menaud's drama of possession to have its full expression, a corresponding subtext is necessary – the *blocking* of his daughter Marie's story. An unequal struggle between a father figure endowed with all the nobility of an epic hero and a daughter who lives only 'for him' (MR57), *Master of the River* recalls the structure of *Angéline de Montbrun*; except that this time the narrative is presented from the point of view of the father.

Marie is not only an image of the feminine element in which – to return to Irigaray's phrase – man 'envelops himself and his possessions,'[26] she is also a character who acts on the structure of the novel, introducing a constellation of themes associated with the flesh, desire, and the happiness of living in the present: a constellation that must be defeated in order to allow the national theme associated with thought, the past, and the Law of the Fathers (also described in the novel as 'the claims of the dead' [MR63]) to triumph.[27] In Laure Conan's novel, the confrontation of these dualities had led to the elimination not only of the father, but also of the fiancé who would have inherited his position of authority. Here, on the contrary, it is the daughter who will be brought into line, and who – faced with rejection by her father and by society – will agree to substitute for the fiancé of her choice one who is more in conformity with her father's ideal. And yet, up to the last words she utters in the text, Marie is a resister.

Marie is constantly diminished by the narrative voice, made into an object of pity and condescension by the repeated references to her as 'poor thing' (MR57, 72, 89, 110), 'poor girl' (MR72, 108), and 'poor little one' (MR130). Denied the possibility of a voice of her own in the text, she is often depicted in the act of crying (MR90, 110, 134) – an unthreatening 'feminine' activity that compensates for the loss of words: 'she began to weep and speak incomprehensibly among her sobs' (MR130). But given the conventions of the novel of the land regarding the exchange of a woman (as typified in the pact between Euchariste Moisan and Père Branchaud), she accomplishes a gesture of surprising autonomy when she agrees to marry le Délié without consulting her father (MR57). This gesture of autonomy introduces a structural break into the text that will continue to grow larger despite the increasing domination Menaud exercises over his daughter's desires on the level of the narrative's surface development.

André Brochu's sensitive reading of the novel insists on the importance of its opening scene, where Menaud listens as his daughter reads aloud to him the 'sacred' pages from the end of *Maria Chapde-*

laine. As she approaches the famous line 'But in the land of Quebec nothing must change,' the text informs us that 'Marie's voice was faltering ... as if a shadow had suddenly fallen over the words' (MR9). Brochu analyses with considerable finesse the importance of this hesitation on Marie's part ('There is nothing surprising in this resistance to a text that is secretly a condemnation of her')[28] and its relevance to the whole set of dualisms that structure the novel. But his article not only fails to follow the implications of this opposition between Menaud and the female universe associated with his daughter to their logical conclusion; it explains in a 'postscript' why it was impossible for Brochu to do so in the Quebec of the 1960s.[29]

Through this hesitation in Marie's voice, it is in fact the whole confrontation between Menaud and the feminine that invades the fabric of the novel. Let us look more closely at the consequences of this eruption of the feminine for 'his story' and for 'her story.' For Menaud, the crack introduced into the narrative by this hesitation opens up a threatening 'abyss of shadow' that will haunt him throughout the novel, and to which he reacts by retreating even further into the rigidity of the dream of enduring forever: 'Menaud stiffened where he sat as if what he had just heard opened an abyss of shadow beneath his feet. "Nothing has changed ... nothing has changed," he murmured' (MR10).

As well, Menaud turns immediately towards the window, towards the view of the 'free mountains' that symbolize his ideal of light and eternal values, to protect himself against 'the thoughts of darkness that were invading him' (MR10). For Marie, on the other hand, this hesitation in her voice will be the first step in a drama consisting of her reduction to silence; of all the scenes in the novel that show her in her father's company, this is the only one in which she speaks (and even then it must be noted that her words are not her own, but the words of the 'sacred' book she is reading to her father). Indeed, Menaud's curt comment to her at the end of this scene is an explicit command to be silent: 'There was fire in Menaud's eye. "Enough," he said to his daughter. She let the book fall to her lap' (MR10).

Rather than a 'confrontation,' this relationship between Menaud and Marie is better described as an exercise of power on the part of the father, leading to an increasing submission on the part of the daughter. Already before the break between them, their relationship had fitted into a well-defined hierarchical order in which masculine rationality is seen to be in a dialogue with the feminine capacity for caring: 'Yet the wordless dialogue of her heart with her father's mind had been pulled apart like a strand of wool' (MR14). After the break, their relationship is characterized by gestures of coldness and rejection on the part of Menaud, and by Marie's growing sense of insecurity: '[Menaud] lowered a dry cheek for his daughter to kiss' (MR19); 'he looked at Marie strangely [and] went out' (MR56); Marie 'went on tiptoe, muffling the household noises that used to overflow through open windows' (MR52).

Having centred her whole life on the devotion she owes to her father,[30] Marie (like Angéline before her) is devastated by this rejection, all the more so because it carries with it the disapproval of an entire society. And yet, in another parallel with *Angéline*, the daughter's deepest desire seems for some obscure reason to lead her in a direction incompatible with this devotion to her father: 'Yet what would this happiness be, bought at the price of treachery? What a weight the hatred of her own and the contempt of her father would be!' (MR79–80).

How can we explain this alliance with a traitor to her race, with this Dé-lié ('the untier') who 'lurks' outside the house while – in a revealing contrast with the imagery of *Maria Chapdelaine* – 'Menaud kept jealous watch at the door of the betrothed' (MR87) and Marie, shut up inside, 'is reassured only by her father's protective presence at the door' (MR88). On one level, there is undoubtedly some misogyny present in this presentation of women as potential 'daughters of Eve,' rendered weak and unfaithful by their female nature. The attraction of le Délié is certainly a physical one, in face of which 'poor' Marie is depicted as helpless: 'Yet what could the poor thing have done against this big fellow who took her by the violence of the spell in his gaze, the high colour in his stormy face, his strength, even his bearing, and whose demands had aroused feelings in her that she did not yet comprehend?' (MR57).

In the presence of her suitor, Marie speaks almost as little as she does with her father ('The poor thing dared not speak,' [MR73]), and even after she has dismissed him 'it was for him that her whole body yearned when not restrained by her will' (MR80). After le Délié's departure, Marie enters into a 'night suddenly crowded with

hate and threats' (MR90), which is not unlike the dark night experienced by Maria Chapdelaine after the death of *her* desire.

But, if we judge by subsequent women's writing, there would seem
to be a deeper logic in this 'alliance' between the female character and
the stranger/foreigner character. Gabrielle Roy's *The Tin Flute*,
Marie-Claire Blais's *Visions d'Anna*, and even 'Speak White,'[31]
Michèle Lalonde's famous nationalist poem, are other examples of
the profound malaise and even repugnance women seem to feel in
relation to the borders that divide human beings and the wars and
violence produced by national struggles. Even after she has given in
to her father's point of view and rejected le Délié, Marie continues
to oppose a resistance within the text to the violence inherent in her
father's project:

At first snowfall [le Lucon] would be leaving with Menaud. Délié would
be going off too ... What would happen on the mountain between these
violent men? Somewhere in the great white wilderness where there was
neither compassion nor moderation, and the heart turned savage and cruel,
she imagined the meeting ... the boiling hatred ... the insults ... and it might
all finish with some unfortunate lying hurt and groaning ... She heard the
sound of the black-flying words that circle around before the hour of
disaster in the minds of men. (MR106)

Even though Marie dares not *express* these fears and forebodings
to her father, the text indicates – by means of the images associated
with her thoughts – the entry into a zone of violence where the
characteristics of the 'heart' formerly associated with woman are
annihilated ('and the heart turned savage and cruel'), and where,
deaf to the voice of the feminine, the patriarchal values of height,
abstraction, and rivalry are pushed to some apocalyptic end issuing
from 'the minds of men.' Following this interpretation, the intervention of nature to block Menaud's forward movement seems entirely
coherent: as woman's more powerful ally, nature paralyses the male
hero's presumptuous attempt at 'flight,' attaching his feet to the
ground just as his wife, before her death, had cut off his 'wings'
(MR12): 'Soon the quavering voice could not be heard beyond the
snow-pit, while the man's feet froze in the shroud he had walked
into' (MR126).

Twice defeated (in the sacrifice of the first object of her desire, and in her silence when her father departs against her will for the mountain), Marie attempts a third time to resist the dream of enduring forever, this time through the agency of the third man in her life – Alexis le Lucon, the fiancé deemed acceptable by her father. The famous sentence she offers to Alexis 'like an invocation of love' before he leaves to join her father on the mountain is a summary of *her* dream, and it resonates in his heart for a long time before being reduced to silence by the voice of the fathers: 'How pleasant it would be to live here ... in peace!' (MR111) To Savard the fervent nationalist we owe this beautiful formulation of the recurrent feminine dream of a world where harmony between peoples and full enjoyment of the present would be possible. And indeed the resonance of the sentence is so powerful in the text that an explicit intervention of the narrator is required in order to make clear its unacceptability. But first it is Alexis who becomes aware of the 'effeminate' nature of this dream of love: 'Marie offered the little life, closed in and locked up like the life of a bear in winter ... As if life could be thus spent, withdrawing and letting oneself be despoiled without putting up some defence. No, that was not the plan of his forefathers' (MR111).

In the closing scene of the novel, Marie herself comes to see that she must give up her dream for the greater good of the country. But, as if a further voice were required to uphold the values of the fathers, her final speech of renunciation is preceded by an intervention of the narrator condemning 'her own dream, her enslaved ideal of life, like those *egotists* who would hear of nothing outside their own fields' (MR133, italics mine). Like Maria Chapdelaine, Marie finally understands – after a long resistance – the impossibility of her own desire for happiness. And like that of Maria, the final image of her in the novel is one of desolation – as well as being as disquieting a 'warning' to the culture as the one proffered by the image of her father's madness: ' "To live here in peace ... to live here in peace, it would be pleasant," she whispered now ... "Yes, it would be! But we have to think of the whole country too. So if you love me, you'll keep on like Joson, like my father." Then, in the refuge of arms he opened to her, she wept for a long time cheek to his cheek' (MR133–4).

'Don't get mad at me, Ma': The life of Alphonsine Moisan

In a scene in *Thirty Acres* that takes place shortly before Alphonsine Moisan's death, the men of the household come into the kitchen after a day's work in the fields, dirtying Alphonsine's clean floor with their muddy boots:

> 'Watch out, 'Charis! Look what you're doing!'
> 'Hey! Don't get mad at me, Ma. That's just good clean dirt!' (TA99)

The cheerful tone of this 'Don't get mad at me, Ma' makes clear who is in charge – even in the kitchen – and contains all the gentle oppression of the life of a 'queen of the hearth' (as the traditional mother was referred to in the ideological discourse of the period in French Canada). Alphonsine does not in fact 'get mad': she remains silent and '[goes] back to her pots and pans,' while around her 'the children were squalling ... Napoléon was pulling little Orpha's hair and she was yelling, and this, added to the clatter of the tumblers and dishes which Malvina and Lucinda were setting out on the table, made a deafening din, typical of *the end of a happy day*' (TA99, italics mine). And yet, pregnant for the thirteenth time at the age of forty, Alphonsine feels an exhaustion she has never experienced during her previous pregnancies.

Unlike Maria Chapdelaine and 'Menaud's Marie,' Alphonsine never expresses any open resistance to her destiny as a woman. Closely tied to her role as wife and mother, she disappears from the text in a few short sentences, never having disturbed the atmosphere of the house with her 'selfish' concerns, as her two predecessors had done: 'It all occurred so suddenly that Oguinase hadn't even time to get home from college. And before Euchariste had fully realized what was happening, he found himself in the big bedroom, where a vaguely outlined form and a waxen bloodless mask were all that was left of his Alphonsine.' (TA106).

On the level of the *textual* fate of Alphonsine, the 'vaguely outlined form,' the 'waxen bloodless mask,' and the absence of her favourite son Oguinase from this deathbed scene are the signs of a slow murder of which this elliptical passage is only the final expression. And as far as her fate in the memory of her family is concerned, it is a proof of the perfection with which she has identified with her role that, with the exception of the black tie her husband begins to wear on Sundays, her death leaves absolutely no trace in the text: 'When Oguinase came home for the summer holidays ... he was surprised to see how little things had changed. It was now Malvina who reigned in the kitchen and she was helped by Lucinda, now almost eleven ...' (TA107).

A perceptive observer of his society, Ringuet has sketched in the white spaces of Euchariste Moisan's narrative a portrait of the life of a French-Canadian wife and mother that provides an explanation for the resistance manifested by Maria Chapdelaine and Marie. From being a young wife and mother happily reigning over the 'separate sphere' of the house, Alphonsine is gradually transformed into the *absent* woman, her face hidden behind the smiling mask of the queen of the hearth, her dry and practical words veiling her anguish.

Unlike Euchariste's story, Alphonsine's is static, its only 'action' consisting of the ravages exercised on her by time and by her female role. Although she does not evolve, she changes – or rather, she *is changed* – getting closer every year to the exhaustion brought about by premature aging. And yet she does not see herself as a 'victim,' and to reduce her to such a status would be to deny the tranquil grandeur of her life. She has a 'good husband,'[32] children, a house, and a role to fulfil that in general it does not occur to her to question: 'She did all this work without pleasure, but without distaste. Weren't all these a woman's usual tasks?' (TA69).

But in the 'without pleasure' of the previous sentence, one detects the presence of the murder of woman implicit in the role of wife and mother: a murder of the body, of the emotions, and of the capacity for speech that gradually reveals its presence as successive brush strokes are added to the portrait of Alphonsine taking shape in the background of Euchariste's story. In spite of her 'brave gentle smile' (TA69) and the habitual reply of 'No, I'm not!' (TA99) that she makes when her fatigue is remarked upon, Alphonsine becomes more and more absent from reality, lost in the ruminations that will finally lead her to the discovery of her lack of power.

During the early years of her marriage, she experiences joys and sorrows that are a sign of full participation in life, and shares with the other women of her community a language that corresponds to the reality of their lives. Like the other women, she lives close to the great mysteries of life and death, those mysteries that are vaguely dismissed by men as 'women's affairs.' Seated in the 'women's corner' at parties, the women speak in 'low voices' (TA61), and always they speak of 'birth, marriage, sickness, death: the main events of their calm even lives. Above all death' (TA38). Frightened at the prospect of her first experience of childbirth, Alphonsine seeks advice and encouragement from the women who have gone before her; and when the moment comes, her instinctive cry of 'Auntie, Auntie, I feel like I'm going to die!' is an expression 'not so much [of] the fear of death, but of the desire for it, to escape the martyrdom that awaited her: this way of the cross whose every anguished station she had guessed in the reticence and the encouragement of those who had gone before her' (TA48).

Afterwards, she knows 'the indescribable joy of creation' (TA49) and a new alliance with her aunt in their shared devotion to the newborn son – a state of affairs that transforms the house into the 'separate sphere' of women, from which Euchariste now feels excluded: 'Now there were questions discussed about which he was ignorant, arguments in which he timidly ventured an opinion only to be told quite clearly that men knew nothing about such things' (TA50).

Very soon, however, Alphonsine's individuality disappears behind a mask of acquiescence through which the text allows us more than once to see her inner chaos. Although she rarely speaks in the novel, her *body* speaks, by means of her 'absent-minded' look (TA76), her habit of 'staring into space' (TA69, 99), and the pregnant woman's gesture that becomes second nature to her: 'From time to time Alphonsine straightened up with a movement of her hips which threw her shoulders back and outlined her prominent girth ... She put her hands to her aching back, for she was more wearied with each new pregnancy by the burden she was carrying' (TA76–7).

Insensitive up until the end to what is happening to his wife, Euchariste continues to see her through the eyes of his desire, despite the 'continued childbearing [which] had already broadened her hips and made her heavy-breasted' (TA69). And although this attention is not displeasing to Alphonsine, her 'brave, gentle smile' gradually becomes less and less frequent (TA69).

Even more serious than the destruction of Alphonsine's body is her loss of the ability to express her emotions. Faced with the unchangeable fact of events like the death of her first daughter, Héléna, she learns to swallow her tears and focus her 'distracted attention' on the newborn child who has already replaced her (TA69). Little by little she becomes a woman who neither laughs nor cries[33] and who lacks the ability to express tenderness to her children, despite the fact that maternal love is her entire *raison d'être*. The text reveals her as more and more absent from reality, even as her body continues to function efficiently within the prescribed tasks. When her favourite son, Oguinase, leaves for the seminary, neither words nor caresses are exchanged between mother and son; simply the dry piece of advice 'Look out for your money' (TA82). And, following the departure, a rare and moving expression of affection for one of the remaining sons:

'Come along, Etienne,' she said in a gentler, more subdued voice than usual.

She gave him her hand, unconsciously wiped away a speck of dust from the corner of one eye, started off towards the house, and then suddenly took Etienne in her arms and hugged him so hard the child began to howl. (TA82).

It is this loss of her favourite son that wounds Alphonsine at the very heart of her mother's love and brings her close to a stance of resistance. In her case, however, resistance takes the form of a futile questioning silenced even before it even begins to take shape by the hard reality of the Law of the Father: 'If it had rested with her, his departure would probably have been postponed indefinitely. Although the priest and Euchariste had settled the matter already, she still thought Oguinase was too young. But how could she, who was only his mother, oppose the concerted wishes of the priest and the boy's father?' (TA77).

By a subtle juxtaposition of the impeccable external behaviour of Alphonsine with the anguish of her secret thoughts, the text reveals women's lack of real power in parenting, in spite of the hypocritical doctrine of the 'separate spheres.' The last time Alphonsine appears in the novel before her death – in the kitchen scene already referred to – she seems lost in another world filled with memories of

Oguinase and worries about her present pregnancy, a world punctuated by an endless questioning of the justice of this removal of her son from her: 'Why had it to be her eldest son who became a priest, and not one of the others, Ephrem, Etienne or Napoléon? What difference could it have possibly have made to God which one it was, while for her ... But no, it must be that things were fated to be that way!' (TA100).

When her husband brings her back to reality by 'tapp[ing] his plate with his knife' (!), Alphonsine 'started up and went over to the stove,' only to see before her, in 'the little nickel-framed mirror on the front of it' the image of 'a woman with lifeless hair and a dried-up face: the Alphonsine of today, who had nothing, or hardly anything, in common with the mother of Oguinase as a baby' (TA100). Behind the mask of the perfect wife and mother, the face is revealed here one last time before being covered by the 'waxen bloodless mask' of death; and its truth is devastating.

The portrait of the French-Canadian mother will be painted in greater detail by a woman seven years later, in the character of Gabrielle Roy's Rose-Anna Lacasse; but it will not be until more than forty years later, with the emergence of feminism in the Quebec literary landscape, that all the incipient madness in such a life of abnegation will be exposed and the experience of an 'Alphonsine' truly shown from within – in Nicole Houde's *La Maison du remous* (The house by the whirlpool),[34] a feminist novel of the land. Already in *Thirty Acres*, however, Ringuet's penetrating gaze has detected the presence of decay in the foundations of the Father's House.

Donalda Laloge: The corpse under the foundations

The archetype of the 'model wife' and the perfect image of 'Christian sainthood' as defined by clerical leaders of the period, Donalda Laloge Poudrier represents the final outcome of the dream of enduring forever: the murder of woman. Totally colonized in body and soul, denied her right not only to love but also to motherhood, Donalda exhibits such total submission that one cannot help thinking of her story as a Québécois, Catholic version of *The Story of O*.[35] And yet her body resists, *speaking* through the illness that devastates it and that represents an unforgivable 'expense' for

Donalda's miserly husband, crying out by means of its symptoms her rebellion against this murder.

In this novel, which plays constantly on the parallels between the two 'cardinal sins' of lust and avarice, there is a minor incident that constitutes a foil to the story of Séraphin and Donalda, offering the reader a more familiar version of the possession of woman by man: the rape of 'young Célina Labranche' by Lemont, a character who borrows from Séraphin at usurious rates and later becomes his victim. In the case of Lemont and Célina, the domination is physical ('Lemont, having enticed young Célina into the barn, had taken her practically by force' WM14) and, when the young girl becomes pregnant (and therefore a cause for expense), she immediately becomes an object of the rapist's hatred and contempt: 'He saw again Célina, so young yet as experienced as an old courtesan ... How violent a craving those bewitching but so brief minutes had enkindled in him! But having to pay $100 for it was decidedly too much. And in his heart of hearts he cursed the fifteen-year-old farmer's daughter' (WM19). Later, we learn that in the eyes of the community Célina has become 'young Célina Labranche the whore' (WM64).

The possession exerted by Séraphin over Donalda is more 'angelic,' and is for this very reason a more absolute possession. After a single act of copulation on their wedding night, Séraphin chooses to deny his young wife all possibility of sexual pleasure and capacity for reproduction, thus ensuring a sadistic control over her mind. Although she is 'meant for the embraces of love, beset by desires which an invincible atavism spread around her like an endless spring' (WM2), Donalda quickly learns to repress her bodily desire: 'and one fine day the ache went away by itself. She no longer craved man, and her flesh was at peace' (WM3). As well, since children represent an expense and expense is unacceptable to Séraphin, Donalda is denied the possibility of the son 'she so desperately wanted' and, fearing her husband's disapproval, she 'never mentioned it again' (WM2). Having been 'brutally possessed' once by her husband, she passes 'without transition ... from her wedding night to the bitter, wearying, gross life of a housekeeper,' becoming 'the robot that could milk the cows, bake the bread, spin the wool, mend stinking clothes, cook, wash the dishes, scrub the floor, tend the sick at night, bank the potatoes, set the fires, work in the field at sowing and harvest time; in a word ... the woman who is expected to do everything but make love' (WM2). Already dead in life at the age of twenty, she works eighteen hours a day, 'frantically ... as if death were too slow in coming' (WM3).

The impact of Donalda's image, like that of Séraphin's, comes from the barely exaggerated resemblance between the two characters and the clichés of the officially sanctioned discourse of the era. Just as Séraphin's greed displaces the values of the dream of enduring forever onto a material object – money – without modifying their basic character, Donalda corresponds to the approved image of the Catholic wife, with the notable exception of the fact that she is denied her reproductive function. Without children to compensate for the absence of conjugal love and justify her arduous labours in the household, her situation brings into sharp relief the maso-chism inherent in the female role as prescribed by the ideology of the period.

While Lemont and Célina Labranche offer an image of the physical and social domination long exercised over women by men, the relationship between Séraphin and Donalda suggests rather the vic-timization of woman by patriarchal *ideology*. Symbolically, Séraphin is not only the husband but the *father*, 'the possessor and the master' (WM27), who addresses Donalda as 'daughter' up until her final death throes, at which point she becomes 'old girl' (WM43). (Subsequently, within a few minutes of her death, he refers to her as 'the defunct' [WM52]). As for Donalda, her psychology is that of the woman under the eye of the father, with all pretence at an autonomous existence eliminated by the presence of this censorious gaze. Like a father dealing with an ignorant child, Séraphin dominates her by his greater 'rationality,' explaining to her that 'eating too much [is] bad for the stomach'; 'And she believed him. She had faith in him as she had in God' (WM6). In the presence of her husband, Donalda reacts with terror, paralysis, and silence; a behaviour that only serves to increase the power of her sadistic master over her: 'On her knees, but straight as an arrow, Donalda was watching this extraordinary man. Her throat dry, speechless, she wished she were dead. She kept silent. Séraphin looked at this vile creature for a moment, and for the first time in his life disdain dribbled from his toothless mouth like foul spittle' (WM4).

In Séraphin's absence, the reproachful gaze is internalized. On one occasion when he goes into town on a hot summer day, his young wife paces back and forth in a house that provides an excellent representation of the Father's House of the larger social and ideological context. Here, even more radically than in *Thirty Acres*, the idea that the house constitutes the 'separate sphere' ruled over by women is shown to be a hollow concept. In the claustrophobic parlour that has served as a 'death chamber' to three generations of Poudriers, the stove (the space traditionally associated with woman and with warmth) is cold, and the ink in the inkwell is congealed. On the walls hang portraits of a number of religious, political, and cultural 'fathers' – Pope Leo XIII, Sir Wilfrid Laurier, Louis Riel, and the pioneering ancestor Damase Poudrier – accompanied by a single portrait of a woman, 'old Aunt Stéphanie, *who had died under atrocious circumstances, poisoned*' (WM7–8, italics mine). In the kitchen, burdened by the memory of her husband's criticisms of her, Donalda despite her hunger 'resigned herself to wait, to wait until death rather than eat' (WM7). Attracted by the coolness of the wing of the house where Séraphin conducts his business, 'she did not dare climb the two steps that stood between her and the greatest happiness which could exist for her just then. It would have meant deceiving Séraphin' (WM10).

But the much maligned body cries out its revolt. As soon as Donalda has become 'accustomed to this life detached from the soul' (WM3), she begins to be tortured by an 'intense thirst,' which soon infiltrates her body and takes the form of an illness. It is a brilliant subversion on the part of the body, for illness is expensive, and it must not be forgotten that in the universe of this novel money is synonymous with 'life, heaven, God. Everything' (WM36). For Séraphin, who 'could not recall ever having needed the doctor, neither for his old father, nor for himself, nor for anyone else,' this betrayal of the patriarchal ideal of disembodied permanence is all the more infuriating because it has been brought about by a woman: 'And now for the first time in his life, a woman was asking for this service that would cost money. No. Anything but that. And as he looked at Donalda from behind, he now despised her, indeed loathed her. He was filled with bitterness and he regretted more than anything else in his life having married this extravagant girl, who was sick ... How unhappy he was and how he cursed the wedded life!' (WM24).

Like many of the other female characters in the novel of the land, Donalda dies 'in the state of grace,' 'asking forgiveness for all her trespasses,' and disappearing from life 'without complaining and without disturbing anyone' (WM37). However, 'dried up ... from within' by fever and thirst during her final agony, she sheds a torrent of tears that seems to carry within it, as though released by a dam that has finally broken, all the unshed tears of the Louise Rivards, the Maria Chapdelaines, and the Alphonsine Moisans of the preceding works: 'Donalda was crying softly, wringing her hands. Her cry was like an out-of-the-way spring in the woods where no one would ever go. Her cheeks were still burning and rosy, rosy as the two most beautiful roses of the most beautiful summer' (WM42).

Given the domination exercised over women and over all the related realm of the 'feminine maternal' in the novel of the land, it seems justifiable to see in Donalda's last words a condemnation that goes far beyond her own case and that – symbolically at least – can be read as the collective reply of all the female characters of these novels: 'I'm thirsty! I'm burning! ... I've been killed ... Mother! Mother!' (WM49). Having died under the signs of water and of fire ('two tears, the last two, from the depths of her being, ran slowly down her burning cheeks' [WM44]), Donalda will have her revenge in the fusion of natural elements (water and fire) that will bring Séraphin's life to an end. After her death, however, her corpse will be the object of a final and grotesque outrage perpetrated against it, one that, like her final words, can be generalized to include the fate of all her sisters. Violently desecrated by a husband determined to make it fit into a casket too small for it – but so much cheaper! – it could be the corpse of all the women characters of the novel of the land, imprisoned within the confines of a role that diminishes them:

Since the knees of the corpse were sticking out, Séraphin pressed on the lid and a sound of cracking bones was heard.

'It'll fit all right,' he concluded. He screwed the lid down himself. (WM67)

CHAPTER THREE

Opening the house to the Other:
The novels of Germaine Guèvremont

Inhabiting is the characteristic most basic to man's being ...

Man never stops seeking, building, creating houses for himself,
everywhere: grottoes, huts, women, cities, language, concepts, theory ...

And what if perception were woman's most characteristic trait? Could
it be that the feminine, that women can remain in a state of perception
without feeling obliged to name or conceptualize? Without closure?
Remaining in a state of perception means remaining open, always
attentive to the outside, to the world. With one's senses always alert ...
But not necessarily divided between two lights and two darknesses.

    Luce Irigaray, *Ethique de la différence sexuelle*

The settler is always threatened by the face of the unknown (the folly
of a song from elsewhere or of an unseen image).

And that is the promise of a work of fiction that disconcerts the reader:
it offers a passage beyond fear.

    Madeleine Gagnon, *Les Fleurs du catalpa*

'One autumn evening, at Monk's Inlet, as the Beauchemin family
was preparing for supper, they were startled by a knocking at the
door. It was a stranger ... '[1] These well-known lines, which open
Germaine Guèvremont's first novel, *The Outlander*, themselves represent an insistent knock at the door of the house that is the novel
of the land – which, thanks to this woman's writing, will finally
open up to the outside world and to all the unexpressed 'otherness'

repressed by the 'dream of enduring forever.' After the edifying chronicle of Jean Rivard's career and the frustrated dramas of possession (with their necessary underside of impotence) played out by Menaud, Euchariste Moisan, and Séraphin, the note sounded in Guèvremont's novels is clearly *different*; her narrative strategy is new.

What happens when a woman begins to write? – she who, according to the dictates of the dominant ideology, has no story, and she who has always been excluded from the hierarchies of identity and possession that shape the representational techniques of the 'traditional novel'? More confident and less alienated than Laure Conan (and also, one suspects, less 'radical' in her vision than her predecessor), Guèvremont does not seem to feel the need to discard the forms of realism in order to grant her female characters a voice. Like her ambivalent Outlander character – who is both 'masculine' and 'feminine,' respectful of the house and its values and yet unable to settle in any one place – she renews the house of the novel of the land from within, basing her novels on a symbolic and cultural world identical to that of her male contemporaries and using narrative techniques similar to theirs. Unlike Laure Conan's work, Guèvremont's almost 'androgynous' writing has been understood and appreciated by male critics since it first appeared.[2] But can a woman's voice express itself freely in the Father's House? There is an ambiguity present in these novels – one that becomes more and more noticeable as we move from *The Outlander* to *Marie-Didace*[3] – and that gradually decentres the narrative until it slides into a fragmentation and violence quite foreign to its original agenda of pleasure.

A woman in the Father's House

Drawing on the same cultural background and situated in the same geographic space as the novels of the land written by men, Guèvremont's writing is a fascinating example of the specificity of women's writing. Like her male counterparts, she builds her plots around the archetypes of the *coureur de bois*, the settler, and the family home passed on from father to son. In her work, however, the familiar universe peopled by these figures is transformed into a sort of liquid image of the novel of the land – the Father's House as reflected in the moving waters of the St Lawrence River, next to which her novels are set. Elements that were unchanging in the earlier novels shift position; their rigid oppositions are deconstructed and further displaced as we move from the first novel to the second.[4] Thus, for example, the formerly warring figures of the *coureur de bois* and the settler 'lay down their arms' in the characters of the Outlander and Père Didace, and are attracted to each other like two complementary halves of a single whole. And the paternal lineage, interrupted by the weakness of the son in *The Outlander* as it had been in earlier novels of the land, opens up in *Marie-Didace* and shifts in a surprising direction – towards the female line of descent.

In fact, none of the dualities to which the novel of the land had accustomed us (the opposition between the *coureur de bois* and the settler, the house and the water, the male subject and the female object) is present in this universe of constant flow and metamorphosis. The house in Guèvremont's work, situated halfway between the river and the road, is no longer a fortress against the outside world but rather a place of welcome and a setting-out point for journeying. And while in the earlier novels of the land the relationship between writer and reader was well symbolized by the reassuring pact between Euchariste and Père Branchaud, here it is the much more disconcerting relationship between the Outlander and the people of Monk's Inlet that offers an image of Guèvremont's attitude to her readers. An invitation, a gift, and a provocation, her writing forces us to shift direction as we read, challenging us to risk that openness to the other which brings about change. But like the Outlander, who teaches Angélina Desmarais how to 'recognize the things that sing on this earth,' her novels invite us, paradoxically, to seek the elsewhere in the here and now, by learning to listen, to see, to touch, and to taste the world around us. This is a writing of pleasure and of risk, with no other message than that of how to live.

The texture of feminine writing

Guèvremont enters the Father's House of the novel of the land just as the Outlander enters the Beauchemins' house, under the sign of water and of pleasure. The first gesture of the provocative stranger on entering the house is to make the kitchen pump work, splashing water over the edge of the sink and onto the floor and laughing at his own carelessness. Then, 'with his extraordinarily alive hands' (03), he washes his face and neck and splashes his hair, offering to the eyes of his disapproving onlookers an image of all that is disconcerting in sensual pleasure. But these initial gestures of the Outlander point to the possibility of renewal as well, to a new type of relationship with people and with objects. 'He seemed to bring fresh significance to an act familiar to them all.' (03). The whole import of the two novels, *The Outlander* and *Marie-Didace*, is already present in this suggestion that possession is not the only way of relating to the world, and that there are other values more nourishing than those of permanence, transcendence, and the sense of duty handed down from the fathers.

Writing 'in the feminine' can mean a *way* of writing adapted to the circumstances of a life divided between family and writing. For Guèvremont, wife and mother of five children (and the only Quebec novelist before the age of modern feminism to have reconciled writing and motherhood), it means a writing that flows with the richness and deep humanity of traditional French-Canadian life, especially as experienced by women. The author's comments on the period when *The Outlander* was written suggest the hectic schedule of a mother's existence: 'There were eight of us in the house, three generations, in the hard times during the war. I wrote wherever I could, whenever I could, on whatever bits of paper I could find. I was carrying *The Outlander*.'5 Such working conditions help to explain not only the fragmented nature of certain parts of the novel (the reader's occasional feeling that some of the author's tableaux of daily life interrupt the plot and bring it temporarily to a standstill), but also the focus on human relations that is central to its vision. As well, Guèvremont mentions to her biographer, Rita Leclerc, that she does not work in a linear mode, but more in the manner of a painter: 'When you paint a picture, you don't start with one corner and then work towards the other. You do a little here, a little there, until the painting is finished.'6

Is it because of this reality of being 'pulled in different directions' so common in women's lives, or for more inner motivations linked to their identification with the feminine-maternal, that women write 'close to the real,' attempting to embrace life in the process of writing rather than to transcend it through a work of art endowed with eternal significance? It is not necessary or even possible to know the answer to this question; what is of interest to the critic is the way this different 'texture' of feminine writing manifests itself in the text. The essence of Guèvremont's vision is found in a density of portrayed life that seems to expand the linearity of the narrative structure: the atmosphere of a warm house, the attention paid to detail (the ingredients of a good meal, or the gestures and laughter, the small yearnings, pettinesses, or acts of generosity that compose the texture of daily life). Often this texture is perceptible in the space *between* words, as in the elliptical conversation between the Outlander and Père Didace, who 'was not much of a talker ... If it had been a question of rounding up a herd of frightened cattle ... in that case, he'd have no problem! But, words you fight against in the darkness?' (o100); or in the marvellous episode, attuned to the silences of male friendship, where Pierre-Côme Provençal manages to console his old rival Didace on the loss of his son without revealing his own emotion (o233–6). At other times, this texture shifts the narrative in the direction of pleasure: like the women's gossip that goes off in all directions (o182–5), communicating a whole dimension of reality excluded from earlier novels of the land. It is in part at least these departures from traditional linear narrative form that produce the ambiguity of Guèvremont's novels, the difficulty experienced by the reader who attempts to extract a single 'meaning' from the constantly shifting relationships of her characters.

From identity to interrelationship

The contrast between Guèvremont's writing and that of her male predecessors also illustrates how the mere presence within the narrative of female characters who exist as subjects results in the deconstruction of age-old concepts of identity and the fictions based on them. It is not simply a question of substituting a female protagonist where formerly there was a male one; on the contrary. Whereas the male novelists of the land had constructed linear dramas of masculine identity in which the female character was relegated to the status of an object to be possessed, in Guèvremont's work the entire dynamic of the narrative is decentred. The preoccupation with identity is replaced by an interest in relationship, unity gives way to multiplicity, and the plot, losing its linearity, becomes a tracing of the stages of desire and loss, focused on the almost imperceptible changes in human beings that constitute the real drama of daily life.

In *Master of the River*, *Thirty Acres*, and *The Woman and the Miser*, the main character is readily identifiable; it is difficult to say who is the main character in *The Outlander* and *Marie-Didace*, however. Certainly the Outlander's arrival sets off a drama that continues to be played out – long after his departure – in the lives of the people of Monk's Inlet. This 'main character' remains veiled in mystery, however; his only role in the plot is his effect on the other characters. Moreover, he is replaced in *Marie-Didace* by another stranger, the Acadian, who acts as his double and asymmetrical reflection. While the earlier novels of the land had advanced in a straight line towards their conclusions, here the multiple perspectives and the defocalized mirror images set up between *The Outlander* and *Marie-Didace* create effects of ambiguity, making the reader suspect that the meaning of the drama before him lies in a place *other* than where he or she is looking. Is the Outlander's effect on the community positive or negative, for example? And what about that of the Acadian, who resembles him in so many ways? In the attempt to answer such questions, the reader is drawn back into the personal dramas of each of the characters and the constant change in their mutual relationships. Twenty years before Hubert Aquin's *Prochain Episode*, the doubling, the ellipses, the asymmetrical and open-ended effects in Guèvremont's novels open the doors of the Quebec novel to modernity.

From patriarchal society to women's world: *The Outlander* and the emergence of the feminine

The Outlander arrives in the Quebec cultural text like an irruption of the whole realm of the feminine repressed by the 'dream of enduring forever.' At the beginning of *The Outlander*, a world is drawing to a close, and it is one clearly dominated by the aging patriarch Didace Beauchemin. By the end of *Marie-Didace*, the focus has shifted to Marie-Didace Beauchemin, a lively and independent little girl who occupies the centre of a world that is devastated but turned towards the future. As a result of the death of her father, her grandfather, and his second wife, and of her mother's madness, all recounted in the space of only a few pages (recalling the violence needed in *Angéline de Montbrun* to clear the patriarchal stage), Marie-Didace is raised by another unconventional and independent woman, Angélina Desmarais – the only inhabitant of Monk's Inlet to have truly absorbed the Outlander's teachings.

The Outlander's arrival is already a sign that all is not well in the community of Monk's Inlet. The embodiment of freedom and pleasure, he arouses desire in all the characters, male or female, who sense something missing in the existing order of things. And one has only to think of Donalda's thirst on her deathbed to understand that the characters most likely to be open to his message are women – Angélina, Phonsine, Marie-Amanda – just as women welcomed Christ's message before patriarchal culture appropriated it and made it a vehicle of its contempt for matter, the body, and woman. Whether a figure of Christ,[7] Eros,[8] or simply a *coureur de bois* looking for a place to rest, the Outlander is clearly the author's spokesman in his diagnosis of the illness of a community that has lost its vitality. For the reader familiar with earlier novels of the land, the symptoms of disease are familiar: a Law that has become inflexible, and a rage to possess that, concerned only with the accumulation of goods, forgets that material objects can also give pleasure.

As Laure Conan had done in the song of Maurice Darville, Guèvremont associates this irruption of the feminine and of Eros into the closed world of her characters with the magic of voice, music, and dance – tangible and fluid signs of a possible *rapprochement* between the body and spiritual values, and reminders of the original corporeal link with the world of the mother. When the Outlander sings, it is this whole repressed universe, and the secret desire of each character, that awakens and insists on being heard: 'His voice was not beautiful; it was quite untrained and yet it spoke to the heart. As soon as it rose, people would stop and listen, their hands unclenched. Everyone who heard it was swept along the road of his own desire, the road where the object of his dreams, warm and welcoming, awaited' (067).

Released by his song, this deep-seated desire for unity is expressed in dance, where the joined hands of the characters speak – as words cannot – of the dream of an experience of sharing and exchange in which the divisions created by culture would disappear: 'Then the dancers gathered in a ring around the room, and girls and men joined hands for the Ladies' Chain. A brief squeeze of hands, and then another, said more than lips dared to express. In their own naïve language, hands, more eloquent than voices, spoke of understanding, everlasting friendship or perhaps indifference' (o68).

To say then that it is the women who welcome the Outlander and the men who reject him would falsify not only the meaning of the novel but also the respect for individual difference so important in Guèvremont's vision. ('Do we expect autumn to be like spring?' asks Angélina as she listens to the other women gossip about Phonsine [o220]). For each of the characters, the Outlander represents the other, the repressed feminine-maternal, the secret desire that yearns to be awakened; and his influence on them is proportionate to each character's capacity for openness. However, in the reactions of the various characters to this disconcerting stranger, it is possible to discern an overall image of patriarchal society as it reacts to the emergence of the feminine. The ambivalent responses of Père Didace and his daughter-in-law, Alphonsine Beauchemin, suggest the state of the Father's House in a period of transition; Angélina's love for the Outlander is that of an independent woman who has finally found a man who is her match; and finally Marie-Amanda, the woman who is already whole (and who lives, significantly, *outside* Monk's Inlet), embodies the same values as the Outlander.

Water / thirst / the absent mother

It is not surprising that, of all the characters, it should be the mayor, Pierre-Côme Provençal (the representative of the Law), who most despises and fears this stranger who has invaded his community. As his name suggests, Pierre-Côme is the patriarchal 'rock,' a symbol of the very rigidity that women's writing rebels against: 'He was more than a man. He was the Law incarnate, inflexible, unyielding. A statue' (o218). Instead of *opposing* this rock, or the house built of stone (*'pierre'*) that is its cultural dwelling place, the words of Guèvremont/the Outlander infiltrate it like life-giving water.

The people of Monk's Inlet, used to spring floods, are vaguely familiar with the idea of renewal brought by water. But of their ancestral myths they have retained only the fear of drowning, an awareness of its destructive power. Anxious to keep the Outlander from leaving when spring comes, Père Didace tells him a series of legendary stories associated with 'the disastrous breakup of the ice on Ash Wednesday in 1865' (073). Moving from the first to the third of these stories (all told from the male point of view), we see how Guèvremont gradually transforms the meaning of the father/children/survival/maternal-sacrifice grouping we saw in the novel of the land, making woman triumph through her closeness to the feared element of water. The first tale, entirely faithful to the tradition, is 'the beautiful story' (074) of a young woman who, about to give birth when the flood begins, begs her husband 'to leave her to her death and escape with the two other children.' The second story also tells of the heroic survival of a man and the disappearance of a woman: Gilbert Brisset 'sees his house split in two and then his wife, his child, his mother, two brothers, four sisters drown before his very eyes' (074), but he himself survives by clinging to a tree trunk. It is the third story that contains a humorous reversal of the tradition. To save himself from drowning, Louis Désy also holds onto a tree, and suddenly he sees his house being washed towards him, with his wife and daughter inside! Ready to follow tradition and sacrifice his 'women' ('*créatures*') he discovers (as had the male novelists of the land) that women are more cunning than he had realized:

'Farewell, wife. Farewell, daughter,' he says, snuffling and raising his arms to heaven. 'I won't see you again, except in paradise.' That said, he shuts his eyes so as not to see them perish. But the two poor creatures – who as usual have misunderstood – instead of replying: 'Farewell, till we meet in heaven!' start to climb out onto the gable end. So that when old Louis opens his eyes, what does he see astride the house? His girl and his wife, perfectly all right, calling out: 'Good morning, little Louis dear.' (074)

The Outlander as well seems to 'misunderstand' the message of the danger of water and the primacy of death. After listening without a word to the stories of Père Didace, he suddenly begins to speak 'in an undertone, as though to himself.' From his words emanate the same thirst for maternal water, the same ecstasy and tenderness expressed in his attitude to alcohol.[9] For him, water is not the threatening Other, but a part of himself, an element of life, a 'loved one' he misses: 'He spoke about the bustle of great sea-ports when they awaken to the life of springtime, and especially about the docker's job. He said nothing of the perils of the longshoreman's life, nor of all the docker had to contend with ... He spoke of the docker's life as one would speak of a loved one in whom one is unwilling to see any faults' (074–5).

Within the Beauchemin family, a similar thirst has been felt since the death of Mathilde Beauchemin, the mother and wife. Without her, the house has lost its 'power to cheer the heart ... that stamp of infallibility which turns a home into a unique refuge against the rest of the world' (09). The curtains hang 'in slovenly folds' against the windows; and the familiar objects, 'once so priceless,' seem to have lost their former value. Another dead mother: but, in contrast to earlier novels of the land, the whole aim of Guèvremont's writing is to compensate for her absence by giving the house, the objects, and the beings within it a new value based on their existence in language. From this new 'fallibility' in the house comes an opportunity for openness, since the woman-object (the mother) who held the old structures in place is now absent.

The Beauchemin family: A cultural microcosm

In addition to Mathilde's death, there is another important death in the Beauchemin family – that of the favourite son, Ephrem, who drowns shortly before his mother dies. In the same line of descent as François Paradis, Menaud's son, Joson (who also dies young), and Ephrem Moisan (Euchariste's favourite son, who emigrates to the United States), Ephrem Beauchemin is the 'positive' son, the one who in another cultural tradition might well become the main focus of the plot and the bearer of the themes of revolt and change. In the Quebec cultural text, however, it is not the son but the daughter who inherits the potential to subvert the Father's order. Like François, Joson, and Ephrem Moisan, Ephrem Beauchemin is forced out of the plot, leaving in the Beauchemin house a group that strangely resembles the patriarchal triangle of father, castrated son, and silent daughter of the first part of *Angéline de Montbrun*. For

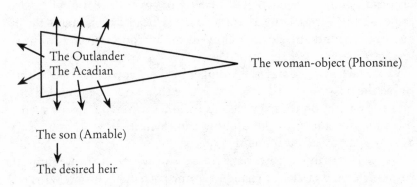

The father (Didace)

The Outlander
The Acadian

The woman-object (Phonsine)

The son (Amable)

The desired heir

Figure 8 *The Outlander*: the shattering of the patriarchal triangle

despite his likeable character, Père Didace is still the patriarch who rules over the house, his son, Amable, the powerless heir of Maurice Darville, and his daughter-in-law, Alphonsine, the daughter dominated by the father's gaze. Since Amable is the impotent son, incapable of any reaction except rejection of the Outlander, it is within the 'couple' formed by Didace and Phonsine that the newcomer's impact is felt. As aging patriarch and rejected daughter, they represent a new version of the archetypal father/daughter couple through which Quebec women's writing engages with its social context and shatters the patriarchal triangle.

THE 'OPENING' OF DIDACE: A CRACK IN THE ORDER OF THE FATHER

For Père Didace, the arrival of the Outlander seems at first to represent the possibility of renewal. In opening the house, Guèvremont also 'opens' the figure of the father, making him a down-to-earth and believable character, more human and fallible than all the fathers who precede him in the Quebec literary text. Through the character of Didace, we realize that the Law can be hard on fathers as well as on daughters and sons. His thirst and his need for tenderness become evident to Phonsine when she finds him sprawled on the floor after an evening of drinking in Sorel: 'She could not convince him to get up and go to bed, so she got a pillow and slipped it under his head, and then went to get a blanket to cover him. But when she came back, he was lying there again, his head on the bare floor, his arms around the down pillow in an attitude that was almost loving' (083).

Once he has welcomed the stranger into his house, Didace begins to see the possibility of a new order, one that would be founded not on the Law but on forgiveness and openness. 'Maybe it isn't such a bad thing for a man to slip up now and then: it shows him he isn't as strong a guy as he thought' (084).

In the last analysis, however, Didace is unable to extricate himself from the closed circle (or triangle) of the patriarchal order. What he seeks in the Outlander is, finally, the narcissistic repetition of an order whose time is past and its perpetuation in 'a son like himself' (0103). Unable to absorb the Outlander's message, he projects onto him the old fantasies of the male 'dream of enduring forever': the desire to conquer, to be the strongest in the hierarchy of Monk's Inlet, to be 'eternal' despite the passage of time. For a moment, when the Outlander fights with Odilon Provençal, the son of Didace's old rival, Pierre-Côme, Didace thinks he has seen the fulfilment of this ancient dream founded on male rivalry: 'A great joy spread within him, his blood ran once more rich and red. His ashen face seamed by age, his failing strength, his aged heart, furrowed by anxiety? All that was a bad dream. He had recovered his youthful strength intact: Didace, son of Didace, has just taken possession of the land. He is thirty again. A first son has been born to him. The reign of the Beauchemins will never end' (070).

Is it this lack of understanding that makes the Outlander's influence on Didace so disastrous? Intending to follow the Outlander's advice, Didace marries the Acadian, who is more of a 'stranger' to the Father's House than any of the Alphonsine Moisans (also seen as 'strangers') introduced into it in earlier novels. Unable to embrace genuine change in the order of things, he enters into marriage with a goal identical to that of Euchariste Moisan in marrying Alphonsine: to produce the son 'like himself' who will guarantee his triumph over death. Having chosen a woman as radically foreign to the house as the Acadian, however, he finds himself confronted by something completely unexpected.

THE ACADIAN: THE 'RADICALLY OTHER'

Like all those who threaten the order of the house in the novel of the land, the Acadian comes from elsewhere. Not only a non-Québécois, but a woman who dares to make her presence felt in the house, she necessarily upsets the existing order of things. Radically 'other,' she functions in the text as a revealer of women's reality and – in the broader Quebec literary text of which this novel is part – as the first messenger from a watery realm that feminist writers will later appropriate for themselves as the realm of women's repressed power.[10] As ambiguous as the novel she dominates, however, she is, in the final analysis, a disappointing character.

Seen in the context of the structure of the Father's House, the Acadian's unforgivable sin is to have supplanted the traditional mother, the woman-object whose presence guaranteed the house's solidity. A pleasure-oriented and somewhat egotistical woman, she makes fun of the Law, unlike Mathilde Beauchemin who upheld it through her self-effacement. This truth is most bluntly expressed by the son, Amable. Furious at his father for having brought this intruder into the house, he compares the Acadian to his own mother, 'Mathilde, the saintly woman, who never spared herself and would go to any length to make others happy,' and says to him, 'You didn't have to get married. Why buy the cow when you can get the milk for nothing?' (0208).

Strong, plump, sensual, and sure of herself, the Acadian is indeed a woman who enjoys life, who has found her voice and is at ease with her body: 'her carnal voice drew out the sound the way wool retains heat' (0149). 'Relaxing' for the men, she arouses suspicion in the other women who, next to her, seem thin, drab, dulled by lives dedicated to duty. Her laughter and her 'smooth forehead' accentuate the rigid appearance of the other women, 'their lips set ominously,' (0166). Reflecting on her way of 'occupying the territory' of the house, Phonsine also thinks of the self-effacement of Didace's first wife: 'Poor shrinking mother Mathilde, always in her little black cape, managing to slip out so unobtrusively when any unwelcome visitor appeared' (0168). But the Acadian's life of pleasure must be good for the health, for a merchant visiting Monk's Inlet immediately notices the difference between her and the other women of the community: 'she doesn't look worn out to me' (0167). In fact it is this very absence of exhaustion that provokes the hostility of the other women: 'a buxom, handsome woman, at her age, must have had a soft life. Too soft, in fact. They, who had always worked so hard, resented her all the more. Besides, their husbands, from sheer perversity, felt free to praise her right in front of them' (0165).

Independent and calm, the Acadian defines the world in her own terms and does not waste her time 'bothering' the men, as the other women do. Next to her, who 'let them smoke in peace ... or talk without ever interrupting them or asking questions' (0166), Laure Provençal, who tries desperately to take part in their conversation, seems 'a nosy woman' (0166).

Always referred to as 'the Other' (0158) by Phonsine and Amable, the Acadian does indeed seem to belong to a separate world, which constantly calls to her and distances her from her husband and from the people of Monk's Inlet. Associated with water, an 'island' and 'dream,' it evokes the liquid sphere to which women have been exiled throughout history, but which can also be seen as a place of Utopian female fulfilment: ' "What can be on her mind all the time?" wondered Père Didace uneasily. "She's never with the rest of us. Like an island away out at sea. Every time she comes back, it's as if she's made an effort, as if she's had to cross water, and a lot of water too. It must be very tiresome" ' (0167).

In spite of the resemblance to the Outlander suggested by her white skin, her blue eyes, and her way of laughing, the Acadian lacks the 'respect for the house' that leads the latter to flee rather than bring misfortune on it. On the contrary, she moves in unhesitatingly, appropriating the title of 'queen and mistress of the house' (0150), rearranging the dishes in the cupboard, and, more symbolically, the old ways of doing things. Her eyes, 'sometimes blue, sometimes green, changing like river water' (0153), recall the Outlander's, but at the same time, there is something in her expression that is 'furtive, dull blue-green, inscrutable,' suggesting a kind of falseness.

What *is* certain amidst all the ambiguity surrounding the Acadian is that the time has not yet come when such an independent woman can exist within the Quebec text. Given the importance of Christian themes in the two novels, it is possible to see her as another Christ-figure, like the Outlander she resembles. But the gospel she brings to women – a message of independence, pleasure, and respect for their bodies[11] – lacks the dimension of love. Thirty years later, Louky Bersianik's Euguélionne will bring a more generous gospel to the 'women of the earth,' and by then they will be ready to listen.

One suspects in fact that not only is the Acadian too 'radical' for the people of Monk's Inlet, she is also too radical for Germaine Guèvremont. Unaware of the values of giving and sharing that made the Beauchemin women of the past remarkable, she communicates her 'truth' through sterile confrontation: 'You're just a bunch of cowards, every one of you ... You're afraid to hear the truth. When someone tells it to you, you run away' (0193). For Guèvremont, the truth is more subtle, more complex, more imbued with love. That of the Acadian has its place, nonetheless, in the tissue of feminine truths she places before the reader.

PHONSINE: THE WOMAN APART

I left because I didn't want to become the queen-mother; although I had all the talents needed for that! Make a divine right for myself out of my failure as a human being? No thanks. And yet, it would have suited others for me to take power and enjoy it ... (Claire Lejeune)[12]

Through the character of Alphonsine Beauchemin, the alienated voice of the French-Canadian woman is heard loud and clear for the first time since the diary of Angéline de Montbrun: the voice of a young girl, a wife, and a mother thirsting for love and rigidly shackled by the force of cultural circumstances. Phonsine does not leave her assigned role as Claire Lejeune does in the words quoted above. On the contrary, she dreams constantly of becoming the 'queen-mother' in the hope that the role will compensate for her failure-to-be. Always distanced from her own authentic selfhood, she clings desperately to anything that promises to give her a sense of belonging in the Father's House, but is unsuccessful. Through her, Guèvremont's writing confronts the ambiguity of its own position in the symbolic order, departs from its itinerary of pleasure, and comes face to face with the Law of the Father.

Moving from *The Outlander* to *Marie-Didace*, the reader notices two not-unrelated phenomena: the greater importance of Phonsine in the second work,[13] and Guèvremont's striking departure in that work from the linearity, logic, and closure typical of the realist novel. Reading the two novels 'in the feminine,' one cannot help wondering if this fragmentation and ambiguity (which have traditionally led critics to conclude that *The Outlander* is 'superior' to *Marie-Didace*) are not rather signs of a woman's writing that, as it unfolds, becomes less and less able to conform to the literary rules of the Father's House. In this respect, the character of Phonsine, whose narrative journey corresponds precisely to the gap between her own desire and the prescribed female roles to which she attempts in vain to conform, provides a *mise en abîme* or mirror reflection of the experience of writing. It is almost as if the author, in creating her, had wanted to make her follow the narrative path traditionally reserved for female characters, only to see her character rebel, insisting that her story be told in *another* way. A daughter rejected by her father, a 'sterile' woman dreaming of fulfilment through pregnancy, and, finally, a mother rejected by her own daughter, Phonsine embodies the impossible female dream of *belonging* in the Father's House. Submitting all her hopes and all her actions to the 'law of the Beauchemins' (081), she convinces herself that, if only she can turn herself into a perfect housewife, loyal wife, obedient daughter, and especially into a mother, she will finally succeed in pleasing the father and find the happiness that has hitherto escaped her. The irony of her fate is that, in acceding to each of these roles, she not only widens the distance separating her from her own needs and desires, but finds herself replaced by the Acadian, a woman of pleasure.

Still a secondary character in *The Outlander*, Phonsine appears timid, insecure, and awkward under the censorious gaze of Père Didace. Like Mina under the scrutiny of Charles de Montbrun, she feels constantly judged and unable to 'measure up.' Her first appearance in the novel, significantly filtered through the perspective of Père Didace, reveals her as a 'little girl' whose clumsiness and nervousness increase as she becomes aware of the father's gaze: 'Frail, with narrow shoulders and hips, her hair in plaits, and sitting there forlornly, she looked like a little girl being punished. As soon as she caught sight of her father-in-law, she busied herself cutting the bread. Sensing the stern look of the master following her slightest movements, she became more and more flustered' (09).

It is only when the men are absent from the house that Phonsine dares to indulge her own desires and pleasures. Then she takes out of their hiding place the 'delicate strips of pale satin and flame-coloured velvet' that she keeps 'for the mere pleasure of gazing at them and feeling their softness to the touch' (024). Her sensual pleasure and delight in beauty are also revealed in the fancy cup she once won at a carnival and that she clings to like a sign of poetry in her monotonous life. The Outlander expresses his approval of these 'forbidden pleasures' when he hands her an armful of sweetgrass (024).

Like other female characters in the novel-of-the-land tradition, Phonsine reveals her relationship to the house and to the paternal lineage in the typical act of washing the kitchen floor. But, being the creation of a woman writer, she is endowed with enough subjectivity that through this act the ambiguities of the housewife's situation are revealed. The scene where, believing she is alone in the house for the day, she washes the floor at her own speed and according to her own standards, stands in sharp contrast to similar scenes in the life of a Donalda Laloge or an Alphonsine Moisan. Unlike Donalda, she sighs with satisfaction at being alone in the house, as if this were the only time she were allowed to be herself: 'During the morning, the time passed quickly. Alphonsine did the housework and prepared the dinner. Then she started washing the floor, perfectly happy to be working unobserved. No one would eye her reproachfully for leaving the soap in the water ... When she turned around, she heaved a sigh of satisfaction at the sight of the floor, shining and clean' (076–7).

Surprised by the arrival of the Outlander, who dirties her floor with his muddy boots, she initially reacts like Alphonsine Moisan, with a burst of anger: 'look at my floor that I've just scrubbed, all over mud! You ought to be ashamed of yourself!' (077). But, unlike the other Alphonsine, this woman-subject can transcend her role and feel tenderness for the intoxicated man: 'But in her heart she was less enraged by the mess on the floor than distressed by the Outlander's condition. In spite of herself, her displeasure was not unmixed with pity for the stranger in his solitude, who thought his bold gestures made him strong' (077–8).

Always distanced from herself, Phonsine reveals that she is learning at last to be 'a true Beauchemin' at the precise moment when she is displaced from her position in the house by the arrival of the Acadian. At this crucial point in her development, she is shown, like Donalda before her, in the presence of the portraits of the ancestors, representatives of the Law and of the name of the Father. But in this female universe, things are no longer black and white, and ironically the Law of the Father seems more human and more worth believing in than it had in the works of the male writers:

Now there are only the three of them left – Didace, Amable-Didace and herself – to look after the ancestral goods. Her gaze wanders from one familiar object to another as though to implore their help ... In the zinc portraits ... reign two previous Didace Beauchemins – six generations of them have borne the name – with bristly chin-beards, brawny shoulders tightly encased in jackets of homespun, but with penetrating eyes, a steady gaze and lofty foreheads. With honesty and with human respect for their sweat ... in lives of bitter hardship ... they have written the law of the Beauchemins. It was up to those who followed them, the inheritors of the name, to observe it faithfully. (081).

To the judgmental eyes of the ancestors, Phonsine responds not with the submission of a Donalda, but rather with a sign that she has become a Beauchemin: a prayer asking 'good Saint Mathilde Beauchemin' to protect her place in the house. It is a prayer that will be answered in the form of a long-awaited pregnancy for this woman who has felt like 'a field-stone, cold and sterile' (082) but who, for all that, will not find her place in the house secured.

In *Marie-Didace*, Phonsine grows as a character, occupying the centre, so to speak, of this decentred work. Once the love-starved daughter, she now becomes the rigid, hateful mother, sterner and more negative than the father who lays down the law in the house. But her inner turmoil is always present in the text – her growing realization that 'There'll never be any peace for me' (0255).

It is through Phonsine's perspective that the novel opens, and that the Acadian's arrival in the Beauchemin house, with all its menacing undertones, is presented. Traumatized by this intrusion, her consciousness is flooded with childhood memories – memories of desertion and rejection that explain her fundamental insecurity. For not only is Phonsine motherless like Angéline, Mina, and Menaud's Marie, she has also been brutally rejected by her alcoholic father, who placed her in an orphanage soon after her mother's death. The image of the six-year-old child watching her father walk away from her eloquently explains the immense need for tenderness she is to feel throughout her life:

'You must be obedient, do you understand? and do everything the good sisters tell you to do. Otherwise, you'll be sent away ... '
    In a movement of long-repressed affection, Phonsine ran to her father. She wanted to throw her arms around his neck as she kissed him goodbye. But, misunderstanding her gesture, he hadn't left her enough time, being in a hurry to get away and only too glad to be relieved of his burden. (0152)

    Motherless and abandoned by her father, the little 'orphan' develops habits of obedience and self-sacrifice in which the contours of her future alienation can be discerned. Always afraid of being sent away, she eats, sleeps, and plays on command. Entering the chapel for evening prayers, she 'offers up her weariness for her father who had made her promise to obey' (0153). Like many another young girl robbed of her spontaneity and her capacity for enjoyment, she finds it more natural to despise herself than to entertain the possibility of anger at the Father.
    As a married woman, Phonsine seeks the affection and the security she lacked as a child, but finds herself, on the contrary, united with a husband who has all the traits of an impotent son. Her desire, already awakened by the Outlander, becomes insistent when the Acadian arrives in the house and she notices the presence of a new sensual pleasure in Père Didace. In the course of one exemplary night, as she lies in bed next to her husband, she experiences all the stages of transformation of the archetypal female character of Quebec literature into the negative mother figure. As she caresses Amable and attempts to console him for the presence of his intrusive new stepmother, she finds herself rejected by a man unable to

respond to her own thirst for love. Longing for shared pleasure, she is obliged instead to play the role of mother, not only of the child she is carrying, but also of her husband. And at that moment she is overwhelmed by an unquenchable thirst, and by feelings of contempt and bitterness that, lacking other means of expression, are transformed into the hardness and resignation typical of many of the mother characters in Quebec literature. The contradictory stages of this swallowing up of the female character by the negative archetype of the mother have perhaps never been so precisely captured in a Quebec literary work, and they are worth noting. First, the offer of tenderness to the weeping husband:

Touched by Amable's distress and at the same time embarrassed by his weakness so nakedly displayed, like a large and shameless body, she held him close to her until he fell asleep, stroking his temples, stroking his hair, stroking his eyelids.

Then, bitterness and scorn:

When his agitation had subsided, one by one her fingers relaxed their grip. And gradually, through her pity for him, came a sense of vague regret, tinged with resentment and secret bitterness ... Was this a man? She lay awake in anguish while he slept, breathing peacefully beside her. All through that day, he had not had a word of sympathy for her, fated, much more than he was, to live in the company of this detested woman. And she was carrying his child, his first child!

The thirst for affection, the loneliness, and the envy of other women:

Something unappeased was tormenting her. Confused images haunted her sleepless hours. She remembered having heard the voices of women in love saying 'You're mine' to a miserable but affectionate husband ... Once more she saw on her knees the sheaf of sweetgrass the Outlander had gathered for her, and she thought of the spontaneous joy she had felt on receiving the gift.

The attempt to push these disloyal thoughts from her mind:

Conscientiously and remorsefully, she banished these pictures from her mind. Amable was a good man, there was no denying that ...

The realization that the only satisfaction marriage offers her is mothering, of a husband as well as of children:

Just as she was about to withdraw her now numbed arm, Amable clutched it. 'He's so weak,' she thought, 'and so defenseless.' From now on, she would have to be brave enough for two. She would have two children, one now lying in her womb, and the other sleeping in her arms.

And finally, there comes a renunciation as painful as Angéline de Montbrun's, one compensated for in this case not by writing but, in much more typical fashion, by motherhood:

Since such was her lot, she would renounce all impossible joys, as she had put aside the remnants of velvet and silk which were not meant for her chapped hands, though from time to time she could not help taking them out and holding the glittering fabrics up to the light.
'But the child who is coming – he'll be mine!'

Before this significant night comes to an end, Phonsine has been irrevocably transformed into the patriarchal French-Canadian mother, the harsh woman filled with bitterness, who punishes those around her for her unquenched thirst:

Before sunrise, she would pester Amable to go to the notary and see they got their rights. If she had to harness the horse herself and put the reins in his hands, Amable would go ... Near the threshold flickered a slant of light ... Brusquely, Phonsine detached her arm from Amable's embrace. Dry-eyed and tight-lipped, she lay awake all night, hatred weighing on her heart. (O155–6)

It is not a coincidence but a textual necessity that, in thus defining herself as a mother, Phonsine renounces pleasure and that in so doing she finally gains the approval of Père Didace. Having finally learned to conform to the Law of the Father, she quickly becomes the shrewish mother, able to relate to her daughter only by possessing and commanding her. 'Only yesterday evening, when it was so windy, Marie-Didace complained of being afraid,' she tells Marie-Amanda. 'It wasn't true ... To get control of her, I told her to lie quietly in her bed. Well, this morning I found her in bed with the Acadian' (0272–3).

Not can it be coincidental that it is at the precise moment when Phonsine becomes a mother that Guèvremont's narrative turns away from its journey towards pleasure and slides into an unlikely series of violent events reminiscent of the second part of *Angéline de Montbrun*. This break in the text is clearly indicated by the division of the novel into two parts, the second beginning immediately after the birth of Marie-Didace. From here to the end of the novel, the narrative pace quickens (with six years elapsing in the first three pages of Part two), leading the reader towards an accumulation of catastrophes. Amable is already dead at the time of the child's birth (having been pushed by Phonsine to leave home in order to prove his 'virility' to his father); and the subsequent sudden deaths of Père Didace and the Acadian, followed by Phonsine's collapse into madness, result in the shattering of the patriarchal family.

While it is possible to describe the cause of the Acadian's death as an excess of 'pleasure' (the lack of discipline that leads her to swallow pills harmful to her health), Phonsine's madness, brought about by feelings of guilt at having been partly responsible for this death, indicates a definitive *distancing* from the message of pleasure brought by the Outlander. The night before she descends into madness, during a visit to Marie-Amanda, she twice refuses her sister-in-law's attempt to calm her by reminding her of the simple pleasures of daily life:

'Look – look at that ship, how deep it is in the water, it must be off to war,' said Marie-Amanda.

'I don't need to look at it. Ships like that go by every day,' replied Phonsine. Nothing outside her could detract from her anxiety ... 'A woman who took my cup! My place! My husband! ... And now she wants to take my little girl! the farm! everything I have! You'll see! I'll be turned out onto the road to beg my bread. All alone.' (0273)

With too fragile a sense of herself, never able to overcome her fear of being 'sent away' from the house, she has constantly clung to objects, to people, and to roles, unable to abandon herself to pleasure. The final image of her in the novel, sitting next to the well with her fancy cup in her hand and staring vacantly into space, is the fulfilment of the recurrent dream that had tormented her since the death of Amable – a dream that she is falling into destructive maternal waters, all the while clinging to her cup and to her daughter: 'She had first dreamed that, in trying to take her cup away from the Acadian, it had slipped out of her hands. As she leaned over the well trying to get it out, she saw that it was not her cup but her little girl that had fallen in. She herself, dragged down by the emptiness, whirled through the bottomless abyss, uttering shrieks that flayed her throat' (O252–3).

For her, and for all the other fragile young girls turned into rigid women by the Law of the Father, another quotation from Claire Lejeune could serve as an epitaph: 'Yesterday, I hardened myself by objectifying their rejection, their discomfort with my thoughts. That is how convexity comes to the spirit of a woman.'[14]

Possession/enjoyment/spending

... without another word, Angélina slipped out the door. Marie-Amanda joined her on the road. They walked in silence, with the calm step of women who have time and space at their disposal. Snow was still falling and it erased the imprints of their footsteps, one by one, on the whitened ground. (O186)

Using the Beauchemin family as a cultural microcosm, I have traced the process through which the family, lacking the presence of the traditional mother who held together the ancient structure of the house, explodes under the pressure of three contradictory points of view: that of the father, that of the 'new' woman of pleasure, and finally that of the daughter destroyed by her attachment to duty. Threatened by the emergence of the feminine, Didace and Phonsine both cling to a past order and lose what security they had. Is there no possibility of reconciliation, then, between man and woman, possession and pleasure, between the dying past and the future that emerges like an orphan in the character of little Marie-Didace Beauchemin? In the novels of the land by men, such oppositions remained gaping, despite the authors' attempt to create unity by silencing the voice of the feminine, of pleasure, and of change.

But perhaps, after all – as two women with 'time and space at their disposal' walk together – something new will emerge. In the play of differing perspectives or voices that constitute Guèvremont's novels, the voices of Angélina Desmarais and Marie-Amanda Beauchemin, and the friendship between them, point to a woman's vision unprecedented in the Quebec text, in which the age-old opposition between possession and pleasure is paradoxically reconciled in the concepts of sharing, giving, and spending. Such a philosophy of the reconciliation of opposites is as old as Heraclitus and as traditional as the Beauchemin women, but it is also modern enough to be relevant to the dilemmas of present-day culture.

Inasmuch as the 'texture' of such a vision can be illustrated by a diagram, it can be seen that Guèvremont's novels represent 'a step forward' in relation to the structure of women's writing outlined in the first chapter. Whereas in Laure Conan's novel the walls of the cloister and the rigidity of the Law had intervened to destroy the links between Mina and Emma S., and later between Angéline and Mina, here friendship between women emerges as a transforming value, symbolized by the independence of little Marie-Didace. What remains after the destruction of the old order is a woman-centred world, one that maintains a continuity with the vitality of its original values.

For Marie-Amanda, who has inherited the 'gift' of the Beauchemin women, but who lives, significantly, *outside* the paternal house, on the well-named 'Isle of Grace,' this reconciliation is found in an attention to the rhythms of nature, to the flow of the river that binds life and death in an unending process: 'It almost seems as if a family is like salt. Rain falls from heaven, soaks into the ground, absorbs the salt from it, then finds its way into streams and rivers and flows down to enrich the sea. The sky pumps up water from the sea and restores the salt to the earth. It seems as if everything starts all over again in this world' (084–5).

In contrast to the 'dream of enduring forever' seen in the male

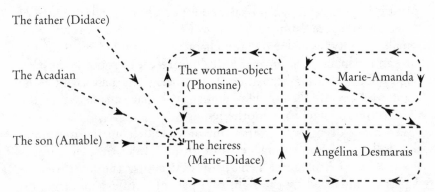

The father (Didace)

The Acadian

The woman-object (Phonsine)

Marie-Amanda

The son (Amable)

The heiress (Marie-Didace)

Angélina Desmarais

Figure 9 *Marie Didace:* the decentring of the narrative towards female subjectivity

novels, Guèvremont is here proposing an acceptance of the death of the individual self and of the pain of loss, made possible through the continuity between generations and through total enjoyment of the present moment: 'A leaf falls from the tree, another leaf replaces it' (o53). Quite the opposite of an abstract dialectic, this female ability to become one with the rhythms of the world does away with contradictions by embracing the continuous change inherent in time. Distressed by the selfish presence of the Acadian within the family, Marie-Amanda tells Angélina, 'It's time. Time brings all things to an end' (o186). Puzzled, her friend replies:

'I don't understand you. The other day you kept telling me that time takes care of everything. Today you're saying the opposite.'
'No, I'm not. I said that everything works out in the end, joys as well as sorrows. Everything disappears as time goes on. (o186–7)

As for Angélina Desmarais, her very name – an 'Angéline' of the marshes? – suggests the possibility of such a reconciliation of opposites: a combining of the mysticism of an Angéline de Montbrun with a rootedness in the elements of earth and water that, for the other Angéline, represented a forbidden realm. Before the arrival of the Outlander, Angélina already lives in these two spheres, but in an incomplete way – a practical woman who manages to satisfy her fondness for poetry by reading Geneviève de Brabant and the 'mystical passages' in her missal, and especially through her love of flowers.[15] It is interesting to note how Guèvremont has broken with female stereotypes in drawing this character, making a lame 'spinster' into an independent woman who calmly refuses proposals of marriage while reassuring her father: 'I guess the right man hasn't come along yet' (O12). Finally, like almost all female characters in the Quebec text, Angélina is motherless.

From her deep love for the Outlander and from the mourning that follows his disappearance from Monk's Inlet, Angélina learns the beauty of Eros and a generosity that allows the loved one to depart. Scandalized by the sight of a pair of gypsies embracing on the roadside, she shows her disapproval in an old Jansenist reflex: 'I don't understand ... that there are people for whom love is ... just that and nothing more' (O108). But, observing the Outlander's respect for the gypsies, she finally comes to understand the circulation of Eros throughout all of nature, and the place of the human body in this creative energy:

Angélina was bewildered. What she had always thought to be a disgrace, a bondage, a weakness of the body, the Outlander spoke of as a glory brought to fullness by an equal glory hidden within another being ... Her eyes were opening up to life. Now she saw this same glory everywhere in nature. This must be the beauty that makes a flower blossom on the stem, beside a barren corolla. A living wellspring, subject to mysterious laws whose secret is known to the Creator alone ... (O109)

That same day, when the Outlander wounds her by laughing at her 'Norman' stinginess, she begins to suspect that the secret of happiness lies not in possession but in spending. But a long period of mourning and the good advice of her friend Marie-Amanda will be necessary before she can stop wanting to 'cling' to the memory of the Outlander and realize instead how much he has enriched her. A few months after his departure, in an attempt to console Phonsine in *her* grief, she decides to bring her the biggest of her famous prize geraniums – but not without inner conflict. For even when they have learned the joy of giving, Guèvremont's characters are far from being entirely saintly: 'But, noticing she had chosen the largest, she changed her mind; a smaller one would do just as well. After looking several times at one and then the other, she took the first' (0220).

If there is to be giving, however, there must be exchange – and Phonsine, feeling sorry for herself as usual, does not know how to receive. Seeing her friend's indifference to the geranium, Angélina shows that she has not completely abandoned her peasant instinct for thrift: ' "It's just about to blossom. You'll have to take good care of it, see that it gets plenty of sun and water, but not too much. You must look after it, do you hear? Because if you let it wither, I'll come and take it away from you, as sure as you're sitting there" ' (0220).

Sub/version

To the extent that the texture of Guèvremont's writing can be situated, then, it is in a space prior to the certainties contained in ideological codes and religious dogma; just as it is in the very imperfection of temporality that her characters seek an incarnation that subverts the Law. No one character in these narratives can be seen as the primary bearer of meaning, for they all come close to meaning without ever reaching it. In contrast to the male novels of the land, here the one has become the many. There is no longer one single truth to cling to, only that of the interrelationship between people and things, of openness to change, and of the richness of sharing. The Outlander, who symbolizes above all the elusive nature of reality, tries to explain to Angélina this contradiction inherent in all things: ' "Listen, my dark one, first you'll have to tell me what you think truth is. Is it what I did to the best of my knowledge? Or is it what I might have done without knowing it? Or maybe what you would have liked me to have done? If you want to question me, go ahead. But don't complain about the answer" ' (0189).

And, more impatiently, he tells Amable: ' "What you give ... is never lost. What you give to one person you get back from another ... Cast your bread ... Oh, never mind!" ' (0118).

CHAPTER FOUR

The defeated son and the rebellious daughter: The poetry of Saint-Denys Garneau and Anne Hébert

By identifying with Christ – through the heroic ritual that is man's word – the son accedes to the sign of the Father within himself. In this way the trinitarian structure that is the basis of our civilization is reproduced. At the moment when the rebellious son identifies with the cruciform word of Christ, he returns – converted – to conformity with the Father's will ... This Christ-centred form is thus ... the linguistic trap by which the Order of the Father/Mother maintains control over the son ... It is the liberation of the poetic word of the daughter that will decisively change this trinity into a quadrature.

Claire Lejeune, *L'Issue*

It would seem, then, that in the area of fiction women's writing allows the entry into language of all the texture, pleasure, and silence of the feminine-maternal realm, making possible a consequent shift in the very form of the novel. When read in conjunction with the male-dominated tradition of the novel of the land, the novels of Laure Conan and Germaine Guèvremont show how the female voice, once it emerges from the silence to which it has been consigned by culture, explodes or decentres the traditional structures of realism, substituting for the artificial unity of the male vision a writing attentive to the multiplicity, density, and detail of the real. While the novel attempts to *re-present* reality in language, the poetic experience can be characterized as a *traversal* of language by a subject desiring to make contact with the real; and it is through the themes, images, and symbols of a given work that sexual difference makes its presence felt. For in the gap between the desire of the writing subject and the world that he or she seeks to apprehend, one can detect the presence of the Law: that is, the ideologies and prohibitions contained in the social codes within which the poet must function, including (and perhaps especially) the prohibition of the feminine.

For the critic seeking to detect the presence of gender differences in writing, the most telling results are those obtained by comparing works in which variables other than gender (such as time period and social class) are as close as possible to being identical. For this reason, the work of Hector de Saint-Denys Garneau and Anne Hébert – two major poets who were not only first cousins, but were raised in precisely the same social and family milieu and influenced by the same Jansenist/Catholic value system – offers a rare opportunity for comparative analysis. Similar in their key images and symbols (water, the house, the closed room, the reduction of the body to its skeletal structure, the gaze of the child) as well as in the external forces that shaped them, these two bodies of poetry demonstrate dramatically the defeat of the son and the transgression of the daughter in relation to the Law of the Father that presides over the discourse of their period.

According to the 'national' focus that has understandably been a major grid of interpretation for the literary works of Quebec culture, the poetic works of Garneau (covering the period between 1937 and 1943)[1] and Hébert (published between 1942 and 1960)[2] have often been seen as symbolizing two consecutive stages in the history of the Quebec psyche: together, the two bodies of work are seen as tracing the passage of a whole culture from 'alienation' to 'liberation,' from 'death' to 'life.' And yet Garneau and Hébert, born in 1912 and 1916 respectively, are representatives of a single generation, and the contrast between the premature disappearance of the former[3] and the longevity of the career of the latter leads one to reflect on the different ways men and women may well have reacted to the stifling cultural atmosphere of Quebec in the period preceding and during the Second World War. The probability that contempt for the feminine and for female values was a staple of the intellectual fabric of the period is suggested by a revealing document recently published by Jeanne Lapointe, a contemporary of Garneau and Hébert who went on to become a professor of Quebec literature and a member of both the Parent Commission on Higher Education in Quebec (1962) and the Royal Commission on the Status of Women (1970). The document published by Lapointe is an extract from her own class notes taken during a course entitled 'The Philosophy of the Sexes' offered at Laval University in 1937 by the eminent Thomist philosopher Charles de Koninck. The notes provide a measure of how institutionalized the idea of women's inferiority had become, and illustrate how it was sanctioned by the church's 'natural law,' which confined women for all time to the realm of matter and nature:

Woman remains a function of the vegetative life to which she is attached by reproduction ... This is the absolute reason for her inferiority ... Woman responds to the need of man, therefore she is inferior to him. This inferiority is natural, says Saint Thomas ... Women are *garrulae* – more precise in meaning that loquacious. It is a sort of incontinence, a delight in futile things ... It must be understood in terms of the superabundance of matter in woman ... Woman has fewer rights than man because her personality is inferior to his.[4]

Trapped in the categories of Aquinas's *Summa* and further hierarchized by the use of the Latin term, one recognizes here a deformed version of certain characteristics of the feminine: the pleasure women seem always to have found in words and mutual exchange, as well as their tendency to remain close to the real, the body, and the material world rather than distancing themselves from it through abstraction. Once we have assimilated the scandalous fact that it was a *woman* who took these notes – who was, in other words, obliged to submit to this discourse of authority in order to obtain a university degree – we can more calmly attempt to imagine what might have been the typical reaction of a young man and a young woman nourished on such intellectual fare. For the young man, the reaction would in all probability be that he would seek refuge in his head, as far as possible from the corruption of woman and matter; hence, perhaps, Saint-Denys Garneau's account in his *Journal* of his 'desire to dwell in the head and the undefiled eyes' and of the grotesque dream that haunted his adolescence: 'Thus, during my adolescence, a kind of desire for my body to end at the waist. To have only my breast, full of light, without any breath of sexuality, without that call from below forever threatening me because of my excessive weakness.'[5]

For the young woman, however, although her instinctive reaction may well have been similar, in order to attain purity it would be necessary to escape herself: a more difficult dilemma. Paradoxically, it may even have been a salvation to be a woman in the dualistic climate of the period, for in a roundabout way such teachings must have kept women in touch with their bodies and with the material world. The same negative association between women and the body is present in a section of the widely distributed *Manual of Christian Parents* (1909) devoted to 'The education of young girls':

To correct your daughter if she is too proud of her beauty, her pretty face, her mind ... remind her that her body, which is her idol, is made from the earth she tramples with her feet; that apart from reason, she is inferior to most animals ... that the flower of the fields is more richly dressed than she will ever be; that an illness, an accident, a wound, or smallpox can disfigure the face she adores, and that soon perhaps death will reduce her to dust. Show her the bird of the barnyard, who preens herself and by so doing only makes herself uglier ... [6]

Products of this period often referred to in Quebec cultural history as that of the 'great darkness' (*la grande noirceur*), Garneau and Hébert reveal its impact in the claustrophobic atmosphere of their poetry. In the work of both poets, the key image of the house offers a symbolic portrait of the Father's House of culture as differently experienced by a man and by a woman. In Garneau's first volume, after a brief initial period of joy and innocence in which the poet feels united through language with the external world, the poetic space narrows to the image of a 'closed house' surrounded by a hostile nature, in which the poet finds himself trapped and stifled:

For a house is dead when nothing is open –
In the sealed house, ringed by the woods
The black woods filled

With bitter wind ...
Alone with the sadness that can find no vent
That you shut within yourself
And that spreads into the room
Like the smoke of a poor chimney
Drawing badly ...
Until you stifle in the sealed house ... (CP50)

Never resigned to this state of imprisonment, Garneau denounces
it in the image of the walls of a city that prevent children from
dancing, and that cut off the desiring gaze before it has been able to
assume shape, rhythm, or embodiment:

My children you are dancing badly
True, it is hard to dance here
In this airless place
Here without space which is the heart of the dance.

How can you hope to dance? I have seen the walls
The city cutting off your glance before it begins
Cropping your maimed vision at the shoulders
Even before one rhythmic movement
Before its race and final rest
Its flowering ... (CP24)

As sensitive, vulnerable, and impotent as a Maurice Darville in the
Father's House, Garneau will however remain a victim of what he
perceives as anonymous forces gradually sucking the life out of him.
Except for a vague 'They are the ones who have killed me' (CP160),
there is never any precision in his work as to the identity of the
figure or figures holding the strings in the drama in which he feels
himself a puppet. In fact, so well has the Father of the dominant
ideology succeeded in masking his presence that the poet describes
himself as the plaything of 'the devil,' who has deluded him with the
dream that life was allowed, and that 'the marvels of reality' could
be reached through the senses:

The Evil One, for my damnation,
Has let me look behind the scene

Through the opening in the curtain.
He has, in playing so with me,
Lifted the corner of the veil
Concealing life ...
Just enough for me to hear
The choir of birds and fairies
The universal harmony
Of these colours and these songs. (CP129)

In Anne Hébert's work, on the contrary, the meaning of the sinister games of power taking place within the house is slowly and painfully explored, until the relative positioning of the man and the woman who occupy the symbolic house are brought to centre stage, and the house itself is exploded from within. Although Hébert's poetic journey begins in the absolute passivity of a woman reduced to the status of an object, it is far from being that of a victim. Carried forward by the erotic energy that accompanies the emergence of the 'daughter's' voice, it moves unerringly towards transgression of the Law and transformation of the symbolic heritage, providing a striking contrast with the poetic journey of the 'son' imprisoned in the same Father's House.

※

What is interesting about Saint-Denys Garneau's poetry from a feminist perspective is the clarity of its demonstration of the various stages of the male journey: the tragedy of the man/poet whose instinctive desire leads him to embrace the world through all his senses, but who, as he internalizes the message of the dominant ideology, gradually moves towards a thematics of the gaze: a poetry that privileges the elements of air and water over those of earth, the vertical over the horizontal, and transcendence over immanence. Step by step, the poems trace the stages of an impossible attempt to *possess* the world that, contradicting the instinctive desire of the poet, soon imprisons him in an impotence reminiscent of that of the protagonists of the novel of the land:

And my gaze goes madly hunting
This splendour disappearing
This clarity escaping through the holes of time ...

My eyes my heart   my open hands
Hands under my eyes   these splayed fingers
Can hold nothing
Can only tremble
In the terror of their emptiness ... (CP64)

If there is one poem where Garneau defines his aesthetic with precision, it is in 'My intention' ('*Mon dessein*'), where the poet clearly distinguishes his art from patriarchal constructions of language and affirms his respect for multiplicity and difference. If one compares this poem to a typical nationalist poem of the 1960s, for example, one is struck by the absence of a thematics of *identity* from Garneau's aesthetic; unlike the later poets, he consciously distances himself from the idea that the poet is a figure of Adam, 'taking possession' of the world through the act of naming. On the contrary, poetry for him is a means of opening himself up to multiplicity, inscribing his relationship to all that is other than himself in a 'balancing game' that is quite the opposite of domination:

I do not plan to rear a handsome building
               vast, solid and perfect
But rather to go forth in the open air

There where the plants are, air and birds
There where the light is and the reeds
There where the water is.
In water and air and on the earth there are
All kinds of things and animals
We need not name them, there are too many
But each of us knows there are so many and so many more
And each is different and unique
You do not see the same ray of light
Falling twice in the same way on the same water ... (CP137)

According to the inner logic of the path on which he is led by his own desire, Garneau is forced to confront the feminine and all the repressed realm of the body that he – the obedient son – has been forbidden to touch. And through an effect of censorship inherent in the language of the period, the transgression his desire and his poetic language have led him to is lived as 'sin' or as a state of paralysis in face of this forbidden realm, followed by an even more negative stage in which the entire universe created by his words seems to turn against him. After the innocent and childlike joy of the early period, he finds himself all too soon cornered 'at the foot of a wall' (CP57), where the only occupations permitted him are those of the male subject in his role as master of the universe: counting, dividing, and surveying a hostile and progressively shrinking world. His resistance – and it *is* a resistance, and deserves to be recognized as such – is in his lucid portrayal of the dead end in which he finds himself. His 'geometric' poems, in which the images come close to pure abstraction, expose all the presumption of the male subject's 'vertical' domination of a horizontal world. Standing alone on the surface of the globe, or imprisoned in the linearity of a journey that leads nowhere, the poet records with growing panic his sense of the circle closing in on him:

It is there that the sequence of points becomes a line
A string attached to us
And there the game becomes terribly pure
With a relentless constancy in its march-to-the-end
                           which forms the circle
This prison. (CP119)

In all these poems, Garneau reveals the presumption and the impotence of a gaze that, assuming an infinite power over the world, remains blind to the urgent matters being 'decided upon' below the surface of things, in the very depths that contain the repressed feminine:

Here is the earth beneath our feet
Flat as a great table
Only we do not see where it ends
(This is because our eyes are weak)

Nor do we see its underside
Through force of habit

And this is a pity
For highly important things are settled there
Relating to our feet and footsteps (CP119)

His tragedy – and in this he is typical of the male writers of his culture – is that he is the too-docile son of a value system that forbids the satisfaction of his instinctive desire for life. Terrified by the feminine that could have been his salvation, he persists in his attempt to rise above matter; 'another Icarus' attempting to reach the sun even while recognizing that his flight will constantly be broken by a link with the earth he cannot bring himself to renounce:

And well we know that across this slender thread we've made,
And these shaky links stretched out across too empty spaces,
There is only one cry that persists
Only one cry
        speaking of a persistent link
Where the stems of the fruits are already broken
And all the stalks of the flowers and petals of the flowers
                      are eaten away
Where these feather-wings of our waxen soul have already
                      detached themselves
Only feathers in the wind feathers floating on the wind
                    above this drowning
With no home port. (CP117)

What form does this simultaneous attraction to and fear of the feminine assume in Garneau's work, then, and what role does it play in the collapse of his poetic universe? Even in his earliest poems Garneau is aware of the central position occupied by woman at the centre of the universe he seeks to embrace through his words. In the image of the 'sun-dappled bathing girl,' which appears typically in poems expressing the poet's union with the world around him, the troubling presence of woman and of the body creeps almost imperceptibly into the liquid transparency of the poet's idealized vision, leaving its innocence at first seemingly intact:

O my eyes this morning wide as rivers
O wave of my eyes ready to reflect all things ...

As a stream refreshes an island
And as the fluent wave curls around
The sun-dappled bathing girl (CP26)

But given the fact that woman and all the material realm associated
with her are identified as 'evil' by the ideological codes that inform
Garneau's language, the whole poetic universe of which she is the
support is open to contamination. Indeed the seeds of this corruption are contained within language itself, by virtue of its inherent
potential for exchange and materiality; and Garneau tries desperately
to retain for himself a space within it where – with no threat of an
'exchange' that might compromise his purity – he can 'welcome' a
silent and disembodied woman, kept distant by his gaze:

Only that I may love you
May see you
And be in love with seeing you

Oh not to speak to you
For no exchange
        or conversation
One thing surrendered, another withheld
For no such half-bestowals of ourselves

But only to know that you are
To love this: that you are. (CP69)

This sterilized universe in which the poet imagines the two solitudes of man and woman coming together, without desire and
therefore without sin, in the comforting enclosure created by a
disembodied male gaze is of course an impossible dream. What will
happen on the contrary is that the garrison Garneau has created for
himself will gradually be infiltrated by a liquid feminine-maternal
element made threatening by the fact of its exclusion from the poetic
universe. Like his predecessor Emile Nelligan, he describes himself
as a shipwrecked vessel ('This child on a voyage all alone / Torn by
the sea before our eyes' [CP66]); but he is closer than Nelligan had
been to understanding the mechanisms of ever-increasing abstraction that have led to his impasse. Torn apart but still lucid, he

observes his own destruction and records with precision his increasing sense of impotence. And yet, despite his apparent lucidity, Garneau never comes close to understanding that the 'void,' the 'abyss,' and the 'sea' that threaten him are his own constructions of the feminine, reduced to the status of a menacing 'otherness,' rather than being welcomed into his poetic universe:

And from the cliff where we stand
Our gaze is on the sea

And our arms hang at our sides
Like a pair of useless oars

Our gaze grieves on the sea
Like two great compassionate hands

Two poor hands doing nothing
Knowing all, doing nothing

What can we do for this heart of ours
This child on a voyage all alone
Torn by the sea before our eyes? (CP66)

Thus the slow death into which the poet enters is experienced as a destruction of his self by the feminine, a drowning to which he gives himself up almost willingly, as if sensing that only the sea can satisfy his thirst for tenderness: 'a drowned man weary of his shipwreck / Who slips into the all-embracing sea / That true sister who embraces us ...' (CP83). At the same time, terrified by the 'sin' associated with these spaces that have been encoded as feminine, he clings desperately to the heights where purity seems inviolate: 'I feel I am swaying on a tree-top / No, you women's voices you will not break / The purity of my song ... ' (CP84). This exhausting internal division will lead him to see the bed where the sexual act is consummated as a 'tomb / Open[ing] itself to our weakened bodies / Like the sea' (CP107), and the two lovers as pure and rigid statues, carefully kept at a distance from each other even as the poet succumbs to temptation:

After the slowest of approaches
The fieriest of caresses
After your body a pillar
Bright and consummately hard
My body a river outspread and pure to the water's edge. (CP107)

Constructed in patriarchal consciousness as the 'enigma' man must penetrate in order to accede to the secrets of the universe, as forbidden knowledge, and as the 'other' whose seduction provides the ultimate proof of his identity and power, woman resists; and as she does so, the whole universe of which she is the symbolic support and foundation withholds itself from man's grasp. In Garneau's work, once the sexual act has been emptied of its essential component of exchange between two subjectivities it appears as a parody of love, followed by an apocalyptic blaze unleashed on the universe – a vision in which the image of woman has become a monstrous reversal of that of the sun-dappled bathing girl. Just as the bathing girl always appears in the 'eyes' of the poet, and 'draw[s] upon herself / all the light of the landscape' (CP85), the vengeance of this hostile universe is directed against the poet's visual sense, and is symbolized by the figure of an enraged animal-woman holding in her claws all the meaning that is slipping away from him:

Under the red sky of my eyelids
The mountains
Are companions of my arms
And the forests burning in the darkness
And the wild beasts
Passing in the claws of your fingers
O my teeth
And the whole earth dying as I grasp it ...

And all the mysteries torn to pieces
In our final cry night has descended (CP108)

It is not surprising that in preference to this state of war the poet chooses the death of all desire; hence his sinister complicity in a drowning in which he imagines himself surrounded by the corpses of silent, distant women imitating the gestures of a no-longer-threatening love:

> I would rather have lost everything
> Would rather be a dead young man laid out
> Under a silent vault
> In the night-light's long unflickering flame
> Or perhaps in the depths of the sea ...
> Beautiful dead maidens, calm and sighing
> Will slide their already-distant shapes before my eyes
> After they've kissed my mouth without a cry
> And followed the dreams of my hands
> Over the serene curves of their shoulders and their loins
> After the voiceless company of their tenderness
> Having seen their shapes approach without hope
> I'll see their shadows vanish without pain ... (CP109–10)

Defeated, he can no longer do anything but turn the knife in his own wounds, pushing away with increasing panic the reality of death, which he sees before, behind, and beneath him. Even his own words, once they take shape on the page before him, become part of the hostile edifice closing in on him. Here again, his words make clear that it is the inability to conceive of relationship in terms other than rivalry and domination that has brought him to this impasse:

> Words on my lips now take your flight
>   you are no longer mine
> Go strangers and my enemies already ...
> Having no power over you since your birth
> I am in conflict with you now
> As with any alien thing ...
> Already you are among the impassible things
>   that ring me round
> One of the barriers made to stifle me. (CP93)

Although Garneau never succeeds in identifying the causes of his alienation with any precision, he comes close to doing so in his final poems, where the image of a family meal infiltrated by a traitor suggests the collective dimension of the problem: 'When did we devour our joy,' he asks, and 'Who is it who has devoured our joy?':

> For there is certainly a traitor among us
> Who took his place at our table when we sat down (CP148)

At this table, it is significant that there is no authority figure against whom revolt can be directed; and consequently no hope of recovering the lost joy. Instead, there is only the eternal rivalry between two enemy brothers, Oedipal rivals pitted against each other by an absent Father:

> Who is it among us that each of us has sheltered
> Welcomed among us ...
> This treacherous brother we have recognized as a brother ...
> And protected with a shared complicity
> And followed to this final place where our joy has been
>   utterly devoured (CP149)

As for the Father hidden behind the scenes and manipulating the strings controlling the action of this drama, it is not difficult to identify him in retrospect. For the 'thee' to whom Saint-Denys Garneau addresses his final and pathetic prayer is a close relative not only of Laure Conan's Charles de Montbrun, but also of the fatherly and seductive figure who, twenty years after Garneau's disappearance from the literary scene, will paralyse the will of Hubert Aquin's revolutionary narrator in *Prochain Episode* and appear to him as well in the mask of an 'enemy brother.' He is the benevolent and sinister Father against whom rebellion is impossible, the Oedipal rival who, at this stage of Quebec's history, communicates his presence through a Jansenist ideology that makes crucifixion the supreme value and love of the earth the ultimate sin. In Garneau's final poems he has consolidated his power absolutely, devouring every part of his victim except his devotion to the Executioner:

> And I will entreat of thy grace to crucify me
> And to nail my feet to thy holy mountain

So that they may not run upon forbidden roads
The roads that lead dizzyingly away
From thee (CP169)

*

A year before Saint-Denys Garneau's death, the first published volume of work by his cousin Anne Hébert appeared. On first reading,
the poems of *Les Songes en équilibre* (Dreams in equilibrium, 1942)
seem so childlike, so docile and obedient, that on making a quick
calculation of dates one is surprised to discover that the author
was already twenty-six years old. What could be more appropriate,
though, in a Father's House that has required of women that they
remain docile children, than this birth of a woman's words precisely
there, in the confined space of her imprisonment? ('She is a child,
and I want her to remain a child as long as possible,' Charles de
Montbrun had said of his daughter.)

Written a generation before the rise of a feminist consciousness
in literature, Hébert's three volumes of poetry trace the solitary path
followed by a 'fallen woman' who passionately reclaims for herself
'the fire and the sword of [her] heritage' (P65). In a 'old,' 'rectilinear'
world that has been 'ordered' along predictable lines for centuries
(S77), the possibility of renewal lies with woman, who possesses
within herself the secret of origins and of desire. But in Hébert's
early poems, she is presented as trapped in the realm of dream,
paralysed by the 'dead gods' who reign over culture – the Christ-
figure for whom she plays the role of Sorrowful Mother, the dead
kings who lie her down and rape her in a vain effort to satisfy their
desire, or the cruel and impotent companions who enclose her in
the dreamlike house of the volume *The Tomb of the Kings* (1953).
Her awakening is rendered doubly difficult by the fact that she has
been betrayed by her female ancestors, powerful matriarchs who
perpetuate the reign of death by preaching the values of gentleness
and loss of self:

Wisdom broke my arms, crushed my bones
She was an envious old woman
Filled with unction, bitterness and bile

She threw her gentleness in my face

Wanting to erase my features
    rubbing them down to a smeared image
Smoothing out my anger like drowned hair (P65)

Descending to the primitive depths where the body rediscovers its link with nature and with language, these poems traverse the multiple layers superimposed by culture on woman's desire before they accede to celebration. Focused at the beginning on the mythology of the male Redeemer and the Sorrowful Mother, they evolve towards a transformed mythology featuring a redeeming woman best epitomized by the figure of Eve, the passionate pagan mother who presides over human history. The elements traditionally described as 'feminine' by patriarchal culture – water, the forest, and the house, the realms of dream and imprisonment – are the privileged spaces of this poetry. It is there that the woman-poet explores the depths of her alienation, awakens, and finally grasps the sacred power that is hers by right as a woman and a poet.

The 'dreams' of a sleeping beauty:
Les Songes en équilibre

By its very unevenness, Les Songes en équilibre reveals the force of the strait-jacket imprisoning the obedient young girl. Its watery universe, pure and dreamlike, acquires a magical dimension through the presence of a choir of fairies who sing the joys of feminine passivity. Little girls described as 'docile to the point of death' (s28), they dance a 'circle of absence' (s12) around the poet. One of them, emerging for an instant from the group, prefigures the mutilation of woman that Hébert will explore to its depths a decade later, in The Tomb of the Kings:

... she has no face
Or even any hands
To put in front of it
Pretending to hide her absent features (s12–13)

There is no discernible rebellion in the numerous edifying poems devoted to the themes of the family and religion in this volume, although one does sense a lucid awareness of the destiny of receptivity, sacrifice, and perpetual childhood reserved for women. In imitation of models like St Thérèse of Lisieux ('The Little Flower of Jesus'), the Blessed Virgin, and her own mother, whose exemplary passivity is mentioned, the poet aspires to be the empty vessel through which an 'other' greater than herself will find expression:

> Dear God, I am afraid
> I am afraid to write ...
> Guide my hand
> Be the hand itself
> I will be content to be the pencil ...
> For in the end you are everything
> And I desire only to be your little nothing (s119)

And yet, in the troubled identification with images like that of Mélisande lost in the forest (s17), the girl frozen in a position of waiting at the window of a Norman tower (s20), and of the 'beautiful stranger ... lost in the mist' (s23–4), there is an erotic power seeking to emerge. In 'Ship's Head' the image of a woman at a window, her hair floating in the wind, is suddenly transformed into that of the figure at the prow of a Viking ship; and as the metamorphosis takes place the house begins to move, like a ship carried forward by the wind. In the ambiguity of this house/vessel that is at once 'in movement and immobile' the poet sees a 'figure of her own drama' (s21–2), and indeed it would be hard to find a more appropriate image of women's age-old dilemma than this challenge of transforming the house into a moving space.

The same unresolved tension between immobility and movement is present in two poems centred on the archetypes that have transmitted Christianity's dualistic vision of woman: Eve and the Virgin Mary. In 'Eve' (s75–7), a transitional poem in which the voice of the feminine-maternal is heard for the first time in Hébert's work, the possibility of a new birth is associated with the image of the original mother. Stifling with boredom in a world she sees as 'old' and 'ordered,' the poet dreams of a primitive world of desire, traversed by the rhythm of jazz – an Edenic world of 'monstrous roots,' 'slithering reptiles,' jungles, and swamps, of which the most notable characteristic is the absence of man. Not only is there no Adam figure present to express his desire for a complementary and inferior companion, there is no tree to introduce the notion of sin, and no God imposing his Law. What *is* present is music, endowed with a seductive power strikingly similar to that associated with it in the writing of Laure Conan and Germaine Guèvremont. In 'three small notes' proffered by a child/woman, the poetic word is born from chaos; and in these three notes, described by the poet as a 'complaint,' an 'appeal,' and a 'seduction,' Eros makes its entry into the poetic universe of Anne Hébert.

This birth and development of the figure of Eve in Hébert's mythology will be accompanied by the gradual disappearance of the figure of the Virgin Mary, a slow death that will continue throughout the following volume, but whose beginning is already present in the poem 'Death.' Here the image of the fairy with the mutilated arms is replaced by that of the *pietà*, whose arms have no function other than that of supporting a dead God:

One by one ...
My fairies have abandoned me,
And I have been left alone
With a great Christ
In my arms (s80)

This identification with the Virgin Mary resonates with a disquieting ambiguity, especially in light of the erotic associations attached to the image of women's hair in earlier poems in the volume. Here the Virgin's hair, caught in the dried blood of the wounds of her son, suggests the paralysing power the traditions of Catholicism have exercised over women's desire. And one has only to recall the reproachful image of the Sacred Heart of Jesus popular in the Catholic imagery of the period to understand the weight of guilt from which the young poet is seeking to free herself:

His heart is bleeding
My long hair
Hangs over his heart
And sticks to his wound.
Even my tears

Are unable to free it
From this blood
From this heart
In which I am frozen (s80)

The corpse on the doorstep of the house:
The Tomb of the Kings

In *The Tomb of the Kings* (1953), the poet goes deeper in her
exploration of the experience of sacrifice and passivity, until a 'ver-
milion fury' (P27) is detected alongside 'the glow of yellow flowers
in blue stoneware' in the house of the faithful spouse. It is in this
volume in particular that Hébert uses themes and images almost
identical to those of Saint-Denys Garneau (solitude, death, the
hands, the house, drowning, bones) and descends to the depths of
the alienation they contain. In her work the greater density and
colour of the images, as well as their subversive dimension, is surely
not unrelated to the very concrete female experience in which they
are rooted. For while Garneau, despite his feeling of imprisonment,
could exhaust himself in a linear voyage 'to the end of the earth'
(CP171), Hébert, being a woman, seems intimately familiar with the
experience of imprisonment in the house, and explores the inner
space of her prison until its walls burst under the pressure of her
desire. In these poems the house becomes the habitation of a dream
woman, a Rapunzel-like figure linked to her fate by a vow of fidelity
older than her will, evoked by the author in conjugal imagery:

Barely a wall
Cipher for a wall
Placed like a crown
Around me

Of course I could leave
Leap over the rose-hedge
Take it off like a ring
Tight around my heart ...

Only my fidelity holds me back.

O hard bonds I knotted
During some unknown secret night
With death! (P21)

Confined to the house, this woman lives in physical and psychic
torment, while the voice of a superego as old as patriarchal culture
reminds her that freedom is forbidden her:

Turn back life of mine
Can you not see the way is closed ...

Turn quickly home
Find the tightest house
The hollowest deepest house

And go live in that pebble ...

Visit your buried heart
Travel on your hand's lines
They are as good as the pathways of the world
Take time to dream of a lovely far-off love
His light hands on their way towards you ... (P28)

As if seeking to distract herself, she attends to the daily tasks of
the household: sweeping, sewing, setting the table, lighting the fire.
But each of these images is bizarrely coloured by her anguish:

The snow – barely a handful –
Flowers in a globe of glass
Like a bride's crown ...

I shall sew my dress with this lost thread. (P25)

My heart placed on the table
Who then has set it with such care
Sharpened the tiny knife
Fascinated, cool,
Without undue haste? (P23)

We force ourselves to live within
Making no noise
Sweeping the room
Tidying away our boredom
Letting our gestures balance alone
At the end of an invisible thread
Coming from our open veins. (P29)

'Ancient patience' (P5), 'relentless offering' (P7), 'marine vocation mirroring my gaze' (P5). This passive destiny traditionally reserved for women is revealed in *The Tomb of the Kings* to be the hypocritical surface of a reality of fragmentation and repressed desire: hearts cut out of bodies (P24), 'fingers without desire stretched outward' (P22), 'veins [lying] open' (P29), and 'one's own ravaged face ... tossed out of sight' (P14). Over the whole volume reigns the figure of the Sorrowful Mother, seated at the foot of a tree in an image that recalls both Eve and the Virgin Mary, the eternal woman who must redeem the world by her tears:

This woman sitting
Makes over stitch by stitch
The humility of the world
With no more than the gentle patience
Of her two scorched hands. (P6)

While this mythic image of the mother remains more or less intact in *The Tomb of the Kings*, the poems progressively unveil the stirrings of anger, self-destruction, and hatred of her impotent companion in the heart of the imprisoned woman. In 'Thin girl,' a strange young girl whose days are spent polishing her bones unceasingly dreams of capturing her lover and 'mak[ing] a silver reliquary of him' (P17). In 'Narrowing,' a 'woman at her window ... watches the passing of bitter crews / And moves not / The day long,' all the while feeling on the back of her neck the breath of a man of salt who 'curse[s] her veins that freeze each time he breathes / Out his slow cold and immobile breath' (P27). In 'The World's Other Side,' the 'blue girls of summer' whose lines of destiny have been sketched out 'from patience and long habit' hold 'strange heavy heads of lovers' in their hands, and finally recognize their own exhaustion: 'Our weariness has eaten at our hearts ... / Our strength has left us ... / Devoured by sunlight / And by skin-deep smiles' (P32).

It is at the moment when the depths of night seem the most impenetrable that a female corpse makes her appearance in Hébert's poetry. In the image of 'the small dead girl' whose body blocks all possibility of exit from the house, the poet confronts the reality of all the 'murdered' women of the past, of the whole realm of the feminine-maternal ('milky night') devastated by culture. And recognizing the little dead girl as a 'sister,' she can no longer remain indifferent to this reality:

A small dead girl
      lay down across the doorsill
We found her there in the morning, struck down
                      on our threshold
Like a fern crushed by frost.

Since she came to us we dare not pass the door
She is a child white in her foaming skirts
From which reverberates a strange milky night.

The life we lead, so minuscule and still,
Lets not one languid motion
Pass through the other side of this limpid mirror
Where this sister that is ours
Bathes blue in the moonlight
While her heady odour swells and rises. (P29)

The growing consciousness of a necessary solidarity among women becomes even more precise in 'The World's Other Side,' where the awakening of the 'blue girls of summer,' Sleeping Beauty figures whose dreamlike lives have been bordered by patience and habit, takes place through the recognition that they are sisters, and that their exile and anguish have been a shared destiny. Unlike Saint-Denys Garneau, who has only a 'treacherous brother' as companion in his attempt to diagnose the collective illness, and who seeks his escape primarily through the activity of intellection, these sister-figures in their attempt to find an exit turn towards the sounds and perfumes of the earth:

> One of us gets up courage
> And softly lays an ear over the earth
> That sealed box buzzing with insect prisoners
> She says: 'The prairie is filled with sounds
> No word-tree puts down its silent roots there
> In the black heart of night
> This is the world's other side
> Who can have chased us hither?'
>
> And she looks in vain behind her
> For a fragrance ...
> And finds this soft ravine of frost
>   in place of memory. (P33)

The shell of alienation encasing the poet is burst decisively in the famous title poem of the volume, 'The Tomb of the Kings,' where female passivity, followed to its ultimate and most terrible consequence, becomes a consent to rape:

> Hungry for the fraternal source of evil in me
> They lay me down, they drink me;
> Seven times I feel the tightening vice of bones
> And the dry hand seeking my heart to crush it. (P41)

In the disturbing eroticism of this transitional poem it is possible to see an allegory of the universal fate of woman in patriarchal society: an 'astonished, barely born' girl-child strangely complicit with the powerful and hidden puppet-master who controls her dream, who consents to being passively led to her destruction 'along muted labyrinths':

> (In what dream
> Was this child tied by the ankle
> Like some fascinated slave?)

The author of the dream
Tugs at the thread
And naked feet are heard

One by one
Like the first drops of rain
At the bottom of a well (P39)

The complicity of the 'daughter' extends as well to her passive consent to a male desire awakened not by the presence of life or Eros in woman, but by the 'source of evil' in her: the 'immobile desire' of the recumbent statues on the tombs that, in exchange for her sacrificed flesh, offers only 'a few tragedies patiently fashioned / On the chests of supine kings / In place of jewels' (P40). The meeting of desire and death is experienced as a strange nuptial, an exorcism perhaps of the last traces of masochism from the female psyche. Prepared for the sacrifice of her flesh and her heart by 'the shade of love,' the victim submits to a ritual that evokes the destruction of her subjectivity:

The mask of gold upon my absent face
Violet flowers for pupils
The shade of love makes up my face with careful strokes (P40)

Behind the exotic decor of this ancient sacrifice one can detect the structure of a French-Canadian culture devoted to the cult of the ancestors, those same fathers who spoke through the voices heard by Maria Chapdelaine and Menaud – and whom Hébert has transformed into dead and powerful kings to whom the daughters of the culture are offered in ritual sacrifice. It is perhaps in order to free herself from their sway that she situates the poem within the mythology of a pre-Christian era, in which there was still a place for *active* female figures. For, in addition to the male 'author of the dream,' there is another important presence implicit at least in the girl's adventure – that of Diana the huntress. It is surely because the young woman/poet holds her heart 'perched on [her] wrist ... / Like a blind falcon' (P39) that this seat of her emotion is able to resist destruction and survive. This renewal of her mythological reference points may well be unconscious on the part of the author at this stage of her evolution. Certainly the final note of the poem, which marks the end of a long period of alienation in Hébert's work, is one of uncertainty as much as of liberation:

> How comes it that this bird
> Trembles and turns towards morning
> Its punctured eyes? (P41)

Mystery of the (female) Word

In the poems that make up *Mystery of the Word*, a final volume of poetry composed between 1953 and 1960, Hébert accedes definitively to a transformed mythology and style of writing. The staccato and anguished verses of *The Tomb of the Kings* are replaced by a triumphal style: long lines of sumptuous density testifying to the existence of a woman's language, which, having broken out of the shackles restraining it, now dares to 'take up space' on the page. At the same time, the frequent use of the past tense and the near anonymity of the biblical tone of these poems suggests that there is a new distance between the author and her poetic drama. One senses that Hébert, having traversed the experience of her own alienation through poetry, is now perhaps more interested in the exploration of the novel form she has already embarked upon during this period, a form that will allow fuller transposition of her experience onto the social level.[7]

The famous preface to this final volume ('Poetry, Broken Solitude'), in which Anne Hébert defines her poetic art, is an important document of 'female' or 'feminine' aesthetics. Not surprisingly, given the date of composition, Hébert uses the masculine pronoun throughout to refer to the poet, but the conception of poetry she puts forward represents a decisive break with patriarchal aesthetics. For her, the very essence of poetry lies in the openness of the poet to the world around him, his attention to 'the call [that] comes from things or beings that have so strong an existence near the poet that the whole earth seems to demand an extra radiance' (P45). The poetic word is born, not in the sort of rivalry with the world that reduced a Saint-Denys Garneau to silence, but in the very heart of silence, in the identification of the poet with a 'mute earth [which teaches him] the resistance of his own mute and quiet heart' (p45). 'The artist is not God's rival,' she goes on. 'He does not try to remake creation. He stays attentive to the call of his gift within. And all his life is but a long, loving wait for grace' (p46).

This identification with the voices that have been silenced by culture – whether those of the earth or of dominated human beings – would seem to be one of the fundamental characteristics of women's writing. Inherent in Hébert's formulation is a political position: a perhaps specifically female way of reconciling art with commitment to the transformation of reality that we will meet again in the work of Gabrielle Roy and France Théoret. The subversive quality of poetry is to be found, according to her, not so much in its 'content' as in the fullness of the act of inhabiting the present moment accomplished by the poetic word. By this insistence on the relationship between artistic creation and the creative rhythms of the natural world, she distances herself from the presumption of an art that would aim to 'possess' or 'direct' the world, insisting on the contrary that the artist's task is to learn to listen to its rhythms:

The artist does not invent, any more than the spider spinning her web or the plant putting forth leaves and flowers. He fulfils his role and accomplishes what he is in the world to do. He must be careful not to interfere, so as not to falsify his inner truth. And it is no small achievement to remain faithful to one's deepest truth, however dangerous it may be, clearing the way for it and giving it a form. It would be so much easier, more reassuring, to direct it from without, making it say what one would like to hear ... (p47)

The poems that follow this preface give shape by their proliferation of biblical images to the 'incarnation' and 'redemption' that for Hébert are primary metaphors of the poetic act. At the centre of their renewed and joyous world reigns woman, the redeemer of man by virtue of the truth and passion she has conserved and transmitted since the beginnings of time. In his terror of the secret depths of earth and sea she contains within her man may want to turn away, but without her, Hébert insists, he will not accede to his own birth:

> I am the earth and the water, you can not ford me,
> my friend, my friend
> I am the well and the thirst, cross me at your peril,
> my friend, my friend (P59)

Fearing mystery, man flees into a reassuring rationalism, but he is invited by woman to a feast of darkness and love, called by her to recognize the female space of his origins and the message of life it contains:

> Hope and ill fortune burn beneath my roof, knotted hard together,
> learn these strange ancient marriages, my friend, my friend
> You flee from omens and in your open hands you press pure
> numbers, my friend, my friend
> You speak in a loud and clear voice, some muffled echo trails behind
> you, listen, hear my black veins singing in the night, my friend,
> my friend
> I lack a name and definite features; I am place of welcome and
> chamber of shadows, pathway for dreams and place of origin, my
> friend, my friend ...
> It took only a morning for my face to flower, recognize your own
> great darkness visited, all the mystery lying bound between your fair
> hands, my love. (P59–60)

The birth of woman's poetic word is accompanied in this volume by a rejection of the patience, the purity, and the tears associated with traditional biblical models of femininity. In full possession of her creative powers, the poet refuses the visit of seven gentle and deceitful virgins carrying 'blue pities' in their jars. These seven girls, who bear with them the time-honoured female values of 'wounded love,' 'bitter hearts,' and 'burnt tears,' include in their number Veronica, the woman who reflects the image of a male God:

> See, the one named Veronica folds large pure sheets and dreams of
> a face to capture in its grimace on veils unrolled like clear mirrors
> of water ... (P55)

No less disrespectful of the mythology of traditional Christianity is the ironic poem 'Annunciation,' in which the conception of Christ by the Blessed Virgin is presented as a rape by the Holy Spirit,[8] and a cruel parody of women's true creative power. To this demystification of the Virgin Mary corresponds the celebration of Eve, in a magnificent poem that bears her name. The Eve of Anne Hébert's maturity is a fusion of several myths: redemptress, witch, sibyl, siren, and mother, she is always the strong woman, 'queen and certain mistress crucified on the gates of the farthest city' (P72). Reversing the traditional interpretation of the Genesis myth, Hébert sees in Eve's desire and transgression a positive model for her daughters:

Tell us the malefice and spell that were the tree's, tell of the garden, of God bright and naked, and sin as fiercely desired as shadow at high noon
Tell us of love unblemished and the first man undone in your embrace (P73)

'Blind mother' who knows the secret of birth and death and of 'this whole daring voyage between two barbarous places of darkness,' she is invoked in the name of all the women who have kept vigil throughout the ages, anonymous spinners and weavers who have helplessly observed the wars perpetrated by the rivalries of their brothers and husbands:

See, your sons and husbands rot pell-mell between your thighs, under the same strong curse
Mother of Christ remember your last-born daughters, those who are without name or history ...
War unfolds its paths of horror, terror and death hold hands ...
See us, recognize us, fix on us your blind gaze, consider the adventure of our hands spinning the mystery like rough wool as we keep our vigil (P72–3)

As the world of the sons of Eve approaches a paroxysm, salvation depends on the strength of these daughters 'without name or history,' and on their accession to the passion and wisdom of the first mother. In 'Captive Gods,' the poem that closes this last volume of poetry by Anne Hébert, it is significant that the dead kings of the preceding volume have become 'captive gods,' and that they too are liberated, thanks to a collectivity of 'life-filled sisters,' 'desired like the mother-colour of the world' (P76). The final image of 'broken solitude' the poet gives us is perhaps the most important of all, for it marks the abolition of the distance that has separated women among themselves:

> Life has begun to move forward again ... the tide breaks on the horizon and the distance between our sisters is broken ... Incarnation, our gods tremble with us! (P76)

CHAPTER FIVE

When the voices of resistance become political: The Tin Flute or realism in the feminine

... she who gives an account of the disaster reveals the syntony between the devastated biological realm and the devastating historical process.
Michèle Causse,
'Le monde comme volonté et comme représentation'

Making someone an object: isn't that the main source of violence? Living, contradictory people and processes fetishized in official declarations, until they are frozen into standardized elements and backdrops: dead themselves and continuing to kill.
Christa Wolf, *Cassandra*

Towards the middle of *The Tin Flute*,[1] there is a remarkable scene, which Gabrielle Roy is careful to present as such. Getting off a streetcar after visiting her son Daniel in the hospital, Rose-Anna Lacasse sees a newspaper headline announcing the German invasion of Norway. She buys a paper and, reading it, feels hatred well up in her:

And this woman, who never read anything but her *Book of Hours*, did an extraordinary thing. She crossed the street, fumbling in her purse for change, and in all haste offered three cents to the newspaper vendor, quickly opening the damp pages he had given her ... After a moment she folded the paper and stared in front of her, eyes heavy with anger. She hated the Germans. She, who had never hated anyone in her life, felt a sudden, implacable hatred for this people she had never known. She hated them, not just for what they were doing to her but for what they were doing to other women like her. (TF163)

The resonance of this scene arises not only from the fact that it presents in an unusual way the fusion of private and public (Rose-Anna buying the newspaper), the feminine and masculine polarities (maternal love and war) that structure the political meaning of this first novel by Gabrielle Roy, but also and particularly from the shock felt by the reader at the way this episode affects Rose-Anna, a woman 'of gentle character' (TF163), who throughout the novel is defined entirely in terms of her love. To be able to imagine Rose-Anna Lacasse – this sorrowful mother whose instinct for life generates the energy of *The Tin Flute* – capable of anger, and even of hatred, is to come close to understanding the radical political meaning of the novel. For by inscribing her feminine, if not feminist,[2] way of seeing within a realist framework, Roy makes explicit the political dimension that was already implicit in the writing of Laure Conan, Germaine Guèvremont, and Anne Hébert. In her hands, the immense social panorama typical of social realism becomes the portrait of a culture rushing towards its ruin – a culture repeatedly drawn back, through the intertwined stories of Rose-Anna and her daughter Florentine, to the reality of the devastated female body underlying it.

In placing the mother at the centre of her novelistic universe, Gabrielle Roy fully assumes the *authority* of realistic representation and, at the same time, transforms realism. Before *The Tin Flute*, as we have seen, becoming a mother in Quebec literature was almost inevitably a fatal blow dealt to the female character. In the ideological text underlying literature, to be a mother meant not to have a story, to be nothing but the other, the reflection and the support of the Father's House; and the absence of mothers in novels was a faithful reflection of this murder.

Thus it is appropriate that it should be by telling the story of a mother that Gabrielle Roy succeeds in bringing realism back to the *real*, offering the Quebec public of the time an unprecedented portrait of its own reality. Unlike that other great realist, Ringuet, who through the distanced gaze of his omniscient narrator had lucidly exposed a disappearing reality, she embraces the painful present of a deprived class and of a whole people, and attempts through writing to open the prison of their present onto a viable future. Her narrative vision, shot through with a love that must be recognized as *maternal*, is brought by its own internal logic to a confrontation with the reality of war, the ultimate consequence and symbol of a power based on the suppression of the weak. This is 'realism in the feminine,' then, and if the omniscient narrator of traditional realism is often compared to 'God the Father,' Roy's narrator is much better evoked by Rose-Anna Lacasse's image of God – a somewhat harassed mother at the beck and call of all her children/characters at the same time, trying to soothe their pain with her loving attentiveness: 'She realized all of a sudden that God knew all about her life, and that it wasn't necessary to remind him of all the details. But then she said to herself: "Maybe he forgets things. There's so much misery he's told about." Thus, the only imperfection in her faith came from this candid supposition that God, as absent-minded, tired and harassed as herself, sometimes got to the point where he could give only cursory attention to human needs' (TF99).

The restrictions of realism and the prison of culture

Dedicated 'to Mélina Roy' and marked during the course of its composition by the death of the author's mother, *The Tin Flute* seems to have been invaded, almost against the wishes of Gabrielle Roy, by the presence of the mother.[3] But beyond the grandeur of the character of Rose-Anna and the nostalgia[4] that Roy undoubtedly felt for her own mother whom she had not seen since 1937 when she left to study in Europe, all Gabrielle Roy's work is permeated with nostalgia for a pre-cultural state of maternal fusion that the act of writing attempts to reinsert into the cultural realm. This voice from the origins – a song of life and of the earth, and an insistent language of love – deconstructs the hierarchies set up by culture and seeks to bring justice to the heart of human history.

It is perhaps in relation to this return to the maternal source that Gabrielle Roy's abandonment of realism after *The Tin Flute* can best be understood. For social realism, with its depth and breadth of vision, the anonymity of its habitual narrative gaze, and its ambition of distilling a single and overriding 'meaning' from the multiplicity of the real, runs counter to all the usual stereotypes associated with women's writing. For example, there seems to be no place in such a vision for autobiography, for a writing of fragments, or for the subtlety of a voice attentive to the truth of the body or of silence – the various ways women have found for espousing the real through writing and for allowing its multiplicity to emerge. By choosing the forms of realism, the writer chooses to enter fully into 'culture,' with all the artifices of construction that implies.

It is not surprising, then, that from *The Tin Flute* on, with the single exception of *The Cashier*,[5] Gabrielle Roy abandoned realism and turned to a literary form more oriented towards becoming than towards the closure of identity: a series of interlinked short stories, autobiographical in content, in which the moment of illumination crystallized in the form of each story becomes part of a temporal process woven from these present moments.[6] In a recent 'biographical essay,'[7] discussing the period of transition separating *The Tin Flute* (1945) and *Where Nests the Water Hen* (1950),[8] François Ricard comments on the astonishment of the reading public when the second book appeared:

People who had read and admired *The Tin Flute*, published five years earlier with great success, were of course expecting Gabrielle Roy to write a second novel that would be a sort of sequel ... But, instead, the author of *Where Nests the Water Hen* deliberately confounded all these expectations: instead of a realistic novel with a strong social message set in a place and time both well-defined and immediate, she produces a book whose universe ... seems to be outside time and space ... instead of a tightly structured, strictly linear narrative, following step by step the changing, problematic destinies of a few characters, she offers a work that is rather diffuse, rather open, juxtaposing three stories that are virtually independent of each other ... '[9]

According to Ricard, the five years separating the two works were a period of painful transition during which the author – living in post-war France and trying to live up to the expectations raised by *The Tin Flute* – was making an effort to write in a realistic framework and painfully putting together a first draft of *The Cashier*. During a visit to Chartres described in a 1956 text, she experienced a moment of 'grace' where 'the country of the Little Water Hen silently awakened in the depths of my memory,'[10] and after which she quickly and effortlessly wrote the text of her second 'novel.' Her description of this return to an earlier time in the depths of memory bears a striking resemblance to the picture of the savage territory of the origins in the first of Anne Hébert's two 'Eve' poems. In both cases, a crucial moment in the writer's development is described, linked to the acknowledgment of the decline or failure of a culture in which the author feels herself to be an outsider, and to the birth of an authentic feminine voice speaking from the space of the maternal-feminine repressed by culture. Gabrielle Roy herself describes this return to the country of the mother as a release of her own voice, beyond realism and beyond the 'deep pain the old nations were inflicting upon each other': 'There, I thought, human beings still have a good chance; there, men could perhaps start over again, if they wanted to ... It was the Tousignants. They seemed young to me, especially Luzina, young as at the beginning of the world ... '[11]

'The mother' and 'war' appear then in Roy's imaginative universe as the two poles of a suffering universe in need of salvation; with nostalgia for the original fusion with the maternal-feminine offering an alternative to the reality of a western culture exhausted by its rivalries and power struggles. What is feminine and profoundly political about Roy's writing is that, rather than remaining torn between these binary opposites, she deconstructs the oppositions they imply – giving a voice to those groups that have been silenced by culture, whether the French-Canadian, Ukrainian, Doukhobor, or Chinese minorities of Canada, the poor, or women. Although this political vision is present throughout her work, it is in *The Tin Flute*, precisely because of the realist narrative structure that Roy later came to see as a constraint, that it is inscribed in the terrain of ideologies and reveals its radical import. Accepting the restrictions of realism, Roy penetrates to the heart of culture and brings a woman's view to bear on its seeming impasse.

A vision that eludes male categories

And yet, in a provocative analysis of *The Tin Flute*, Guy Laflèche attacks the novel's political stance by approaching it precisely from the standpoint of its narrative technique. The narrator, he maintains, is neither 'objective'[12] nor 'innocent;'[13] on the contrary, 'he' is guilty of spreading a 'rhetoric of confusion and mystery'[14] that is no less than an 'ideological obfuscation'[15] of the situation presented in the novel. 'In fact,' writes Laflèche, 'the narrator is overwhelmed by the story he is telling, just as the characters are crushed by the universe they inhabit. This is why such a simple story appears so complex: incapable of analysis, the narrator disorients his reader and bewilders him.'[16]

But what if 'the narrator' were, as I have suggested, a *woman*? And what if her political stance were a *woman*'s position? As Laflèche is aware, this narrator is not 'innocent,' and she is definitely not indifferent: as a result of the many shifts of perspective made possible by the 'free indirect' style of narration Roy uses so frequently in this novel, she seems in fact to help her characters to speak, as a good mother would, allowing all the contradictions of their often confused reactions to emerge and weaving them together into a whole that respects the autonomy of its fragments. This is not to say that she does not take a stand: on the contrary, her woman's viewpoint, extremely precise and attentive to detail, ruthlessly reveals the mechanisms of power that objectify individuals, especially women, and illustrates their cultural consequences.

If I have given space to Laflèche's analysis, which is, after all, only one point of view among many on the political meaning of the novel,[17] it is because by its very failure to understand the novel it reveals the impossibility of explicating women's political vision according to the accepted categories of patriarchal society. 'Every woman who has given birth,' says Madeleine Ouellette-Michalska, 'knows that a thing can be itself and its opposite, itself and something else that is infinite, multiple, where the notion of boundary is inadequate.'[18] Rose-Anna knows this too; she recognizes her solidarity as mother and wife with women of all ages and all countries, 'women like herself, women of the people, as needy as she was. For centuries they had seen their husbands and sons march away' (TF231).

Hence Roy's refusal to separate reason from emotion, the public from the private, and abstract technological culture from the bruised women's bodies it treads on in its march towards an unattainable 'progress.' *The Tin Flute* is an exceptionally *emotional* novel, and already this courage to feel and not just to analyse the situation it presents would be a clue to the untutored reader that the author is a woman. And it is precisely this emotion, which extends beyond purely rational categories, that Guy Laflèche describes as 'confusion,' 'disorient[ation] of the reader,' 'inability to analyse.' Admittedly 'bewildered' by 'the multiple, changing focus'[19] of the narrative, this male reader chooses to respond by an aggressive attack on the novel.

While indeed a product of feeling, this work describing the suffering of the women, men, and children of the Saint-Henri district of Montreal at the beginning of the Second World War is also a novel of ideas. Not only does Roy situate the impasse facing her characters in relation to then-current ideologies of class and nation, but she lets them discuss politics, so often that the review in *Le Devoir* at the time of the novel's publication expressed strong reservations regarding 'the pages and pages of political-social discussion ... which could have been limited to a few short sketches, broadly summed up, dealt with more briefly.'[20] Roy's characters suffer because they are French Canadians, because they belong to a working class deprived of its traditional trades by technology and capital, and because they are poor. And among them, those who suffer most are women, because they cannot escape. What the logical (and male) categories of Laflèche's analysis fail to account for is that this denunciation of war and of the totalitarian machine that crushes those whose voices are too weak to be heard is the expression of a woman's political vision, which – while including the dimensions of class, nation, and sexual difference – cannot be reduced to any one of these categories. Not only are the multiple voices of resistance in the novel political; they are perhaps the only effective opposition to the oppressive unity of the Law of the Father.

Behind the image of the father/mother: Battered bodies

'Radical' in the original sense of the word, this female vision goes back to the sources of the 'deep pain' Roy later described as sapping the universe, and demystifies the images of the father and mother that underlie the dominant ideological codes and ensure their perpetuity. As in the writing of Laure Conan and Germaine Guèvremont, the very fact of putting a woman – or women – at the centre of the novelistic universe subverts the image of the 'Holy Family' sanctioned by the dominant ideology. In place of the patriarchal triangle of the father, the woman-object or symbolic mother, and the son or suitor whose function is to ensure the continuation of the family lineage, she substitutes a shattered structure based on the reality of a family where father, mother, and children are all victims of an anonymous power that uses them for purposes they don't understand.

Once again the hidden Father appears, then, at last revealing his economic, technological, capitalist identity. Although none of the characters (except perhaps Emmanuel Létourneau) manages to identify with any certainty this face behind the 'system' they know to be crushing them, together the polyphony of their voices, carried by the voice of the narrator, identifies and denounces him.

Moreover, Roy introduces another important structural element in the gradual transformation of patriarchal structures by women's writing: the relationship between mother and daughter. For it is only when mothers and daughters begin to see each other as sisters and allies, and not the enemies they were decreed to be by the statutes of the Father's House, that the statue of the symbolic mother holding the whole structure together will collapse. At the heart of Roy's vision of culture lies the reality of the wounded reproductive bodies of women and the vicious circle of the maternal role transmitted from mother to daughter down through the generations – the circle that must be opened if the transformation of culture is to take place.

THE DEFEATED FATHER

Demystified, the family is seen to be a cell of suffering, loving beings, broken by their roles but – resisting – always greater than these roles. In the place of the patriarch enthroned by ideology, Roy presents the reality of the defeated father: the very human Azarius, who resists his own destruction by keeping alive within himself the identity of an eternal son. As sensitive as Maurice Darville, as idealistic as Saint-Denys Garneau, and as great a lover of nature as François Paradis and the Outlander, he is, like them, the man the Quebec text seems to prevent from growing up, the man imprisoned in linearity and abstraction[21] who seems threatened by the concrete reality associated with women's lives. For him, as for his predecessors, words – which he uses with great eloquence – function as a safety valve or a screen separating him from the real. He is the 'do-nothing big talker' (TF145) who feels comfortable only in the male world of The Two Records, where there is no woman's gaze to force him back to unbearable reality: 'He was in his element here. They'd listen to him in a minute when he started talking. Sam would contradict him but he'd listen. Above all he'd hear the sound of his own voice reaffirming his confidence in himself' (TF147).

Even more clearly than Guèvremont, Roy shows women's mistrust of this male tendency to satisfy themselves with words and ideas at the expense of the real. The contemptuous 'Sing, you beautiful robin' that Phonsine hurls in the Outlander's face in Guèvremont's novel of the same year can possibly be interpreted by the reader as the frustrated words of a woman insensitive to the magic of masculine speech; but in Roy's novel it is the reality of mouths to be fed and rent to be paid that deflates male rhetoric. Back home in the bosom of his family, his 'chattiness ... gone,' 'his boastfulness ... vanished' (TF89), Azarius is 'without resilience, as if he were in a nest of thorns, trying to pluck them away one by one as they multiplied around him. Even his voice was not the one he used outside ... ' (TF90). When his wife, who knows from bitter experience the price he pays for deluding himself, looks at him, he can only 'bow his head' (TF155). Ironically, then, for this man deprived by technology and economic crisis of the real freedom of satisfying work, and of the possibility of sharing responsibility with his wife as in the early days of their marriage, it is the family that seems an unbearable prison and woman's love that seems the greatest blow to his fragile identity. Like his nomadic ancestors, he wishes only for escape and the illusory freedom of a linear journey leading nowhere: 'He saw himself packing his bundle and making off before his wife returned ... he'd take the highway until fortune smiled on him at last, a man born to high adventure ... He wished he had no wife, no family, no roof over his head ... he wished for the dawn that would find him a free man with no ties, no cares, no love' (TF159).

MOTHERHOOD REINVENTED

Friendship must be reinvented, but for that to become possible, first motherhood must be reinvented. (Claire Lejeune, *L'Atelier*)

Through Rose-Anna and the other mother characters who appear in the novel, Roy paradoxically succeeds in demystifying the symbolic mother figure while at the same time making her novel a hymn to maternal love. In contrast to the traditional realist novel, where the characters are made to blend entirely into their roles, serving as 'types' and not simply as individual cases (like Alphonsine Moisan in *Thirty Acres*, who represents 'the mother' and never deviates from her role), Roy presents a multiplicity of mothers, each *different*, and each devoured in a different way by the maternal role. On the one hand, she shows that the maternal devotion glorified by male ideologues really exists; through their sacrifices mothers hold together not only the symbolic order but the everyday reality of families. But the price paid for this devotion – in exhaustion, in bitterness, in the obliteration of woman's subjectivity, and in the negative attitudes conveyed by these mothers to their children – proves exorbitant both for women and for culture.

Each of the secondary mother characters – Mrs Létourneau, Mrs Lévesque, and Rose-Anna's mother, Mrs Laplante – reveals a different aspect of the destruction caused by the so-called matriarchy. Confined to their roles of mother and wife, these women see their vital energy blocked and channelled into self-destructive attitudes, or else they direct it outside themselves, in negative form, to their children. Mrs Létourneau, Emmanuel's mother, who 'chat[s] endlessly in a nervous, cooing voice' plays her role perfectly. But, after a whole life spent being the mediator between her husband and her son, she has become the very archetype of the woman-as-reflection: 'her timid soul, weak and loving, had tried for so long to reconcile these two that she had become like a mirror that gave an exaggerated reflection of her son's vivacity and her husband's dignity. She wavered between childish effusiveness and a sudden and unexplained rigidity which seemed to express her respectful devotion to Mr Létourneau' (TF127).

In one of those symmetries Gabrielle Roy excels at,[22] Jean Lévesque's mother represents the other side of maternal alienation. While Mrs Létourneau effaces herself by giving too much love, Mrs Lévesque is the mother who holds back her love, and her wronged son – the most negative character in the novel – is an example of the selfishness and desire for superiority through which such men seek to distance themselves from the maternal-feminine. The whole drama of this silent, embittered woman is, however, played out within the bounds of the maternal role. Having adopted Jean as part of a 'transaction with God,' carried out so that her own sick daughter would recover her health, Mrs Lévesque withdraws into a shell of pain when the daughter dies, becoming 'distant [and] inaccessible' and condemning her adopted son to 'a loneliness worse than that of the orphanage' (TF201–2).

For all these women, even Rose-Anna, complaining is their everyday language. In a revealing passage, presented from the point of view of the daughter Florentine, Roy suggests that this negative attitude, which goes hand in hand with the maternal role, combined with the feelings of rejection, revolt, or resentment it creates in children, is perhaps what best defines the family as an institution – and, by extension, one might add, the culture of which the family is the linchpin:

Oh, that was her mother, thought Florentine, starting right off with their troubles! Away from home, she always had an embarrassed smile, and she didn't mean to dampen youthful spirits – on the contrary, she liked to warm herself by their fire and often adopted a forced gaiety – but her words of complaint came out automatically. They were her real words of greeting. And perhaps they were the right words to reach her family for, apart from their worries, what kept them together? Wasn't that what, in ten or twenty years, would best sum up the family? (TF116)

At the heart of the novel's radical message, then, lies this terrible observation: that in the social and cultural form consigned to it, maternal love almost inevitably turns into its opposite, the mother being driven by the force of circumstances towards the temptation of being a destroyer as well as a giver of life. Contained in the words '*almost* inevitably,' however, is the dramatic tension that animates the entire novel: the constant struggle against the forces of death and resignation that constitutes its meaning. And it is perhaps the image of Rose-Anna's relation to her own mother that best sums up this struggle: the simultaneous revelation to the reader of the truth that she is becoming more and more like that woman-martyr, along with the certainty that she will never allow herself to be drained of her love in such a way.

This mother, Mrs Laplante, is at once the icon of maternal negativism and the perfect incarnation of the teachings of the dominant ideology. In her, all hint of affection has been killed by duty, all love of the earth by the false comfort of a religious doctrine that assures her that she has 'put up with her purgatory here on earth': 'She liked to think that she was on her way to her Creator laden with indulgences, her hands filled with good deeds. It was almost as if she saw herself stepping into paradise like a careful traveller who has taken lifelong precautions to ensure herself a comfortable stay when she finally arrived up there' (TF193).

Offering a striking image of immobility as she sits in her creaking rocking chair, she is the symbolic mother, the 'priest's wife,' the martyred woman against whom the sons of the next generation will rebel. Careful, however, not to confuse this 'negation of all hope' (TF193) with real motherhood, Roy denounces the ideology responsible for such an aberration: 'She had held fifteen round heads against her breast, fifteen little bodies had clung to her skirts; she had had a good, affectionate and attentive husband; but all her life she had talked about the crosses she had to bear, her trials and burdens, her Christian resignation and the pain she must endure' (TF194).

The harshness of Mrs Laplante's message to her children – 'You mark my words: poverty finds us out' (TF195) – is occasionally repeated in Rose-Anna's dealings with her own family. In fact, an only slightly modified version of her mother's message is found in her words to Florentine: 'There's nothing we can do about it ... We don't do what we like in this life, we do what we can' (TF90). The multiple perspectives of the narrative allow Gabrielle Roy to show from both the inside and the outside all the nuances of woman's imprisonment in this maternal role that – *almost* inevitably – turns her into a martyr or shrew. Despite everything the novel shows us about Rose-Anna's gentleness and love, we still see her criticizing her husband with words (TF89), through silence (TF146), and through looks (TF153). Like her mother, she has never learned to express her affection, with the result that 'she was not often demonstrative, either with her children or with Azarius. Her tenderness was almost always concealed behind a look that was discreet or words that were so common as to be unnoticeable. She would have been embarrassed to express herself in any other way' (TF164). For each of her children and for her husband, her ceaseless refrain about their problems has become a living reminder of the house, of poverty, of the origins they are trying to escape. In Eugène's memory of his mother's 'drawn white face' (TF234) on the day when he as a teenager had stolen a bicycle, there is an echo of the image Rose-Anna herself had of the 'white, angular' face (TF193) of Mrs Laplante. For this eldest son of Rose-Anna, his mother's very goodness and her sacrifices are paralysing, and he dreams constantly of escaping from her perpetual complaints: 'He looked away. He couldn't bear to hear her talking about rents and poverty. Would the two of them ever talk about anything else? Was that what he'd come home for? To hear more complaints?' (TF235).

Similarly, Azarius, in a rare burst of anger, tells her her complaining is enough to 'drive a man to drink' (TF146). Even young Daniel is relieved to be at the hospital far from the nocturnal whisperings about 'money, about rent, about expenses, words vast and cruel that came to his ears in the darkness' (TF226).

Counterbalancing all this negativism are Rose-Anna's love and her tenacity – a refusal to give up hope which, along with that of her daughter Florentine – is literally the energy that propels the novel forward, through the growing horrors it reveals. During her twelfth pregnancy, Rose-Anna is several times tempted by death and resists it only through the conviction that her children need her. As soon as her child is born, however, she is revitalized by a maternal love that – like the narrative technique adopted in the novel, and like Roy's all-embracing political vision – has no need to choose among her children, loving each of them as if he or she were unique: 'It seemed to her that this was not her twelfth child but the first, the only one. Yet this concentrated tenderness did not exclude the others' (TF363–4). The themes of love and of the instinct for life that appear here and throughout the novel are crystallized in the image of the old woman in black who appears as an answer to

Emmanuel's anguished questions on the meaning of war, telling him simply: 'Some day there'll be an end' (TF378). One feels sure that this woman, doubtless a mother, knows whereof she speaks and understands the love towards which the world must seek its way.

From object to subject: Florentine's narrative journey

From the first sentence of the novel on, Florentine is presented in the situation of vulnerable expectation that is characteristic of the woman-object: 'Toward noon, Florentine had taken to watching out for the young man who, yesterday, while seeming to joke around had let her know he found her pretty' (TF7).

Prisoner of a biological reality she would prefer to deny in order to have access to a position within culture, Florentine embodies the contradictory situation of the daughter in the Father's House of representation. Dreaming of a linear ascent like that reserved for male characters, she finds herself, much against her wishes, confined to the prison of her reproductive body. But from the moment she contravenes the Law of the Father by becoming an unmarried mother (that is, a woman who reproduces the species without having been exchanged between father and suitor), a gap opens up in the patriarchal text that will never again be closed. Almost unwillingly, she is forced to evolve from the status of object to that of subject, to move beyond her destructive relationship with Jean Lévesque to a love/friendship with Emmanuel Létourneau, bearer in the Quebec text of the 'good news' of a new relationship possible between women and men.

The reader will recall that in the larger Quebec 'text' containing both men's and women's writing, the mother has no story, and the daughter's story ends at the point when she becomes a mother. To the straight line of 'his story' corresponds the vicious circle reserved for women's bodies, 'her story' having been written in advance and destined for eternal repetition. Despite the fact that her maternal love is the unifying principle of the novel's structure, Rose-Anna does not contravene this law. Constantly struggling to keep her family together, she has no goal other than that of maintaining a status quo threatened by the forces of disintegration, and she undertakes no narrative journey other than this marking of time, which is in itself a victory. Unlike her mother's, Florentine's ambiguous narrative journey leads to a possible break in the repetitious circle of women-objects holding up the cultural edifice. The possibility is fragile but tenacious, like Florentine herself. It is through a selfish 'pride' completely unlike the maternal sacrifice of the preceding generation that Florentine begins to open the circle. But paradoxically it is in facing up to the hopelessness of her female condition that she sees herself for the first time as a subject, a woman linked with other women.

MAKING THE SILENCES SPEAK:
THE DAUGHTER-MOTHER RELATIONSHIP

In the tradition of novels written by women in Quebec, Florentine is the first daughter who is not motherless,[23] and in her relations with her mother she exhibits all the ambivalence inherent in the complex daughter-mother relationship. In putting this relationship at the centre of her novelistic universe, Roy shows how the feminine role as defined by patriarchal society separates women from each other, thus perpetuating the status quo of a culture founded on their subjection. In this war, which pits Florentine against her own mother, against the other women of her milieu, and against herself, lies the knot to be undone if cultural transformation is to be possible.

In the scenes where Florentine and Rose-Anna appear together, Roy's narrative technique reveals with remarkable finesse and subtlety a deep-seated love between mother and daughter, but a love frustrated by the constraints imposed by language and culture. Despite the stubborn realism and sense of responsibility for the family that bind them together, Florentine and Rose-Anna are made enemies by their common female condition. Each scene in the novel where they appear together depicts a situation of failed communication, but one that the narrator, by presenting to the reader the thoughts and emotions the characters are unable to put into words, at the same time reveals as attempts to reach each other. It is *between* the words that women's bodies speak, in their silences, gestures, facial expressions, and hesitations that one perceives the distance separating women from themselves and from each other.

A sequence describing a rare visit by Rose-Anna to the Five and Ten where her daughter works can serve as an example of this 'loving' use of narrative point of view. Instead of distancing the characters, the narrative embraces their reactions in the smallest detail, insisting throughout the sequence on the love they find so difficult to express in words. Surprised to see her mother approach the counter, Florentine silently observes the exhaustion and age etched on her face. Moved, she suddenly decides to give her a small gift of money, but her mother's complaining words ('Your father's at home, as you know. And out of work!' [TF116]) irritate her so much that she wants to strike back, then hesitates: 'Florentine frowned, irritated at feeling her good intentions weakening so soon, but she caught herself in time and answered kindly' (TF116). In the few minutes separating Florentine's decision to give her mother the money from the actual gesture, a whole series of words and looks are exchanged between the two women, awkwardly expressing the desire of each of them to please the other. Florentine offers to buy her mother a meal, the 'forty-cent chicken' on special that day. Her mother hesitates, pretending she is not hungry. It is not Rose-Anna but the narrator who, observing her closely, expresses the words that 'you could almost hear her murmur with dread: "Forty cents! That's a fortune!"' (TF117). Through Florentine's exhausted patience, disguised by a false gaiety, and Rose-Anna's awkward efforts to 'put on a happier front' (TF118) as she realizes vaguely 'how imprudent it was always to bother Florentine with their troubles, casting her shadow on this girl's youth' (TF118), the reader is led to see the humdrum, everyday, but very difficult route travelled by a mother and a daughter seeking closeness:

This compliment was like balm to Florentine's heart.
   'I'm ordering chicken. You'll see, it's good,' she cried, back to her first resolve to be kind to Rose-Anna ... Then Florentine, seeing her mother relaxed and almost happy, felt a ten-fold desire to add to the joy she had already given her. (TF118–19)

The gulf between the two women is usually conveyed in a more brutal way. When Florentine learns she is pregnant, she needs to communicate with her mother. But Rose-Anna, perhaps as scandalized by the biological trap that has closed shut on her daughter as by her 'sin,' rejects Florentine in her moment of need: 'She stared wide-eyed, with an expression of mute horror. Without pity, without affection, without kindness ... the two women stared at each other like enemies' (TF261–2).

As if in revenge, the daughter turns away from her mother on her wedding day when Rose-Anna tries to explain the seriousness of the vows she is about to take: 'You're always preaching' (TF344). Later, Florentine changes her mind, but too late: 'She came close to running to her mother's arms, but Rose-Anna turned away, hesitated and went to the kitchen' (TF345).

Perceiving her mother's life as 'a long, grey voyage which she, Florentine, would never make' (TF116), Florentine plays her only trump card, her 'physical charm,' in 'a frightening gamble for happiness' (TF16). Her original 'strategy,' the one typically used by women in a society where all power belongs to men, is to reject all friendship with other women, her rivals in the race to 'catch a man.' Drifting aimlessly and alone,[24] refusing to be part of the 'entirely female, chattering herd' of young girls who go to the movies together (TF17), she concentrates on the make-up, clothes, and appearance that will make her an object acceptable to male eyes. Before she meets Jean Lévesque, her only relationships with men have been dates at the neighbourhood movie theatre, where she has found herself reduced to being a commodity: 'Sometimes, not often, she had gone out with young men, but ... they expected to be paid off in kisses for such a miserly evening; she'd be so busy fending them off that she didn't even get to watch the movie' (TF17).

THE SEDUCTION GAME AND THE STAKES OF POWER:
JEAN AND FLORENTINE

As soon as Jean Lévesque sits down at the counter of the Five and Ten on the first page of the novel, Florentine feels 'disconcerted, vaguely humiliated' (TF8). Between her and the young man is established a relationship that is absolutely familiar and recognizable for any Western reader and yet blatantly sado-masochistic: the relationship of desire between man and woman as stipulated in the patriarchal text. An unequal struggle for power that is also called a 'game of seduction,' this relationship of mutual fascination constantly reduces Florentine to the status of an object controlled by the dominating gaze of her partner. The recurrent image of wind and snow associated with Jean and Florentine makes the sado-masochistic nature of their relationship explicit: 'The wind was master with his whip, the snow was the wild, supple ballerina running before him, spinning on command and, at a word, prostrating herself on the earth before him' (TF27).

The dynamics of this game of power and seduction, which will eventually lead to a sexual scene with all the characteristics of a rape 'invited' by the victim, clearly emerge from the first meeting at the counter of the Five and Ten. The narrator's gaze, far from being 'neutral' or 'unbiased,' ruthlessly follows the sequence of gestures and non-verbal messages establishing the power of the man over the woman. Always in control, Jean skilfully moves through the stages of the seduction, manipulating his victim through the tone of his voice, through the use of the familiar 'tu' to which Florentine, the waitress, answers with 'vous,' and especially through the power of his gaze: 'His eyes hardened' (TF8); 'Once again his look had that brutal familiarity' (TF9); 'As he stared at her, his eyes narrowed' (TF9); 'Elbows on the counter, eyes staring into Florentine's, he was waiting, as if in a cruel game, for a move from her to which he could react' (TF10).

In this power game, closer to mutual hate than to love, the man's hold increases to the extent that the woman – overwhelmed – comes to feel contempt for herself. For Florentine, whose dominant character trait is pride, the effect of 'the unbearable, mockery of [Jean's] dark eyes' is first and foremost indignation at herself. 'How could she have spent so much time in the last few days thinking about this boy?' (TF8).

In this relationship, the young woman cannot act, but only react. Aware of the power game taking place and the clever aloofness of her adversary, Florentine wavers between paralysis ('She stiffened under his brutal scrutiny' [TF10]), irritation, and 'helpless anger' (TF18). Like a mouse trapped in a cat's paws, she in turn tries to provoke him, using her body, the only weapon she has, against the superiority of male language and the male gaze. In doing so, she simply walks straight into the trap set by her partner's destructive desire: 'she forgot herself and rested on one thrust-out hip, hiding her nervousness in a sulk. But he was no longer seeing her as she was before him. He saw her dressed up, ready to go out in the evening ... a girl in a strange get-up, flighty, fretful in her desire to please him. Something arose in him like a gust of destroying wind' (TF10–11).

Presented by a female narrator, the rules of the seduction game are thus very unlike the patriarchal stereotype of the seductive woman's power. When Jean asks Florentine to go out with him, he is careful to do it with seeming reluctance, 'as if he wanted her to refuse' (TF11). 'Normally,' he insists, 'I'd take another three days at least ... But since you've more or less invited me to ask you ... ' (TF9). Aware of being caught in the position of a victim, Florentine feels viscerally the humiliation and helpless rage of one reduced to the state of an object: 'Florentine's cheeks had flushed red. That was what she hated about this guy: the way he could, after dragging her out of her depth, banish her from his mind, leaving her like an object of no interest. Yet it was he who had, for the last few days, been making the advances ... ' (TF11).

PATRIARCHAL MAN, THE NEW MAN, AND
THE FEMININE-MATERNAL

Far from being an isolated incident, the relationship between Jean and Florentine is a metaphor for the mechanisms of power exposed by the novel as a whole. Jean 'possesses' Florentine on the old couch in the Lacasse living-room under the portrait of a Madonna that has disturbed him since he arrived. All the biographical details associated with Jean, particularly those dealing with his relationship to the feminine-maternal, make him the patriarchal man *par excellence*, the man who must 'possess' and abandon the female otherness he sees as a threat to his identity. The author repeatedly contrasts him with Emmanuel, a 'new man' in his need for affection and his ability to love women.

Ready to sacrifice everything in his rise to success, Jean 'likes work not for itself but for the ambition it feeds' (TF24). His fragile identity is betrayed by a need to dominate and be recognized ('They'd see that Jean Lévesque was somebody to be reckoned with' [TF24], and he welcomes war as an opportunity for personal profit. Diametrically opposed to him, Emmanuel departs from male stereotypes and proves to be the strongest male character in the novel. The only male character to recognize the horror of war, he differs from Jean as well in his ability to love Florentine while seeing her as a subject.

With a clarity unprecedented in the Quebec novel, Roy shows the link between male desire for success, as seen in a Jean Lévesque, and a misogyny rooted in a problematic relationship with the feminine-maternal. Not only orphaned but rejected by his adoptive mother, Jean despises women, whom he sees above all as obstacles to his rise in society: 'When those girls get their hooks into you, they never let go' (TF23), he muses as he walks through Saint-Henri. In a parallel sequence, Emmanuel is seen wandering in the neighbourhood, tormented by 'a need for tenderness' and trying to 'recall the features of the girls he had taken to the movies or met at parties' (TF62–3). The contrast between the two characters and the key to their differing behaviour becomes clear in their conflicting attitudes to Ma Philibert, who played a maternal role in the adolescence of each of them. Although he recognizes in her 'the most maternal and gentle influence in his life' (TF31), Jean fights off the temptation of giving in to the sweetness of these memories with a generalized scorn for 'mothers' that, significantly, extends to their bodily aspect: 'If anyone around there could write about that strange time ... it would be Ma Philibert ... But there it is ... These big, red-faced happy mommas probably see nothing and understand nothing, and think everything's just lovely' (TF32).

This does not stop him from wanting 'to be seen ... by her ... in all his new importance' (TF36). Emmanuel, in contrast, is confident enough to behave in a spontaneous and physical way with this maternal figure: ' "Ma Philibert ... you're just as fat and round and heavy as ever ... and just as beautiful," he added, chucking her under the chin' (TF49).

TO ACCEPT ONESELF AS A WOMAN:
BECOMING ONE WITH ONE'S IMAGE

A woman who discovers she is pregnant against her will sees her fate take shape irrevocably, at the command of her body. The pages of literature describing the anguish and terror of this common female experience are surprisingly rare; and yet that is where Gabrielle Roy instinctively places Florentine's moment of truth.

Knowing she is pregnant, Florentine traverses a 'black night' of fear, anguish, and hatred aroused by the inescapability of her biological condition. Her woman's fear is experienced as a surging up in her body of a truth her mind rejects: 'her fear began to sound an alarm within her like a runaway bell that refused to stop, ringing louder than all the church towers in the city – the fear that she had felt approaching for days, for a long time, perhaps ever since Jean had been at her house' (TF247).

A deep resentment – 'so strong that she felt her whole being poisoned by it' (TF251) – grows in her at the intolerable vision of 'this man's life which was unfolding freely, without any regrets' (TF251), while she is left to bear the burden of their act. And yet – like Angéline de Montbrun after her father's death – she is thrown into a state of emptiness by the withdrawal of the sustaining male gaze. Even while hating Jean and even going so far as to wish him dead (TF251), she remains the woman-object, dependent on him for a sense of her own existence: 'In her heart she felt a muted lament, a low cry, a prayer asking that Jean should love her still, despite the leaden hate she felt for him. In order for her to be freed of hatred, freed of fear, he had to love her. And she searched her memory for small proofs of tenderness in things he had said. She clung to these words as a beggar clings to a penny, turning it over and over, hoping perhaps to see it grow' (TF251–2).

But perhaps, more positively, this is what it means to be a woman, this inability to live without love or to be detached from the other. The long description of a freighter moving up the canal that Florentine 'stops to watch ... because she now perceived everything with a painful acuteness, and found it paralyzing' (TF249) is invested with a symbolic resonance that goes far beyond the simple image of phallic penetration seen by Gérard Bessette.[25] Jean's penetration of Florentine, suggested by the freighter 'gliding between the barriers' (TF249–50), is, in a broader sense, an image of the freedom of man's voyage through life and of the ravages left in his wake by his insatiable search for 'distant horizons' (TF250). With no other aim than that of reaching its goal, such a voyage reduces the people and things encountered along the way to simple 'obstacles' to be triumphed over, and to be abandoned in the race towards new horizons to conquer.

It was a tramp steamer ... which ... had completed a long journey between two horizons so distant that they were lost in mists and, now following its narrow path through the city ... it had only one goal: passing from obstacle to obstacle, from barrier to barrier, to reach the open St. Lawrence and the swell of the Great Lakes ... with its crew members standing on deck ... the ship slid quietly, lazily along. And it seemed to have come to impose on that poverty-stricken neighbourhood a life indifferent to the contingencies of the earth. (TF250)

The narrative journey Roy is describing here can be seen as that of a culture and not simply of the individual Jean Lévesque. Given the context of the novel, it is not exaggerated to see in this image the *political* consequences of a dream of the absolute as old (in the Quebec text) as the golden ship of Emile Nelligan's famous poem. Encoded as feminine and maternal ('the open St. Lawrence' and 'the swell of the Great Lakes') since the beginning of recorded culture, this absolute by definition eludes the male subject just as he believes it is within his grasp. And Roy's novel shows that in his thirst for this absolute, 'impos[ing] a life indifferent to the contingencies of the earth' on those in his path, man will go as far as the ultimate irony of killing and being killed.

Such a collective, cultural interpretation of the disaster experienced in Florentine's body seems even more justified if we examine the images used in her own understanding of the damage that has taken place: she bitterly observes that a 'war' has invaded the private domain, transforming the desire between men and women into a mere 'truce' in their 'ancient hostilities.' This war of the sexes is experienced by the woman trapped in the position of object as a war against herself. The defeat of love by 'war' at this critical moment in Florentine's narrative journey is paralleled by the image of Rose-Anna's love conquered by war in the other main plot, and offers a striking illustration of the 'syntony between the devastated biological realm and the devastating historical process' that Michèle Causse identifies as a characteristic of patriarchal culture:[26]

And so this was what made the world go 'round: this was why man and woman, those two enemies, called a truce in their ancient hostilities ... why the night air could turn so soft ... She ... saw nothing but the trap that had been set for her weakness, and this trap seemed coarse and brutal to her, ... she felt, stronger than fear itself, an unspeakable contempt for her fate as a woman, and a self-hatred that left her amazed. (TF252)

Always ambiguous, torn by her inner contradictions, Florentine never attains the linearity of the male narrative journey. And perhaps it is precisely this that constitutes the feminine version of 'his story': a succession of advances and of retreats into the real that, better than the narrative journey of the male protagonist, corresponds to the progress of a life. And yet, despite this fact, the awareness Florentine comes to during her walk along the canal, and later in the little restaurant where she stops on her way home, can be considered a turning point in the history of the female character in Quebec literature. For not only does she experience in her own body the brutal transformation from being an 'object of desire' to a 'mother without a story' that forms the basic structure of the patriarchal text, but she understands, viscerally, the power game that has led her into this 'trap.' Even more important, she begins to extricate herself from this situation by accepting her own reflection in the mirror.

The mixture of superficiality and depth that makes the character of Florentine a novelistic *tour de force* is important here, since the young woman's evolution in this scene is due, at least in part, to her vanity: a delight in the pleasure of clothes and appearance that indicates an irrepressible taste for life. This enjoyment first emerges in her body and her heart in response to the renewal in nature – 'the charms of spring' (TF246) to which, at the beginning of the sequence, her anguish had made her immune. It is strengthened thanks to a musical tune on the juke-box that, despite her dark thoughts, awakens her body to the rhythms of life: 'beneath the table her feet tapped to the rhythm of the feverish music' (TF255). From music to the pleasure of the body and then to the mechanical gesture of taking out her comb and mirror, the progression is automatic and paradoxically liberating:

to the accompaniment of a deafening boogie-woogie, she took out her comb, her compact and her lipstick, and began to apply her makeup with great care ... A last look in the glass and she was satisfied. She was pale, it was true, but pretty, prettier than ever, with her hair down ... She looked down at her slim body as if she had never seen it before ... She stretched out her hands to admire her delicate fingers with their carmine nails. Seeing her youth, her fine hair, and the whiteness of her arms, she began to love life once more. (TF255–6)

From the first image of Florentine as a young woman who 'had never been able to enjoy the possession of the most insignificant thing, or of a passing friendship, or even her scanty memories, except through the eyes of others' (TF22), the journey towards this ability to be one with her image, to live at last according to her own gaze, has been a meaningful one. The closed circle opens into another spiral loop with the beginnings of a closeness to Marguerite, the friend from the Five and Ten she had previously scorned.

BETWEEN WOMEN: TOWARDS A SHARED VOICE

The first instinct of the woman-subject, borne by the rhythm of life awakened in her, is a feeling of tenderness for her mother, with whom she wishes to share from now on her new-found strength: 'Yes, from now on she'd be a real help to her mother. What did it matter if Eugène and Azarius didn't do their share? She'd never leave her mother to their tender care!' (TF256). Standing in the light from the window of the family house, she sees 'Rose-Anna's courage' shining 'like a lighthouse beam before her. Home would take her in, home would cure her' (TF257).

But could it be that the time has not yet come in the Quebec text for the voices of mother and daughter to come together? As she opens the door, Florentine sees the chaos of a hurried move, with the new tenants already there even before her parents have found other lodgings, and Rose-Anna, overcome, reduced to the state of the 'complaining mother.' Between the two women – one of them exhausted and at her wits' end, and the other terrified by her still unrevealed pregnancy – words attempt to trace a path as if between two impassable chasms. To the daughter 'who seems to hear nothing,' the mother asks a question, but without even 'waiting for a reply' (TF259). In face of so much suffering, women's speech is reduced to a cry in the void, immediately swallowed up by silence: 'Were there any answers to be had in this abyss that so engulfed them you could scream for days and hear no response but the echo of your own despair?' (TF259).

An almost identical image is used with respect to Florentine, who 'herself was sinking into a suffocating darkness in which no help, no counsel came from any side' (TF261). Their voices defeated, nothing remains between the two women but the distance of their looks, the mute appeal of eyes eliciting no answer in return.

She [Rose-Anna] stopped short, and the two women stared at each other like enemies ...

Florentine's eyes gave way first. She blinked back her tears, her lips quivered and her whole body was in anguish. It was the one time in her life that her face expressed this call for help, the call of a hunted creature. But Rose-Anna had turned away. (TF262)

Fleeing from the house and from her own terror, Florentine then runs blindly (TF263) towards the home of her friend Marguerite, where she finds a welcome that is a first step in the breaking of the ancestral solitude between women. Here again, the narrator's voice insists on the distance between the two female characters and the cultural forces separating them. It is in spite of herself that Florentine, from the depths of her loneliness, has turned towards another woman, for 'She had never made any effort to cultivate the friendship of girls of her own age. She had always imagined that they envied her and might play her some unpleasant trick, or had simply found them boring ... But she knew that Marguerite had a kind heart, and in her present dejection she needed to be with someone – even someone a little simple-minded – who would take her in and care for her' (TF263).

The two young women are separated as well by all the distance created by Florentine's transgression, the irreparable act that must remain *secret*, unspoken. It is the distance between innocence and experience, and it 'terrifies' Florentine and leads her to seek a physical contact outside language: 'Terrified by the gulf she sensed between herself and the other girls of her milieu, she dug her nails into Marguerite's shoulders as if to transfer her own unbearable anguish to the other, to unburden herself onto another human being' (TF266–7).

Still more secret, even unspeakable, is the possibility of abortion, implied but never openly expressed in the words of the two young women. In the conventional Marguerite, who has guessed Florentine's secret, her friend's suffering awakens a deep maternal urge that leads her in turn to transgress the facile moralism of her milieu: ' "Good God, is it possible?" she thought. And she was surprised to feel no contempt for Florentine, though she had always been severe in her judgments on love outside marriage ... And here she was, thinking only of protecting Florentine from the ruin she saw strewn all along her path' (TF267).

Alone, the narrator's voice seems to suggest, women are condemned to a narrative journey that can only be a path strewn with 'ruin.' Together, there is perhaps hope of 'getting through' (TF268). Friendship between women leads to transformation, while demanding the courage to leave the secure enclosure of the father's house. But for this friendship to be sealed and for real transformation to take place, 'secrets' must enter language and shared speech must shatter the inherited structures. While Marguerite seems to sense these new possibilities, Florentine is not ready for such a commitment to another woman. At her friend's offer of money and invitation to share confidences, she draws back, retreating into the shell of her habitual disdain for women. The invitation to talk as real friends comes from Marguerite: 'Listen, Florentine, there are ways, you know ... I'll be with you, Florentine, I promise. And I'll stick up for you, ok? It'll be a secret between the two of us' (TF268).

And the rejection comes from Florentine, scandalized precisely by the entrance into language of her bodily secret, her transgression of the Law. 'Petrified with surprise that her secret had been found out so easily, and especially that Marguerite dared speak of it' (TF268), she falls back into the ways of thinking that have always separated women from each other: 'What a fool Marguerite was! What a great idiot! A stupid fool! ... above all, she must destroy this idea the big ninny had got into her head' (TF268).

It is alone, then, that Florentine will traverse the rest of her 'dark night' and face the terrifying idea of abortion, quickly rejected as a violence she is unable to inflict upon herself: 'She toyed with the idea, stiffening at the thought of physical pain, knowing she could never accept it' (TF269). As a final irony, she chooses to make of her scorn for women a link in the armour of solitude that encloses her: ' "Women!" she thought, contemptuously. Could one woman help another? ... But who, who would help her? – ... ' (TF270). This last question comes not from Florentine but from the narrator, and the ellipses in the text, exceptional in the narrative style of the novel, seem to indicate that this question is yet to be resolved.

Emmanuel: Thought rooted in the real

When Florentine and Emmanuel dance together, the image of their two bodies united to the rhythm of a jazz tune provides a moment of lightness, a pause paradoxically full of movement in the inexorable progression of events outside. A man and a woman meet in the joy of their bodies and minds; caught up in the music, he is released from the prison of his head, she from that of her body, forever tired and at the service of others. On Emmanuel's face shines 'a new smile, like an offering of his joy' (TF129), while Florentine, accustomed to having to defend herself against men, can finally abandon herself to harmony with another and with her own body: 'From the very first steps, Florentine followed Emmanuel in perfect harmony. She who was so rebellious and strong-willed showed an astonishing docility to the movements of her partner when she danced, a submission to the rhythm of her slender agile body, and a passionate, childlike, almost primitive abandonment to the music' (TF129–30).

It is significant that this release of Eros – a song of life and of the body that Roy's whole vision attempts to make heard despite its repression by culture – takes place under the disapproving scrutiny of Mr Létourneau, Emmanuel's father and the spokesman for conservative nationalism.

They jumped in a jerking rhythm, face to face, breath to breath, mirrored in each other's eyes. Florentine's hair, floating free, flew from shoulder to shoulder and blinded her when she whirled ...

'This is madness!' muttered Mr. Létourneau, twisting his moustache. 'That boy will never keep up his station in life.' (TF130)

At odds with his father and his 'conservative ideas: the survival of the race, fidelity to ancestral traditions, the cult of the national holiday' that for the son are no longer anything but 'fossilized rituals' (TF298), Emmanuel is also the character in the novel who best represents the author's thought. A man of tenderness who loves women, he embodies a 'woman's way of thinking' that makes its way through the various ideological explanations of 'misery,' always measuring them against the reality of the suffering beings he meets – all different despite their similarities of class, national origin, or gender. Far from being an abstract 'universalism,' too respectful of difference[27] to be considered a simple 'humanism,' this way of thinking moves forward, pauses, moves forward again, feeling its way, in an attempt to 'make sense' of the cultural catastrophe while remaining open to the contradictions of the real.

Emmanuel is the man who knows how to listen and wait, whose gaze at a woman is an encounter with another subjectivity and not the possession of an object. Florentine notices this gaze, which 'seemed to be looking for something ... then ... fell on her, recognized her and brightened' (TF128). She cannot help comparing it to Jean's expression: 'Just now Emmanuel looked at me as if he'd known me forever ... while Jean always looks as if he's trying to remember who I am' (TF128).

For Emmanuel, looking, listening, and thought are one, traversed as they are by the looks and voices of the marginal ones of culture: 'His thought couldn't detach itself from these ... beings ... revealed to him in all their solitude' (TF314). In order to reconcile his 'ideal of justice, beauty, brotherhood' (TF315) with a reality marked by economic crisis and war, he knows that he will have to 'embark upon a long voyage through his thoughts, to channel them into something that would be his own truth' (TF299). His voyage into thought is also and above all a voyage into the real, in search of an understanding of Alphonse's face, 'striped with black, as if he were seeing him behind bars' (TF309), of the 'ancient weariness' he reads in Florentine's face, and of Pitou's haunting voice 'soaring in a song that told of the soft prairies, the freedom of the deer, gentle fawns with wide,

innocent eyes ... and then was lost in the wild cry of the wind'
(TF61).

In his only moment of anger, as he walks among the 'princely
mansions' of Westmount, he sees these faces and voices of life
crushed – not simply by human beings of another class or another
nation, but by an anonymous power for whom possession is the
ultimate value. Here again we see the face of the hidden Father,
masked by the imposing capitalist structure that has become his
cultural dwelling place and now uttering his censoring word through
its fetishized objects:

The stone, the wrought-iron grills, tall and cool, the doors of solid oak,
their heavy brass knockers, the iron, the steel, the wood, stone, copper and
silver seemed to come to life with a sneer that was taken up by the luxurious
bushes and trimmed hedges, making its way to him across the night: 'What's
this you're daring to think, poor creature that you are? How dare you try
to put yourself on our level? Your life? Why, that's the cheapest thing on
earth! Stone and steel and iron, gold and silver – we're the things that last,
and cost the most.' (TF320)

In this most frightening of his mutations to date, the Father has
pushed the linear journey of his sons to its apocalyptic outcome: in
a mad journey 'to the end of the world to shoot and be shot at'
(TF377), during which the sons realize, with good reason, that they
have 'at last become men' (TF375).

CHAPTER SIX

The corpse under
the foundations of the house:
Violence to women in the
contemporary Quebec novel

... the pornographic mind is the mind of our culture. In pornography
we find the fantasy life of this mind.
Susan Griffin, *Pornography and Silence*

I have killed, yes! And I can write about it fifty or even a hundred times,
covering the page from left to right, as long as I don't *speak* about it ...
Hubert Aquin, *Blackout*

As it enters the modern age during the Quiet Revolution period,
Quebec literature begins to confront the repressed psychic traces of
its former dream of domination. Once the ancient and reassuring
structures of realism have collapsed, the voices of the body, of
nature, and of the whole feminine realm held in contempt for more
than a century begin to invade the literary text, making it the site of
a struggle to the death between a threatened male ego attempting to
maintain its mastery over the world and this 'otherness' erupting
into the text. Behind the anarchic, apocalyptic violence of the works
of this period lies an unspeakable reality whose shape resembles the
corpse of a woman.

Veiled by the political crisis that shook Quebec between the first
bombs of the FLQ in 1963 and the October Crisis of 1970, this
violence in the novel appears at first glance to be simply the predictable reflection of a social situation. A society dominated from
without and held captive from within by an officially sanctioned

opposition to progress was in the process of exploding, and it would have been extraordinary if the tremors of its revolution had not been felt in the writing of the period. Several writers of the early and mid-1960s explicitly acknowledged the impact of the political violence on their works. According to Jacques Godbout, the plot of his novel *Knife on the Table*[1] was transformed during the process of its composition by the first bombs of the FLQ, while for writers like Gaston Miron, Hubert Aquin, and Paul Chamberland the very possibility of writing was thrown into question by the political situation. As Chamberland writes:

> It only took a single day, everything was blown to
> pieces
> there's nothing I can do about it I possess neither
> rhyme nor reason
> the time of the bombs surprised me and the time of
> the prisons
> the time of things becoming obvious
> and here I am on the first floor of my life
> exactly like the humblest of our people.[2]

While a feminist analysis does not deny these obvious parallels between literature and society, it does begin to question in a new way the myths and psychic forces underlying the violence present in the literature – and persisting in it long after the era of dramatic social unrest has come to an end. For even a superficial analysis of the literature of the 1960s and 1970s reveals a troubling phenomenon: in almost all the novels written by men, it is a woman who is victim of the violence. Both Claude Jasmin's *La Corde au cou* (The noose tightens)[3] and Hubert Aquin's *Blackout*,[4] for example, open with the murder by the protagonist of the woman he loves. In Jacques Renaud's famous 'joual' novel, *Broke City*,[5] the protagonist jealously watches the comings and goings of his girl-friend, Mémène, whom he considers his sole possession, and he beats her brutally when he can no longer tolerate his own social frustrations. The entire novelistic universe of Hubert Aquin tends towards mystical fusion with an archetypal woman identified with country, revolution, and death, and is traversed by sexual violence. In Aquin's first novel, *Prochain*

Episode[6] the object of the narrator's desire for violence is still unfocused, although there is a suspicion that the woman he adores and idealizes is perhaps his real enemy. In the subsequent novels the violence against women is explicit and central to each novel's meaning. The symmetrical structure of *Blackout* is based on mirror reflections set up between the murder of the protagonist's lover in the first half of the novel and the rape of the murdered woman's sister in the second half; *The Antiphonary*[7] can be read as a series of jealousy-related rapes and murders; and *Hamlet's Twin*[8] recounts the murder and ritualistic mutilation of a young woman by her husband during their honeymoon. The same configuration of murder and sacrificial mutilation constitutes the entire subject of Victor-Lévy Beaulieu's *A Québécois Dream*,[9] which the author presents to the reader as a literary transposition of the 1970 October Crisis.

The relationship between violence and sexual mysticism is, however, far from being a uniquely Québécois literary phenomenon. For Georges Bataille, sexual violence is the literary subject *par excellence*, since literature, like mystical experience, represents a transgression of social codes and a refusal of all limits. Bataille sees the dream of Sade, the 'divine Marquis,' as the dream of all philosophy: to realize the union of subject and object in a mystical 'fusion' consisting of the frenetic and violent destruction of the resisting object by the subject seeking to possess it.[10] Needless to say, the subject is male and the object female.

Particularly interesting from a feminist point of view is the extent to which the nationalist project in the literature of the 1960s is linked to a similar dream of absolute power and excludes women by the very terms in which it is formulated.[11] In these texts the revolutionary project is that of the son rebelling against the mother and seeking a 'virility' seemingly achievable only at women's expense. The image of birth is frequently used to evoke the bringing-into-existence of the longed-for nation, but it is a birth conceived of as a refusal of and defence against the all-powerful and suffocating figure of the mother. Sanctioned by the revolutionary conjuncture, the violence of the period perpetuates male values as ancient as patriarchal culture.

And so we find ourselves once again in the presence of an all-too-familiar figure: the mythical mother fantasized as overwhelming and 'castrating' by the patriarchal mind. Although she is probably more of an ideological construct than a reality, this mother is nonetheless threatening to her sons – particularly in the context of Quebec culture, where the power of the father has always been concealed behind the image of her *supposed* power, and where the son has felt blocked by external circumstance in his own growth towards autonomy. As early as 1950, Anne Hébert captured the ravages wrought on both the male and the female psyche by this fetishization of the mother in the figure of the gigantic Claudine, whose presence intervenes between her son's subjectivity and a world she has presented to him as a forbidden realm. The opening lines of *The Torrent* evoke with brutal simplicity the transposition from the psychic to the ideological plane that transforms the mother (the original experience of totality known by the infant) into a symbol of the Law that condemns him to 'dispossession' and fragmentation:

As a child, I was dispossessed of the world. By the decree of a will previous to my own, I had to renounce all possession in this life. I related to the world by fragments, only at those points which were immediately and strictly necessary, and which were removed from me as soon as their usefulness had ended ... I could see the large hand of my mother when it was raised towards me, but I could not perceive my mother as a whole, from head to foot. I could only feel her terrible size, which chilled me.[12]

In an article suggestively entitled 'The Colonial Oedipus,'[13] Pierre Maheu inserts this myth of the mother into the political conjuncture of the 1960s and heralds the birth of a revolutionary project defined as a confrontation of her power over her sons. Although he insists on the fact that in reality traditional French Canada was a paternalistic society, Maheu demonstrates how on the levels of religion, history, and family life its existence was dominated by the maternal myth. According to him, the systematic opposition to progress, the valorization of the period prior to the Conquest, and the emphasis on spiritual and moral values at the expense of action that characterized this society are all manifestations of the 'feminization' of its value system. In a colonized society, he argues, the passage from adolescence to adulthood is experienced not as a confrontation with the father, since the latter is 'non-existent,' but with 'a prohibitive presence ... that is global, overwhelming, and maternal.' (Maheu is of course generalizing on the basis of what he considers to be the typical *male* psychological pattern, although he sees no need to make this explicit.) 'Authority doesn't threaten to strike us,' he continues, 'but to engulf us.'[14] The 'depersonalization' that accompanies colonialism is experienced as 'a state of social chaos in which we feel sucked into the quicksands of the Mother.'[15] Using the thematics of birth and rebirth common to the poetry of the same period, Maheu reveals the potential for violence it contains: 'Revolution is a paroxystic act, as dangerous as a return to the origins or a descent into hell ... In the course of this return to the origins, we must traverse the night. Our adventure is that of Orpheus: to descend to the underworld of colonial alienation and to conquer the maternal and castrating monsters that lurk there ... '[16]

Maheu distinguishes carefully (albeit unconvincingly) between the need for this war against the mother in the psychic and symbolic domain and real relationships between men and women. The confrontation with the mother will, he insists, simultaneously 'make women our lovers and wives and free us from the Mother as we emerge anew from her womb.'[17] Nonetheless, his analysis remains trapped within the limits of 'his story': the familiar quest of the male subject for identity through a series of initiation rites marked by violence and confrontation. And it is in light of its relation to these initiation rites (the traversal of the night, the vanquishing of a female monster, and the symbolic 'birth' that results), that the sexual violence in the novels of the period reveals its coherence.

The male protagonist of these novels – a son and an extension of such early heroes as Menaud, Euchariste Moisan, and Séraphin Poudrier – is Oedipus on the brink of manhood, but still trapped in the triangle of traditional male desire. Feeling mutilated, impotent, unsure of his identity, and ill at ease in his body, he dreams of a woman in whose embrace he can allow his identity to dissolve, and yet at the same time whom he can dominate, using her submission and humiliation as a proof of his power. The list of these 'mythical heroes' is scandalously long, and includes such well-known characters as the narrator of Aquin's *Prochain Episode*, who dreams that he 'penetrates, an absolute terrorist, into every pore of [the spoken] lake'[18] of his lover's body; and that of Godbout's *Knife on the Table*, who seeks to lose himself in the 'otherness' of the character Patricia, a symbol of 'Americanity' and of anglophone reality. François Galarneau, Godbout's otherwise good-natured hero, muses on the possibility that after making love with his girl-friend, Marise (who bears the same name as his mother), 'perhaps I could strangle her, or break her back the way we did with the grasshoppers on the steps of the priest's house.'[19] As well, there are all the exhausted and impotent heroes of André Major's trilogy *Les Déserteurs*, in particular Inspector Therrien, the inveterate voyeur who compensates for his impotence by using his camera to freeze reality and fragment the female body.[20] And Victor-Lévy Beaulieu's Barthélémy Dupuis, the symbol of absolute dispossession, who before brutally murdering his wife forces her to carry him in her arms and dreams he is 'a big blue baby in his mother's arms.'[21] Finally, in a female transposition, there is Réjean Ducharme's Bérénice Einberg, the strange young heroine of *The Swallower Swallowed*, who lives her entire life according to the inexorable logic of the equation 'to exist = to destroy.' The opening lines of the novel make explicit the link between this equation and the perceived power of the mother from which Bérénice is determined to free herself: 'Everything swallows me. When my eyes are shut it's my insides that swallow me, it's in my insides that I stifle. When my eyes are open I'm swallowed because I see, it's in the inside of what I see that I suffocate. I'm swallowed by the river that's too big, the sky that's too high, the flowers that are too fragile, the butterflies that are too timid, by my mother's face that is too beautiful.'[22]

When identity can be conceived of only as a reduction of all 'otherness' to a reflection of self, that self will be constantly threatened by the very existence of the other. In order not to be swallowed, one becomes a swallower; in order not to succumb to the temptation of a regressive desire for fusion, one destroys the desired object. Pierre X. Magnant, the mad revolutionary and murderer who is the main narrator of Hubert Aquin's *Blackout*, points out the political and the specifically Québécois dimension of this sexual alienation: 'My sexual behaviour is the reflection of a national behaviour whose hallmark is impotence: the easier the going, the more I want to rape. Normal love-making interests me less and less ... My disenchantment is too close to being a phobia of impotence. Weary, I dream of the plenitude of rape – as the mystics must aspire to divine ecstasy ... '[23]

From the 'grandfathers' to the grandsons:
A continuity in violence

For those who would doubt the continuity linking this recurring theme of the murder of woman to the less obviously violent 'dream of enduring forever' that inspires the novel of the land, Victor-Lévy Beaulieu's novel *Grandfathers*[24] is a revealing document. Published in 1971, it can be read both as the last gasp of the rural tradition in Quebec literature and as a statement of the impasse faced by contemporary men's writing. In the nightmare world inhabited by its protagonist, Milien, all the repressed underside of the novel of the land emerges: the hatred between men and women, the fear of and fascination with the body, the obsession with an 'evil' that is both threatening and ardently desired and that enters the body from 'below' and propels it towards the abyss of a triumphant obscenity. Once the reassuring codes and behaviours that kept the old order in place have disappeared, the whole world seems to disintegrate into a chaotic state of violence that extends beyond the rural boundaries of the novel to evoke a more universal cultural apocalypse. The formerly impregnable Father's House is invaded and torn apart by its own inner demons: 'the devils were coming up from the cellar and between the walls, their powerful tails like noisy whips and their forks red with hell-fire, piercing hard into the flesh, tearing apart his body as it twisted on the bed' (G157).

Milien's crisis is that of a culture whose sons have 'destroyed the image of the Father' (G115), and of a house swept away in 'the slide of the whole country into the anarchy of spring' (G90). Once the protective guard-rails of paternal authority have been removed, the destructive (and maternal) waters formerly held in check begin to overflow, in the 'furious madness of the Boisbouscache [River]' (G90). The entire earth is experienced as a huge 'diseased womb' inside which the protagonists are 'alone in the thick night, falling into emptiness' (G99). In response to this revenge of the scorned feminine-maternal element, the male ego only becomes more unyielding, sensing in the chaos of these new times the opportunity to unleash at last its unquenchable thirst for mastery: 'Negative times were coming, times that would be the reverse side of the known world ... And maybe we would finally be allowed to be incestuous and sadistic and happy' (G100–1). During his wife's final moments, old Milien fantasizes the arrival of death in her body as its progressive reduction until nothing remains but her buttocks, the site of his desire. The fragmentation of the female body by the male gaze present in all the novels of the land reaches its culmination in this passage, where the psychic motivation behind this murder of woman is finally exposed: the need to destroy that which in the female body is perceived as a threat to the male ego, even as that same body is conserved as a fetish to sustain phallic power. 'He would see life slowly leaving Milienne, slipping away from the fatty pads in her neck, her arms, her breasts, her stomach; only her buttocks would remain enormous, and her legs would be a vice in which he would no longer be smothered ... One word was possible and this was the word Milien was saying as he looked at his wife's rosy bum: "Beautiful, beautiful, beautiful" ... and now he was nothing but an overly-stiff phallus' (G102–3).

This cultural apocalypse emerging at the very heart of the narrative provides a black, post-modern version of 'his story' – now become an unrelenting advance towards 'something that would be horrible and malicious' (G94), for 'what could there be beyond [the house], if not the end of all that was possible, if not murder or some terrible settling of accounts?' (G101). Deprived of the paternal law that had formerly governed its course, the male journey persists in its mad rush forward, refusing renewal and continuing without a goal until it finally comes face to face with its repressed fantasy: the obscene dream of an apocalyptic murder of the mother/wife. The entire structure of Beaulieu's novel in fact corresponds to a walk – the pathetic wandering of a husband fleeing the house where he has abandoned his dying wife, after having brutally beaten her as she lies on the kitchen floor. Like the image of Donalda Poudrier, the image of his wife that haunts Milien as he wanders through the village and the territory of memory is charged with guilt: 'His last vision was of Milienne lying in a small pool of blood, her eyes shut, her legs folded under her: Milienne in a humble posture which was itself an act of accusation, despairing in its motionlessness' (G19).

Fleeing this vision (like Pierre X. Magnant in *Blackout*, who writes in order to forget the fact that he has murdered the woman he loved), Milien roams through the village and the surrounding countryside, seeking distraction from the accusing truth of his own violence. It is hard not to see in him the image of the male writer roaming through the territory of language, tormented by the memories of sadism and hatred that are gradually revealing themselves as the repressed truth of his 'dream of enduring forever.' For the aged Milien, this dream has been fortified by the reassuring image of the couple and the unchanging gender roles that protect the smooth surface of appearances and 'free [us] from anxiety': 'Great tenderness rushed through him, for nothing could really change; they were made to last forever and they would age in this calm slowness, and their aging would bring them only more intensely toward ... this very childhood from which they would draw their continuance' (G81). The illusion of immortality is also associated with the authority of the father, now threatened by the sons' awareness of its hypocrisy: 'How could his sons guess that it was his immortality he wanted to save? Was the Father's need so strange to them? "My sons, my sons," he said to them, "this is our only chance to be" ' (G115).

The parallel between Milien's impasse and that of the male narrative is made even more explicit in the tale of an archetypal 'Journey' that he recounts to his dying friend Chien Chien Pichlotte – a 'dog-man' who provides yet another grotesque image of the bestiality and madness that threaten the male protagonist. Sitting in the dark at the bedside of this dying, filthy, and almost unconscious friend who masturbates under the covers as the story progresses, Milien tells his story, and the text is explicit about the fact that it is because he is a 'father' that he is qualified to tell it (G106). In this pact or exchange between two dying men achieved through the magic of a shared tale, there is an image of the long process of myth-making shared by men and founded on the objectification of woman that constitutes the tradition of male narrative. The story Milien tells is that of a journey formerly endowed with 'privileged meaning' (G106), but that can no longer be told without an awareness of 'the enormity of the lie that had to be perpetrated' (G105). In it, Milien and three of his friends are in a huge automobile hurtling through the countryside towards the city – vulgar and childlike Ulysses figures in flight from the house and from woman; they are presented as 'foetuses' (G107) in an aborted birth and overgrown children amusing themselves by 'noisy farts' (G108) and jokes as the car moves through space. Like all the earlier versions of 'his story,' this journey through the male imaginary landscape takes place under the sign of the gaze and its ability to dominate the world: 'the car was an animal that would disfigure the landscape, accelerating the speed of images coming at you. Everything the eye saw would be dressed up in some alarming meaning ... after seeing, you had to recreate decomposed things' (G107). And as in earlier versions, its goal is a state of unity made possible by paternal authority ('the reassembling of the clan'). Far from reaching this goal, however, it leads Milien to a state of frag- mentation, hatred, and betrayal by his sons, who arrange for a prostitute to distract their father from his 'quest.' It is in the pathetic act of possessing the despised female body that Milien finally con- fronts the long-repressed truth that undermines the noble enterprise of the male quest and topples the edifice constructed by the Father's authority: 'His sons knew that after that, after having kissed her lips, caressed her breasts, patted her buttocks, lain on top of this woman and spurted his seed into her, he would not dare to appear before them again. They had killed him, they had destroyed the Father image. What remained to be done after that? ... He knew that noth- ing was possible any longer' (G115–16).

The scene of the murder

Incapable of going any further in his story, Milien falls asleep and dreams of an orgiastic act that places him 'right at the centre of his bliss' (G119): the murder of his wife and children. The pornography and the hatred of women in this murder scene brutally reveal the presence of the corpse of a woman at the foundations of the entire representational and cultural edifice based on the economy of male desire. The fear and contempt of woman's body implicit in all the male narratives we have examined so far are here precisely identified as the repressed content and the ultimate outcome of 'his story.' By the very logic of the male quest, Milien's story makes clear, the female body must be dominated, dismembered, and mutilated, pre- cisely because of its power to arouse male desire, and hence to threaten the complete mastery of the male subject over the world. Moreover, since according to this same logic woman's gravest 'sin' is to have been a mother – that is, anterior to man and more powerful than he – she must be struck down in her maternal love in order for male pleasure to be complete.

The pleasure evoked by this dream of murder is explicitly associated with the sense of power it gives Milien: 'he was content because wicked thoughts were coming to him: in his dream he murders Milienne and all his children. It is so easy to do' (G118). Indeed, it is not only the act of killing, but of killing *his own family* – the 'others' who according to the patriarchal hierarchy are the possessions of the father and husband – that releases in him a sensation of power and immortality: 'It seemed to him that he had never been so great as that night; the idea of killing his family so that he might be the only one with some chance of surviving eternally is not yet very clear to him, but it comes from far down inside him and nothing now can repress his desire' (G118–19).

This feeling of being immortal – the 'dream of enduring forever' finally achieved – is an integral part of Milien's sexual pleasure. Having first taken off his clothes 'so that the blood, the spurts of pink liquid, would gush only over his skin, touching his hairs and his flesh so as to assure his immortality' (G119), he proceeds to decapitate the nine children asleep in the attic of the house with an axe, piling the mutilated bodies and heads in a pyramid in the centre of the room and seating himself in the blood: 'Something is rising within him, an extraordinary feeling of joy that gives him great pangs in the stomach. He is ... right at the centre of his bliss' (G119).

After the children, it is the turn of the wife, who will be struck down and punished in the position of Sorrowful Mother, despairingly kissing the corpses of her children. While for the male subject observing her she is an object to be despised, for the reader she seems the archetypal end point of the long list of anonymous and silent woman-objects of earlier narratives: 'she is like some kind of nameless deformity he must put an end to' (G119). In fact it hardly seems an exaggeration to see in this image of a nude man *observing* the spectacle of destroyed maternity he has created and hating the woman, even at this ultimate moment, for the 'provocation' her body represents, an image of all the repressed content of patriarchal society's system of representation. Could it be that *to kill the mother in order to exist* is the hidden structure of all these male narratives?

In this regard, the following passage from Beaulieu's novel, with its precise allusions to motherhood as the primordial threat ('milky breasts,' the 'big blind cow bellowing') and the apocalyptic fragmentation of the female body that concludes it, is important enough to be quoted in full:

... she walks up to the pile of corpses, lies on top of her children and begins to weep because she understands that the axe has taken them from her forever. She embraces the blood, the arms that are under her, the chopped necks, the open eyes staring at the vision of the axe slicing the air. Naked beside her, he looks at her: why was she provoking him with her overly-big buttocks? He undresses her. Oh, no longer to see those milky breasts dragging so obscenely in the blood. He slips her nightgown over her head – she is a big blind cow bellowing on a pile of refuse. The axe rises, rises in the black sky, making flashing whirlwinds. He misses his mark, shattering only the shoulder. The axe must strike again and again on the big body, bloody and broken, whose bones are flying all over the room. (G120)

Consciousness as a way out:
Hubert Aquin and Réjean Ducharme

Is this violence against women inevitable, then, and inherent in the very process of representation as experienced by the male subject? Or could there be a way to undo the patriarchal triangle, to enter into language *otherwise*? In order for the sons and daughters of culture to free themselves from the symbolic father/mother and find their way out of the Father's House, women must first begin to exist as subjects and men must begin to listen to their words. It is only with the advent of feminist writing in the mid-1970s – the collective project of women consciously seeking to inscribe themselves as subjects within language and undertaking the laborious deconstruction of the patriarchal symbolic order – that such change will become a real possibility. But before that the novels of Hubert Aquin and Réjean Ducharme constitute a turning point, a moment of transition. For in the elliptical, enigmatic narrative strategies used by both writers one can almost hear a call for other voices and subjectivities to emerge and to propose new values capable of revitalizing culture.

For the two novelists, the way out of the present impasse, if one exists, is to be found in consciousness: consciousness of the representational traps that perpetuate the subject-object dichotomy and of their origins within culture; and consciousness of the role played by active reader participation in the creation of new modes of intersubjectivity. And yet the work of both these writers is marked by a violence and sado-masochism from which the authors seem unable to free themselves, and which they can only display to the reader as a symptom of the cultural malaise the works are attempting to expose. To propose an 'anatomy of the illness' – to borrow the term Aquin himself uses to describe one of his novels[25] – is already a considerable step forward.

An ardent admirer of Sherlock Holmes and of detective novels in general, Aquin early detected the presence of a corpse buried beneath the edifice of Western culture that all his self-conscious and history-centred novels explore. That this corpse was female there was no doubt; and one of the most striking contrasts between his second novel, *Blackout*, and Hans Holbein's painting *The Ambassadors*, of which it is constructed as a mirror reflection, is the existence of this female corpse and the presence in the novel of the violence that has destroyed her. In Holbein's work, the anamorphosis of a skull puts the entire edifice of the medieval arts and sciences into question, reminding the spectator that in face of the reality of death all these glories are but vanity. In Aquin's novel, the corpse of Joan Ruskin[26] occupies a similar position, emphasizing not only the self-reflexive character of Aquin's creation, but also its relation to a cultural tradition based on violence to women: 'She is the unverifiable focus of a story whose only function is to disintegrate around her mortal remains. The book is no more than an accumulation of vanities, multiple masks of the atrocious fact which we can, by a simple shift of viewpoint, designate as murder' (*Blackout* 116).

Could this murder be the source of the guilt that haunts all Aquin's protagonists and drives more than one of them to suicide? And could it be related to the trap in which the narrator of *Prochain Episode* mysteriously finds himself ensnared when he ventures into the château of his adversary, H. de Heutz? The paralysis he experiences on that occasion is not surprising, given the fact that he is at last face to face with the elusive and invulnerable father figure, who is not only his rival for the woman he loves but also a double and an 'enemy-brother' in whom he recognizes his own image. Following *Prochain Episode*, where this Oedipal structure of desire and rivalry is revealed as the unresolvable cultural enigma, Aquin's work slides into an increasing darkness and violence. The unending and narcissistic mirror reflections, the increasing despair of the attempt to uncover the source of the problem somewhere in the historical past, and the violence and self-destruction of the characters are all indications of the circularity of the quest of the male subject imprisoned in the Father's House. Condemned by the dualistic ideology of patriarchy to 'live in his head,' it would seem that the son can only search for an exit there, in the hyperconscious lucidity of his writing.

Unable to free himself from this dualistic heritage, Aquin can do no more than offer his readers an anatomy of the cul-de-sac of Western culture, and encourage them by means of highly self-conscious techniques inviting reader participation to enter into a process of 'co-creation,' by which each reader in his or her own way will begin to fill the void Aquin has opened up before them. It is significant that in two of his novels, in the devastated space that remains after the suicide or the disappearance of the male protagonists, it is female characters who assume responsibility for the narrative. In *Blackout*, it is Rachel Ruskin, the sister of the murdered Joan, who organizes the text and presents it to the public once she has recovered from the traumatic effects of her rape by the male protagonist, thus becoming an image of the reader involved in the creative process. Transformed by her reading of the novel, she lives 'alone' and 'at peace,' carrying a child whose birth she sees as a sign of the advent of a new world, free of the violence that has consumed the child's father. Similarly, at the end of *Hamlet's Twin*, after a scene of violence as apocalyptic as any of the scenes in Victor-Lévy Beaulieu's novels (but far more explicit in the cultural references that situate the violence and attempt to explain it), the two female characters who have survived come together in a mystical lesbian embrace from which violence is absent – a parthenogenesis[27] based on a true exchange between the partners, unlike the possession and destruction of the other that characterizes the heterosexual relationships in Aquin's work. The author seems to be suggesting that the path to

Undensacre, the place of non-violent and immanent sacredness for which the entire novel yearns, will be opened by the emerging voices of women who have become subjects.

Réjean Ducharme goes even further than Aquin in his demystification of the modes of domination underlying the literary edifice, and in his identification of the maternal archetype to which this male violence is linked. By endowing his first and most famous heroine, Bérénice Einberg of *The Swallower Swallowed*, with a dual Jewish-Christian ancestry – and by presenting that ancestry as inseparable from the thirst for violence that leads her to Israel and to the sadistic pleasures of war – Ducharme locates the reality of violence within a Judaeo-Christian heritage that pays homage to the archetype of the mother but is in reality dominated by the image of a vengeful father. When one is possessed as Bérénice is by desire for the mother, there is an obvious and all-too-frequent solution: to free oneself from her spell by transforming her into a negative image – a witch, or a 'dead cat ... something as hideous and repulsive as possible' (ss19). But Bérénice is conscious of what she is doing, and behind the myth of the monstrous mother the face of her real mother is perceptible in the novel, challenging the reader to deconstruct the myth. Terrified by sexuality, Ducharme's young heroes and heroines seek a world in which men and women could come together in tenderness and equality. 'Be satisfied with being my sister, with being *with* me; don't try to *belong* to me,' says Mille Milles to his friend Chateaugué in *Le Nez qui voque*.[28] But they are prisoners of a world where the body is identified with sin and violence, and like their favourite writers, Emile Nelligan and Saint-Denys Garneau, they choose to remain in childhood.

For these two transitional writers, the thematics of desire are still based on distance, the gaze, and a destructive fascination with the other. And although the Father's House of realist representation explodes under their destructive blows, the modalities of the relationship between author, text, and reader in their works remain trapped in the male space of rivalry and domination. Here again Aquin and Ducharme, unable to transcend the cultural and historical moment in which their works are situated, can only expose the problem to their readers and laugh about it.

However, the complicated games of irony and the sado-masochistic teasing of the reader that characterize their works have the merit of making explicit the male rivalry implicit in earlier works of the realist tradition. Whether perceived as a male rival or a female object, the reader must be dominated and humiliated in a game of seduction in which the author holds all the cards. 'I was on the verge of recreating the world, but I stopped, for I was irritated by the rivalry of God the Father,' wrote Aquin as early as 1950. 'It's clear that he will always be stronger than I, and I'm a poor loser.'[29] Ducharme addresses the reader as follows: 'I hate you. There is also the élite of humanity; not only you, the dregs.'[30] And elsewhere: 'Do not adjust your set ... Leave it alone and go away.'[31] There is no question that such zany interventions add to the pleasure of reading these 'post-modern' works, as well as serving to demystify the realist illusion. But the problem of the apparently indissoluble link between representation, domination, and violence that they bring to light remains unresolved. Aquin reminds us of the urgency of this problem when he intervenes at the moment when the suspense in *Hamlet's Twin* is at its peak, informing the reader that he/she is in the process of being raped:

The present, which has been employed from the outset, is the time of the screenplay because it does not relate anything, but transmits an intention – and not just any intention: that of an abduction! The account of an imaged rape is rather unexciting if we compare it with a plan for rape ... That goes without saying; but what is less obvious is the relationship between this violent terminology and the situation of the viewer of the film ... Perhaps the viewer will suddenly be offended when he realizes that he has done everything to be raped; offended, too, when he deduces that the spectacle he is watching is hypocritically penetrating him ... [32]

The corpse as seen by a woman:
In the Shadow of the Wind

Discovered by a woman a few years later, the corpse has become double, even multiple ... and it has escaped toward the sea/the mother (*la mer/mère*), where it refuses to remain silent. Anne Hébert's *In the Shadow of the Wind*[33] is the story of the rape and murder of two young girls, Nora and Olivia Atkins, by their cousin

Stevens Brown; and despite the fact that it is written by a woman it presents the same portrait of male desire demolishing its object, the same cultural impasse, and the same apocalyptic violence as do the novels written by men. But under a woman's gaze the metaphor of murder is made the focus of a writing of resistance, affirming the existence of a *different* desire and pleasure than that which seeks to kill its object, and insisting on the need for cultural transformation.

In the work of the male novelists, the emergence of the body and of the 'semiotic' or 'maternal' dimension of language (rhythms, sexual drives, fluidity, senses other than the visual) that accompanies modernity clashes with the male subject's desire for domination, producing an 'exploded' style of writing – but one that is *negatively* exploded, so to speak, like a fortress assaulted from without. In other words, in spite of its *apparent* modernity, this writing is still under the control of a powerful Jansenist superego, simultaneously obsessed with and horrified by the body, which it has always seen as the greatest 'occasion of sin.' Hence the excremental vision of Victor-Lévy Beaulieu, where the body speaks through farts, belches, and bad odours that arouse sexual pleasure,[34] and the tense sexuality of Hubert Aquin, where in a typical scene malaise with the body is expressed by an almost torrential gushing of sperm that covers the sexual act with ridicule.[35] In contrast, the flow of Anne Hébert's writing seems to espouse desire, emerging multiple and polyphonic in the gaps of a suspense-filled narrative that advances inexorably towards the act of destruction that forms its climax.

This subversion of the Word (the discourse of mastery) is announced in the opening pages of the novel, in the image of the disorder introduced by the twins, Pam and Pat, into the portrait gallery of their uncle, the Reverend Nicholas Jones. The portraits of male ancestors, which Nicholas has painted in black and white, recall the portraits of the ancestors in the novel of the land, although Hébert is far more explicit than earlier authors about their symbolism. They represent a linear retracing of the male past on the part of a man 'without issue' (sw10), haunted like his forbears by the 'dream of enduring forever': 'I, Nicholas Jones ... set up a gallery of ancestors so as to proclaim that my blood would endure ... I who had no sons beget my fathers unto the tenth generation ... ' (sw10). Unlike *their* forbears, however, Pam and Pat, who can be seen as the 'mad' and 'haunted' daughters of the female characters of the novel of the land, no longer submit to the reproving gaze of the portraits. Armed with brushes and brilliant colours, they 'discover the pleasure of painting,' 'turning chronology upside down, inventing for themselves grandmothers and sisters galore' (sw11) – subverting 'his story' in a mad joyful excess that suggests something of the texture and non-linearity of women's creativity:

Set loose with brushes and paint, shut away in the portrait gallery for a whole day, the twins have slathered the walls with cascades of lace, with flounces, checks and dots and multicolored stripes, with flowers, leaves, red birds, blue fish, crimson seaweed. A few heads of women emerge from it all, wearing hats, quills, ribbons, some with only one eye or lacking a nose or mouth, and more alive than any dream creature who has haunted Griffin Creek since the mists of time. (sw11)

But along with the bliss, madness, and overflowing of Pam and Pat's art, their canvas also contains the revelation of a hidden crime, cried out in 'a single endless graffiti: 19361936193619361936193619361936 1936,' and in 'three women's heads [a]drift upon a seagreen background ... Nora, Olivia, Irene [Nicholas Jones's wife, who commits suicide in the novel]' (sw11). In a similar fashion, Hébert's writing also subverts traditional literary codes based on domination and reveals the repressed truth of the murder of woman they conceal. The six 'books' that make up the novel are presented by five different narrative voices – two male (the preacher and the murderer), two female (the two victims), and the voice of the idiot Perceval, 'whose desire, surpassing the limits and bounds of language, can only be expressed in unbearable cries.'[36] These voices are amplified by a polyphony of other voices emerging from long silence – those of the inhabitants of Griffin Creek, those of the women of the past, and those of a nature unleashed after centuries of domination (the voice of the wind seeping under the doors of the closed house, the voice of the enraged sea, and the piercing shrieks of the gannets, the fous de bassan of the novel's original French title).[37]

This is a writing of jouissance,[38] then, but also a committed and a subversive writing, a passionate indictment of a culture that strikes down pleasure in its earliest bloom, at the precise moment when the young girl stands on the threshold of the adult world, 'eyes barely open but already filled with all the energy in the world' (sw81). All the world's song can be heard in the words of little Nora Atkins, before she reaches the age when culture teaches her guilt for inhabiting a female body: 'I like days that are white with heat, when the water and sky reflect one another, a fine warm mist covers everything, and on the soft, oyster-colored sandbar, footsteps are erased as they are formed' (sw82). Nora's words are the expression of a young body awake to the rhythms of the earth and made powerful by 'the promise of ten or twelve children with ultramarine eyes that nests ... in the hollow of [her] belly' (sw86). Affirming along with feminist writers like Louky Bersianik that the flesh precedes the Word,[39] Nora's words dare to stand in place of the biblical Word used by her uncle, Nicholas Jones, to reduce the village to silence:

He talks about God and about the men and women of Griffin Creek who owe obedience to God and to him, uncle Nicholas, God's representative at Griffin Creek ...
And the Word was made flesh and dwelt among us. And I, Nora Atkins, I too was made flesh and I dwell among them, among my brothers and cousins ... The word in me has not been uttered or written down: it is only a secret murmuring in my veins. (sw85–6)

Later, however, after being exposed to her uncle's caresses and her cousin Stevens Brown's insistent gaze, Nora loses this assurance born of an innocent sensuality; 'He says that I'm wicked ... He seems to want to hit me. He says that through me, sin has entered Griffin Creek ... I did something dirty too, with the preacher' (sw93–4). Originally presented as 'the new Eve' (sw86), she is transformed by her culture into an adept practitioner of the war of the sexes; so much so that Stevens, later recalling the rage that pushed him to rape and strangle the two young women, remembers Nora's provocation most of all: 'Nora's mouth vociferating within reach of my mouth. Repeats that I'm not a man. Tells Olivia to watch out for me. Throws back her head. Her peals of laughter' (sw180).

While this war between the sexes is familiar to readers of Anne Hébert's earlier work, it is revealed in *In the Shadow of the Wind* to be a confrontation between two previously scripted stories, the cultural texts assigned to men and to women from early childhood on, in which each in a different way is forced into the role of victim. The novel's entire structure can be seen as a confrontation between these two narratives – 'his story' (that of Stevens Brown) and 'her story' (that of Olivia Atkins) – and one made all the more tragic by the fact that it is also a frustrated love story. Each of the two stories goes back to the same moment of overpowering desire felt by a little boy and girl on a beach in the morning sunlight – a moment cut short by the brutal words of their parents, who call them back to the names and identities assigned to them by the patriarchal text. This moment of desire exchanged in innocence and equality – a meeting of the separate spheres of sun and shadow, in which the stereotypical associations of male and female are reversed – shines forth in the text as a revelation not only of what could have been, but of what *could* be. It is significant that in this passage it is not the boy who looks, and affirms by his gaze his desire for the other's body, but the girl; and that it is not the girl who touches with tenderness, and admires the other's creativity, but the boy:

The little girl blinks, takes a long look at the little boy, from his feet to his head, luminous and golden, suffused with pale light, his head half lost in the wind and sky like a pale disheveled sun, she thinks ...

Now he is crouching in the sand beside her. Looks closely at the sand castles. Looks closely at the little girl. Doesn't know which he admires more, the sand heaped up in tidy rows or the little girl herself, who has built it all. She is breathing against his shoulder, hiding behind her bangs. With his fingertips he grazes the little girl's cheek ... Who will be the first to shout with joy in the wind ... ? (sw153)

All of this lasts only an instant, before the return to the gender roles that imprison and separate: ' "Stevens! Olivia!" says one of the mothers over there, knitting on her folding stool' (sw153). In the image of young Stevens hurriedly departing, swallowing his instinctive desire for freedom as he prepares to face his father's brutality, there is an explanation of all the brutality he will himself display when he reaches the age of adulthood. It is important to note that in Hébert's universe mothers are the all-too-willing spokespersons of this brutality of the fathers, communicating the rules and codes that govern behaviour: 'Someone says that the boy is unmanageable and must be taken in hand' (sw154).

Although they are equally stifling for their subjects, 'his story' and 'her story' differ significantly in terms of their relationship to the feminine-maternal. Tyrannized by unfaithful or brutal husbands, the wives and mothers perpetuate culture's vicious circle by preferring their daughters and rejecting their sons. The die is permanently cast when the sons, once they reach adulthood, become obsessed with 'subduing' women as a means of compensating for their perpetual thirst. Nicholas Jones, kissed by his mother, Felicity, for the first time at the age of twelve when he tells her of his decision to become a minister, will become the incarnation of the Law of the Father in Griffin Creek: he who 'in the name of God and the law of the Church ... knows how to put women in their place' (sw63). And yet it is his mother, once she is freed from her years of marriage and mothering, who becomes the symbol of the power and sensuality associated with the feminine-maternal realm: 'She reigns over the sea. Her dressing gown with its brown-and-red pattern of leaves drifts about her. Like a giant medusa' (sw24). Felicity shares her morning bathing rituals with her granddaughters Nora and Olivia, and not with her grandson Stevens. And he, knowing full well that he is a disappointment to the grandmother he adores, becomes more and more susceptible to the cultural role prescribed for him: 'She declares that I'm just like my grandfather, can't be trusted, and that all men are pigs ... my grandmother has always preferred girls' (sw54). Stevens' rape of Olivia is an attempt to possess the feminine-maternal element that has always eluded him, to freeze its movement[40] and to usurp its power by degrading the female body. His penis is

a weapon that stands erect in the fishy sea conch in the middle of Olivia like deep mud that must be reached at any cost ... The real problem was how to immobilize her altogether. To abuse her in peace. Call her a slut. Unmask her, the girl who was too beautiful and well-behaved. By playing angel so much you ... Make her admit that she's hairy under her pants, like an animal. The hidden flaw in her fine and solemn person, that moist black tuft between her thighs, where I fornicate just as I do with whores ... (sw182–3)

To immobilize woman: the goal of 'his story.' To escape from immobility: the starting point and the goal of 'her story.' Interwoven from the very beginning, the stories of Stevens and Olivia both extend beyond the moment of the murder, creating an openness and textual ambiguity that may well be one of the most common characteristics of women's writing. Having reached its goal with the destruction of Olivia, Stevens' tale continues for a time, acquiring a collective resonance as it traverses the apocalyptic violence of the Second World War. In the image of the rows of hospital beds where languish the young men destroyed in battle, Hébert denounces war as a triumph of the cultural values of linearity and permanence – a tragic imitation of the 'dream of enduring forever': 'When their bodies were torn to shreds they were twenty years old. Were shipped home, taken in hand by society, laid in neat rows of white beds in big bright sterile rooms, growing old like everyone else, drop by drop, day by day, year by year, while nothing around them changes, only this smooth whiteness ... ' (sw170).

For these anaesthetized and mutilated men, only one dream of happiness persists – that of a return to an at last welcoming maternal breast: 'At times the sister of charity bends very low over an invalid's bed, half-opens her bodice, shows her breasts which shine in the night. The man with no hands or arms weeps. The sister of charity consoles him, bends ever lower, brushes the soldier's cheek with her rosy nipples. Puts them right in his face. In his mouth. He sucks gently, closing his eyes' (sw170). And one nightmare – that of a war they have experienced as an apocalypse of sexual climax gone wrong, an explosion of all the senses where nothing survives but reason, the unshakable seat of patriarchal thought: 'It comes, most likely, from what my eyes have seen, what my nose has smelled, my ears have heard, my palate has tasted, my hands have done – with and without a gun. A real feast for the senses. Nerves frayed. Reason, which persists when it should have shattered long ago, under the repeated shock of images, odors, and sharp-beaked sounds' (sw169–70).

Like numerous other narrators and protagonists before him, Stevens offers an image of the male writer trapped in the mechanics of the patriarchal text. From the moment of his arrival in Griffin Creek, he puts on the air of the all-powerful author or the omniscient narrator, distancing himself from the entire village by his gaze and

by the power of his crushing boot: 'Arms folded under my head ...
I raise my leg, blink, move my foot, shod in its dusty boot, over the
village ... My foot is huge and the village under it is very small ... I
could crush my grandfather like a cockroach. But I leave him there
to sleep and dream under my sole ... I know what my grandfather is
thinking, as well as if I'd drunk from his glass' (sw45–6).

Like other contemporary writer-protagonists (Aquin's Pierre X.
Magnant and Christine Forestier, Beaulieu's Milien, and Ducharme's
Mille Milles come immediately to mind), Stevens writes to exorcise
the memories of violence that haunt him. And like them he feels the
need for a 'travelling companion' in his narrative journey, a pact
with another character that will give him the necessary strength to
continue on to the end of his unspeakable story. For Stevens this
'implied reader' – the other without whom he would be unable to
complete his tale – is Michael Hotchkiss, the old friend from Florida
with whom he spent his time 'chasing women':[41] 'What's important,
old Mick, is that you read my letter right to the end ... It's as if I
was asking you to come along the road with me, till there's nothing
at all ahead of me, nothing but the abrupt cliff, the void, the leap
into the void' (sw179).

Given the rather surprising order of the various 'books' that make
up the novel (the second-last book is narrated by one of the two
victims from beyond the grave, and the final one by the murderer,
from the temporal perspective of 1982, the year of the novel's
publication) it is clear that the novel's structure corresponds to the
linear quest or journey of the male subject, and that Hébert is seeking
to establish a correspondence between that journey and the present
situation of our culture. The novel ends with the scandalous image
of the corpses of the two young women, that of the younger one
frozen in a pose all too familiar to the reader of this group of novels:
'Poor little Nora fallen so fast onto the sand at my feet, one leg
folded under her ... Didn't have time to take my pleasure from her.
From her furor. From the smell of terror in her armpits' (sw180).
And it is to the uncontested power of a Law that condones such
sexual violence that Hébert gives the final word: 'P.S. You may be
surprised if I tell you, old Mick, that at the February 1937 assizes I
was tried and acquitted, my confession to McKenna having been

rejected by the court and considered to have been extorted and not in accordance with the law' (SW183–4).

And yet the preceding section of the novel, the astonishing book of 'Olivia of the High Sea,' provides another meaning, a possibility of subversion, and a way out of the impasse of 'his story.' In it the voice of culture's repressed rises up from the depths of the sea/ mother (*la mer/mère*), speaking through the multiple voices of the 'great liquid women' (SW163), all those women of the past who have been murdered by culture, imprisoned in the strait-jacket of the role of wife and mother as defined by male power. While it has long existed as a muffled complaint, a lamentation washed away by the sea's rhythm, this voice of the 'mothers and grandmothers' becomes an insistent demand when it merges with Olivia's desire to be a 'full-fledged woman' (SW160) – a desire that has survived her individual death and that returns with urgency to the shore along with every tide. It is the same hunger for life as that of the 'black woman' evoked at the end of *Kamouraska*,[42] here become powerful enough to explode not only the limits of the character of Olivia (whose desire speaks even after the female role which limited her in life has been left behind), but also the closure of the text. In the memory of the reader after he or she has closed the book, it remains as a burning demand for cultural transformation.

It would seem, then, that in the cultural text containing all these stories there is a single narrative pattern that repeats itself *ad infinitum* – as if 'his story' were unimaginable in any other terms than as an annihilation of 'her story.' And yet the quotations Hébert uses as epigraphs to two of the 'books' in her novel – the first by Hélène Cixous, and the second by Shakespeare – suggest another possible intersection of these two narrative journeys. If 'his story' were to open out to hers, in such a way as to permit her 'to be able to laugh in cascades and belly to the earth / and at full force and with abandon and in a torrent / and as she intends' (Cixous, SW80), then that story might become something other than 'a tale told by an idiot, full of sound and fury' (Shakespeare, SW100), in which the characters turn unendingly in the vicious circle of the identities assigned to them by culture.

CHAPTER SEVEN

What Oedipus sees:
Hamlet's Twin *and the*
impasse of 'his story'

The root problem behind the reality of men's relations with women is the way men see women, is Seeing ... He sees nothing at all except what he represents to himself. Under his aesthetic gaze, any woman, known or unknown, turns into the 'stranger,' that object of no interest except for its capacity to stimulate the subject's feeling of life.

Susanne Kappeler, *The Pornography of Representation*

Narrativity endlessly reconstructs the traumatic moment of an Oedipal drama ... All narrative cinema, in a sense, is the making good of Oedipus, the restoration of his vision by the film's representation (re-enactment) of the drama.

Teresa De Lauretis, *Alice Doesn't: Feminism, Semiotics, Cinema*

Nothing is free here ... Something tells me that an earlier model [of this story] is plunging my improvisation into an atavistic form ...

Hubert Aquin, *Prochain Episode*

Near the end of Hubert Aquin's final novel, *Hamlet's Twin*,[1] which is written as a film scenario, appears the following description: 'the body of Sylvie Lewandowski slides slowly and falls into the void. Nicolas moves away, but he is seized by vertigo. High angle shot of him backing towards the precipice in terror, as though he can't stop and as though the precipice were exerting an irresistible attraction over him. He staggers, falls backward; his head is very close to the precipice. Fade to black' (HT196).

With his uncanny ability for producing images of our contemporary cultural malaise, Aquin here places in conjunction the spectacle of a woman's body, the abyss to which she has been consigned by male violence, and a man's head: the male character riveted by the fascination and terror of the abyss into which he has thrown the corpse of the woman he loves. Fade to black.

Unlike a real filmic image, this one is described in words and therefore, paradoxically, it exists on the page framed by silence: the equivalent of a slow-motion shot in which meaning is crystallized. It is not accidental, I think, that the male protagonist in this shot is *backing* towards the precipice, as Aquin himself, in a series of novels that extended his range of exploration farther and farther into the Western cultural past, seemed to be backing closer and closer with each novel to a point of no return. In this final work, written three years before the author's suicide, the intertext is Shakespeare's *Hamlet*; and in it Ophelia's lament becomes an obsessive refrain ('Woe is me / To have seen what I have seen, see what I see!'). Behind this tragedy of vision, one detects as well the shadow of Oedipus – that drama of Everyman that ends in an apotheosis of knowledge as intolerable sight.

What did the hyperconscious Aquin see when he looked into the gap in history that separates Shakespeare's enigmatic work from his own? And why did he privilege *vision* in this novel, to the point of writing it as the scenario of an unproduceable film? The experience of reading *Hamlet's Twin* was compared by one male critic to the sensation of reading 'the last book of all time.'[2] Aquin himself told an interviewer of the feeling during the novel's elaboration of being 'close to the end,'[3] and in fact his inability to continue writing after *Hamlet's Twin* was certainly an important factor in his suicide in 1977. Always extraordinarily lucid about the implications of his writing, he was undoubtedly aware that in *Hamlet's Twin* he had pushed the narrative function to its imaginable limits, thus confronting both the possibilities and the constraints of 'his story.' Like his previous novels, *Hamlet's Twin* focuses on the post-modern male subject, surrounded by mirror reflections and multiplying the effects of illusion and reality in a frenetic attempt to escape from some unnamed truth lurking in the depths of those mirrors. The voyage, a recurring metaphor of the narrative journey in Aquin's work, reaches its geographic limits in this novel, which shifts from Montreal to Spitzbergen in the Arctic circle, where an act of absolute violence transforms the snow into a 'vitrified black texture' (HT126), and then to Natchez-under-the-Hill in the American South, where the turbulent waters of the Mississippi carry a liquefied evil out to the ocean: 'At the end of the street the walker may gently enter the waters of the Mississippi and baptize himself by immersion until his body, purified of the spirit of evil, turns liquid and rolls like the waves of the great river as far as Bâton Rouge, Plaquemine, Chalmette, Evergreen ... ' (HT183). Behind all these frantic shifts in location, one senses the presence of an inescapable anxiety: the pain of feeling the approach of death while one remains outside 'the impenetrable shell of the real' (HT152).

The novel's basic structure is one of incest: the artist as Oedipus, whose quest for the impossible narrative culminates in the discovery of the incestuous relationship between the woman he loves and her father, and in a scene of intolerable violence in which he 'punishes' her for having thus evaded his own attempts at possessing her. The structure is identical to that of the patriarchal or Oedipal triangle seen in previous works, except that in this case the situation of the son and the daughter in the Father's House of representation (and the power relationship between them) at last becomes clear. Nicolas Vanesse, the symbolic son, is a post-modern descendant of Maurice Darville: a new figure of the artist attempting to affirm his autonomy in relation to a domineering father. The first figure of this father in the novel is Stan Parisé, the condescending director of the play Nicolas is acting in, from whom Nicolas frees himself by renouncing his acting career in order to write the scenario of an autobiographical film (thus acceding to the status of a 'father' in the hierarchy of classical theatre).[4] This film scenario within the novel, which is being written as the narrative advances, is encased in an authorial commentary on art, time, love, and the sacred – or what a post-modernist would describe somewhat less poetically as representation, desire, and the unrepresentable. In the final scene of the film scenario (towards which the author leads the reader in a process described as 'rape' in the text), Sylvie is ritually murdered and her body dismembered and devoured by her husband, Nicolas – and this on a honeymoon trip to the North Pole that is presented as an image of the cultural and epistemological journey to the mythical 'Ultima Thule' that has haunted the Western imagination.

As well as pointing to the Oedipal triangle as the foundation of Western representational practices, Aquin adds to that triangle a variation rich in potential for change: the introduction of a second female character, Eva Vos, who replaces Sylvie in Nicolas's affections after the latter's disappearance during the honeymoon. Like Sylvie, Eva will experience the temptation of complicity with the Father and with the violence of male desire, but unlike her she will succeed in achieving the status of a subject, withdrawing from 'his story' and affirming an alternative desire that will have significant narrative consequences.

Thus *Hamlet's Twin* can be read as a sustained reflection both on patriarchal discourse and its structures of representation and on the violence to woman that seemingly cannot be divorced from the 'penetration' of the real that the male subject has regarded as central to his cultural project. Unlike many of the other self-referential narratives of post-modernism, where the mirror reflections and *mise en abîme* techniques create an illusion of openness while maintaining the supremacy of the male subject, Aquin lucidly confronts the emergence of the female subject and the implications of that emergence for 'his story.' And what the novel suggests is that integrating the feminine into patriarchal discourse is no simple matter – that to see lucidly and confront the implications of the emergence of woman as subject is to confront the impasse of the male subject, the end of his narrative. One is reminded of Luce Irigaray's ironic observation on contemporary psychoanalysis, one that might also serve as a comment on literary post-modernism:

Subjectivity denied to woman [she writes] provides the ... backing for every irreducible constitution as an object: of representation, of discourse, of desire ... The male subject can sustain himself only by bouncing back off some objectiveness, some objective ... And her possession by a 'subject,' a subject's desire to appropriate her, is yet another of his vertiginous 'failures.' For where he projects a something to absorb, to take, to see, to possess ...

a mirror to catch his reflection, he is already faced by another specularization ... The quest for the 'object' becomes a game of Chinese boxes. Infinitely receding ... [5]

And Irigaray continues: 'But what if the object started to speak? That is, also to "see", etc. ... What disaggregation of the subject would that entail?'[6] The importance of Aquin's final novel is that it leads precisely to this point of conjuncture between patriarchal culture and feminism. His gaze into the post-modernist mirror is lucid enough to make it shatter; and what emerges from the shards is a plea for women's voices to carry the culture out of its impasse.

Who is Sylvia?

Who then is this woman in fragments, this Sylvie Lewandowski thrown into the void while Aquin's narrative, which contains within it a dream integrating all the narratives of history,[7] attempts to continue on its course? Reading *Hamlet's Twin* from the point of view of sexual difference, it becomes clear that she is the idealized and objectified woman who has been the support of patriarchal discourse, the Woman symbol who, as Nicole Brossard has pointed out, must be killed in order for real women to exist as acting subjects within history.[8] When the camera focuses on Sylvie, the words of the scenario specify that this is 'the first icon of Sylvie Dubuque' (HT36), a woman 'in tears' (HT35), whose beauty is defined in terms of vision, painting, and the sacred:

Sylvie has been crying or is about to start crying: yes, she goes through life with wet eyes, masked, in a way, by a transparent secretion. Her gaze, even more than her other corporeal properties, epitomizes her ... Constantly shifting, it is what most connects her to the invisible. But how to give a precise idea of her body? Invoking Titian or Tiepolo is a reference to fixed images. And yet these points of reference are not completely ineffectual, for a halo of splendour suffuses Tiepolo's airborne women ... (HT36–7)

Identified later in the novel with 'the Alpha and the Omega,' Sylvie is defined entirely by characteristics that make her the archetypal projection of male fantasy – the idealized other with no voice of her own whose function is to 'carry' the film and link it with centuries of cultural symbolism:

Sumptuous, captivating (her rather broken voice only adds to this quality), embodied with a connotation of plenitude, unvarying in her attractive force, Sylvie is the ultimate woman, the mirror of love, the hollow vessel of Snaebjorn, the work of works. From the beginning – and for some time yet to come – Sylvie is the carrying structure of the film: everything refers to her, is grafted to her skin, everything is measured in terms of her. She is the origin and the end of all successions, and the allusive symbol of duration. (HT36–7)

Despite this idealization, or rather as an essential part of its meaning, Sylvie is presented as the castrating woman. Her pendant, 'a convex plexus with numerous bars that join the eruptive and ambiguous core to its crown' (HT31), is at once a symbol of the female sexual organ and of the sacred,[9] and is also the weapon she uses to wound Nicolas's penis when he forces her to participate in fellatio (HT35). As 'son' and 'daughter' of the patriarchal symbolic order, Nicolas and Sylvie (like Maurice Darville and Angéline de Montbrun) seem equally 'wounded' in their attempts at mutual love. Sylvie is obscurely conscious of this when she says to Nicolas: 'I'm not like the image of me that you've built up ... But because you love me, Nicolas, you're unfair, because you want me to be like the woman of your life' (HT59). This mutilation of the human by the symbolic is emphasized in a scene showing the young couple in a taxi on their way to Dorval airport at the beginning of their honeymoon. As the taxi moves along, the image of a giant poster showing the body of a naked woman fragmented by the vehicle's movement unfolds at a hallucinatory pace behind the lovers:

the gigantic poster of the reclining woman goes past in the opposite direction, from the hair to the feet, as Nicolas smiles affectionately at Sylvie. Reverse shot: Sylvie in right foreground responds to Nicolas's loving smile in a slow fade which makes the poster-woman appear from feet to head (because the taxi has just changed direction). However, it is as though the poster has been torn at irregular intervals: some pieces are missing from the horizontal representation of the naked woman. (HT26)

Essential to the symbolic power of the Sylvie image is the movement of the camera, which attempts to 'possess' and to 'penetrate' this female body fantasized as the container of the enigma that haunts the male imagination. The entire novel, presented through the voyeuristic gaze inherent in filmic representation, in fact hovers on the ambiguous border between pornography and eroticism. The camera lingers over Sylvie's body in sleep, 'her right hand ... at the top of her thigh, at the most vulnerable place on her body, as though to veil the invisible' (HT5), focuses on 'a small rivulet of sweat [that] flows between her breasts' (HT5) as if in a desire to penetrate her mystery, and emphasizes the Medusa-like quality of her magnificent blonde hair, 'spread over the pillow like an octopus' (HT12). Is this an 'objective' recording of reality, or a projection of male fantasy? Aquin's choice of a filmic form exacerbates through its visual imagery the play of desire and the unconscious that is present in all narrative; as many feminists have pointed out, and as he seems to be discovering in this novel, patriarchal culture finds its privileged expression in the specular, visual possession and destruction of the desired object – the representation that kills. Sylvie herself seems physically conscious of this fragmentation of her body by the male gaze, complaining of the sensation of being literally torn apart from within: 'Everything's shattered inside me. All the little pieces of my body are coming apart. It's terrifying, you know. I could feel my belly splitting inside me ... and inside my skull I was watching myself dissolve' (HT58).

Hamlet's Twin is not a film, however, but a novel, and it is the conjunction of word and image that makes the reader conscious of the symbolic and real significance of what he or she is experiencing through the image. The novel's opening lines, apparently narrated by a traditional omniscient narrator, are an example of the ambiguity of the narrative gaze throughout the novel: 'The city is sweltering, as it has been all summer. Montreal is like a vast open furnace: apartment windows are wide open, offering solitary voyeurs countless low-angle views. Bare shoulders, backs exposed to the sun, thighs spread open, faces coated with sun-tan lotion, white stomachs: so many components of dizzying allusive images!' (HT5).

With no explicit mention of either men or women, the above passage compounds the ambiguity of the apparently genderless voice in which it is narrated – for the typical reader in our culture, whether male or female, will in all probability imagine the solitary voyeur as male and the shoulders, backs, thighs, faces, and stomachs as female. Unease increases as the reader gradually becomes aware that the action he/she has the illusion of seeing directly is in reality being mediated through the gaze of a hidden and voyeuristic observer: the camera? the author? or the reader him/herself who of necessity espouses the vision of this observer?

Killing this woman-symbol in a feminist text, as Nicole Brossard does in *These Our Mothers*, is one thing; killing her violently at the hands of a male protagonist in a novel written by a man is decidedly another. On one level, Aquin's novel is a complex, modern version of the all-too-familiar pornographic aesthetic.[10] Like Baudelaire's famous liminary poem in *Les Fleurs du mal* it justifies its violence by accusing the reader of complicity: 'Hypocrite lecteur, mon semblable, mon frère!' As the novel's suspense intensifies, the author intervenes in the filmic narrative to point out to the reader that s/he is being raped, violated, pushed to the edge of the abyss as Sylvie herself is being pushed, and that, like Sylvie, s/he is a willing partner in this game of cat and mouse. In fact, insists the narrator, this 'pact' between writer and reader in which the reader necessarily occupies the position of victim is an essential component of both literary representation and cinema:

the author puts off the moment when he must summon up his strength, move on to the attack. He waits for the viewer to find his aptitude for diving into the unpredictable the way one dives into an inky night. The dialogue resides in that. The viewer, the interlocutor, chooses to ignore the processes that are used to cast a spell over him. Life is probably too short to let us keep in touch with the latest techniques for abduction; it's enough to be carried off. Better yet: it's enough to want to leave ... (HT134)

Of course the viewer hesitates to perceive himself as a succubus when he is sunk in the obscurity of a movie theatre, and to admit the troubled complementarity of the film and of the person who watches it right to the end. Something hard to admit is linked to any freely consented obscurity, even that of a cinema, and for that very reason people should wear masks to the cinema. (HT129)

What saves the novel from being simply pornography and manipulation is precisely this awareness of the deep-rootedness of the fantasies and the power struggles embodied in the act of representation itself. There is a despairing quality to this awareness on the part of the author, who uncovers the origins of this violence in gender-based concepts of identity and knowing, which reify woman in order to consolidate the male's position as subject. To tell a story, to invest it with suspense, to capture the reader's interest, and to play on his or her desire all appear as modes of domination linked to pre-scripted cultural responses skilfully brought into play by the author – responses that he reveals as essential to the dimension of mystical love the novel seeks to awaken in the reader:

At this point in the film the viewer might experience a sense of security if he could see this sequence through to its logical conclusion ... But it is necessary to interrupt this process of being swallowed up, transform the two feverish bodies into pillars of salt and leave the viewer to his own unsatisfied desires ... Instead of spreading through Eva's mucous membranes, nectar will flow through the serpiginous paths of the viewer's imagination and rise up to the invisible heights of his being ... (HT144)

Thus the desire for mystical fusion that gives the novel its lyric intensity is shown to be inseparable from the desire for penetration and possession of the real and of all 'otherness,' and therefore to be doomed to failure. Hence the sense of infinite sadness that permeates this part of the novel: 'We believe that we enter the loved person: all we do is slide on the shining skin of her legs. Love, no matter how deliberately intrusive it is, is reduced to a velar approximation of the other, to a desperate cruise on the roof of a sea that can never be pierced ... It's not time that flies, it is being which eludes us ... ' (HT152).

When impossible to imagine except as the expression of a 'solid' identity threatened by the 'liquidity' of the feminine-maternal, the acts of both knowing and loving necessarily meet up with the resistance of the 'object': 'All existence unfolds on the fringe of time and on waves that threaten to open, but never expose more than what a consenting belly exposes to the one who invests it' (HT152). Writing and all attempts at representation appear as a continuation

of the Cartesian *cogito* – an impasse for the desiring subject that the
narrator evokes in an image strikingly similar to the one in the earlier
quoted passage by Irigaray:

The cantata in a mirror has just shattered under the devastating action of
the *Cogito cogitatem*, only the shards of an unreflecting mirror remain. No
one knows anything, decidedly ... If there is no way to convey the sorrow
contained in this last assertion, if the bumpy travelling shots don't acutely
render the pain of being on the impenetrable shell of the real, then the
image is worth nothing. It is nothing and all that remains is to invent a
musical substitute to express the great sorrow that we feel; a cantata for
the valley of death. (HT152)

Nicolas/Hamlet/Oedipus: Narrative as HISTORY

Is there no way, then, for the male subject to escape from the
Oedipal drama and to make his story into something other than a
tragedy? *Hamlet's Twin*, which is traversed from beginning to end
by an unresolved tension between narrative openness and closure,
between the 'unpredictable' and the 'irreversible,' is the author's final
attempt to break out of the tragic Oedipal configuration present in
his work from his earliest writings. For it is the Oedipal 'knot' that
constitutes the irresolvable enigma and the basic structure of the
narrative journey of each of Aquin's protagonists – from the novella
Les Rédempteurs,[11] permeated by the nostalgia for a pre-temporal
state of unity and structured around the rivalry between two brothers, through the yearning and tragic love stories of the author's
television plays, to his novels. In the novels, the impotence and
violence of the protagonists clearly seems an internalization of the
prohibitions of an all-powerful father figure – that same figure whose
'sun-edged silhouette' stands between the protagonist of *Prochain
Episode* and the landscape where he 'dreams confusedly of fleeing,
following the streams to the wonder-struck lake.'[12] In *Hamlet's
Twin*, however, the author seems to have given all possible advan-
tages to his hero in the struggle against the father: early in the novel
we learn that Nicolas has already married Sylvie, that he has decided
to abandon his career as an actor (and the condescending father-
figure of Stan Parisé) in order to work on the writing and production

of his film, and that his honeymoon trip with Sylvie is imminent.
Presently playing the role of Fortinbras in a production of *Hamlet*
for television, he seems as likely to 'become' this victorious son,
who 'avenges his father by winning back the kingdom of Denmark
in his name' (HT8), as to identify with Hamlet, the tragic son who
is unable to undo the Oedipal knot linking him to his mother and
his uncle.[13]

Corresponding to this sense of possibility in the plot is an initial
openness in the form of the novel. The reader is encouraged to seek
meanings not in a closed one-on-one correspondence with *Hamlet*,
but in the defocalized gap between image and referent: 'Where is
this sight? Where is this sight? Where is this sight? (HT11) says
Nicolas, practising his lines from *Hamlet*; but 'the two images are
never in focus at the same time, as if they were seeking each other,
but in vain' (HT14–5). Playing constantly on the tension between
indeterminacy and closure in narrative development (HT10, 13, 17,
24, ff), Aquin leads us to see that openness in narrative is not as
simple a matter as some critics would have us think.[14] Whether we
like it or not, we are made up of our past experience; and narrative,
like life and like history, can reach a 'threshold of irreversibility'
(HT133) where the accumulated weight of its past dramatically
reduces its possibilities. Interspersed with flashback shots that suggest a menacing past hanging over their story (scenes of Nicolas
binding and gagging Linda Noble, the actress who plays Ophelia in
the TV *Hamlet*; a scene of Sylvie in a rage attacking Nicolas's penis
with her sharp-edged pendant necklace; a scene of her in bed with
an unidentified man), the camera follows Nicolas and Sylvie on their
honeymoon to a deserted spot on the island of Spitzbergen, then
cuts abruptly to a distraught Nicolas explaining to Norwegian rescu-
ers that his wife has had a fatal accident. The murder of Sylvie takes
place in a blank space in the narrative, and not until the end of the
novel is the reader confronted with the horror of what took place
by the precipice. Following that ellipse or blank space, Nicolas's life
appears to go on normally, and in fact he immediately enters into a
relationship with another woman, Eva Vos, who will eventually
emerge as Sylvie's positive double.

But despite this appearance of openness in the unfolding of his
story, Nicolas carries with him a suitcase which is 'Sylvie's symbolic

coffin ... the weight of the body drags him along, determines how he will walk and what his destiny will be' (HT97). Although he continues to work on his film scenario, it will be invaded by reality, thrown off its original course by the accumulated violence of 'his story.' It is only at the point when the scenario – trapped by life in a hallucinatory series of events reflecting the plot of *Hamlet* – is finally completed that the destiny to which Nicolas acceded at the edge of the precipice is revealed to the reader: neither Hamlet nor Fortinbras, he is the reverse mirror image of each of these two 'enemy brothers.' Unlike Hamlet, he has penetrated the enigma that obsessed him and has destroyed its mystery. And like Fortinbras, the one who 'doesn't die' (HT44), he will continue to live, although without having become the 'victorious son' (HT8). In *Hamlet*, the play within a play is a trap to 'catch the conscience of the King.' In *Hamlet's Twin*, the film scenario is a trap for the characters and for the reader, who together are caught in its suspense and accelerating violence. But in turn the scenario is trapped by an intersection with reality (the violence of the cultural text in which the roles of Nicolas and Sylvie seem to have been determined in advance) and transformed into something beyond the author's control. The apparent freedom that marked the beginning of its composition has led, after a series of detours and illusions, to its inevitable insertion in the text of which – unknown to the author – it was always a part. As we shall see, this paralysing intersection of Nicolas's story with its own past and with the surrounding cultural text takes place in a highly significant place: the Father's House.

Inventing a musical substitute: The emergence of woman as subject

If Nicolas, the film-maker, is gradually walking into a trap constructed by his own past, Aquin, the author, has other resources than image and other escape routes to explore for his narrative. Following the ellipse in the plot, the story seems to begin again in apparent symmetry with the first section of the novel, only now music emerges as an alternative to the closure of the image. On Nicolas's return to Oslo after the 'accident,' he is met at the airport by Eva Vos, a friend of Sylvie who gradually assumes the same role that Sylvie had played in his life. But while Sylvie was associated with the image, Eva is music:

When we see Eva on the Lille Grensen, the film's musical theme is introduced ... Generally ... the music in a film is subdued, but here, when [it] bursts out it becomes supreme ... Eva ... makes the Orphic hymn which is dedicated to her extend onto Lille Grensen. The way she moves, her graceful walk, the beauty of her motions refer the viewer to the invisible stretto underlying all these visual insertions ... It is important in this passage to let the image flow, not compose it too much, leave it partly undetermined, so that the weight of the music is not contested by any detail of the visual treatment ... (HT113)

As music 'extends' into reality without 'capturing' it, Aquin is seeking a new mode of narrative coextensive with music rather than film, one that would play on repetition and variation and allow the reader to create his or her own meanings outside the text. The word 'stretto' in the above passage is a clue to the fact that *Hamlet's Twin* is not only a film built on suspense and closure, but a fugue, with Sylvie as subject or main theme and Eva as counter-subject – the woman-centred woman whose presence will transform the whole structure of the work.

Eva's independence and her association with movement are emphasized on her first appearance in the novel, an event that takes place before Sylvie's death. Already at the age of twenty-five she occupies a senior enough position at the public radio and television station in Oslo to have her own secretary, and she drives her little Renault 15 with confidence: 'In the parking lot, she handles her R15 skilfully' (HT40). A stranger and a foreigner (thus fitting both definitions of the French word 'étrangère') she steps into the plot in much the same way as Mina Darville arrives at Charles de Montbrun's ancestral dwelling – an 'intruder' in an Oedipal triangle that, unlike Mina, she will eventually succeed in breaking apart: '(For the spectator, Eva Vos's appearance is more disconcerting than mystifying. She gives the impression of having been parachuted completely unexpectedly into the plot. Eva qualifies as an intruder in this world where she has not been subtly inserted.)' (HT40).

It is during this first appearance of Eva in the novel that the name of Michel Lewandowski is mentioned for the first time. At the end of a meal between the newlyweds and their Norwegian friend, Nicolas leaves the table momentarily, and the conversation between the two young women immediately turns to the previous summer in Montreal, and to the question of a sexual affair between Sylvie and this mysterious Michel, which she insists Nicolas must not find out about. It is only on a second reading of the novel that the reader, having learned that Michel is in fact Sylvie's father, can appreciate the significance of this scene and its structural parallelism with *Angéline de Montbrun*. In each of the two novels the main characters form an 'Oedipal' triangle made up of the father, the son or suitor and the woman-object; and in each a *second* female character emerges and offers the woman-object the possibility of a different kind of desire from the one that imprisons her in the Father's House:

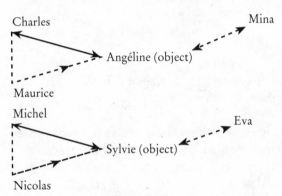

Figure 10 Structural parallels between *Angéline de Montbrun* and *Hamlet's Twin*

As in *Angéline*, extreme violence will be necessary before the patriarchal triangle can be destroyed. This time, however, it is not the father who is removed from the narrative, but the daughter who is complicitous with his power. The attraction shared by Sylvie and Eva for Michel Lewandowski makes their relationship structurally identical to the relationship between Angéline and Mina, another pair of 'sisters' made rivals by their shared desire for the father. As in Conan's work, the relationship between the two women makes possible the emergence of a *different* desire, one which if allowed to take shape would give rise to a new version of 'her story':

EVA

Does Nicolas know Michel?

SYLVIE

Don't ever mention Michel's name in front of Nic, I beg you.

EVA

Don't worry. You know, I can tell you now, I was jealous of you in Montreal ... because of Michel.

SYLVIE

You like him?

EVA

I thought he was very handsome and charming ... Is it painful for you when I talk about him? I'm an idiot. Oh, I'm angry at myself. Please forget it, Sylvie, and forgive me for being so tactless.

SYLVIE

I'm not annoyed at you, Eva.

Sylvie takes Eva's hand affectionately and brings it to her lips so suddenly that they are both disturbed by it. (HT42–3)

This desire and feeling of sisterhood between two women offers the possibility of a sharing and an eroticism functioning according to rules other than that of the destruction of the 'object,' and for that reason it represents a key moment in the structure of the narrative. And yet it seems to hesitate to enter the text, as if the fascination exerted by male desire were still too powerful to resist. Sylvie will pay for this hesitation with her death, and after her Eva too will experience the fascination and paralysis emanating from Nicolas: a sado-masochistic eroticism expressing the son's obsessive need to triumph over the maternal breast that has always eluded his possession:

Nicolas sticks his hand into Eva's blouse and rubs her breast, taking it out of its lacy envelope. With the tip of his thumb Nicolas makes the nipple stand out, be reabsorbed, come out again. Close shot of Nicolas: he is staring and his face is the ascetic, even painful mask of ecstasy.

EVA

You're hurting me a little.

Flash closeup of Sylvie, open-mouthed, stupefied, horrified. Series of shots of Nicolas: he goes on caressing Eva's breast with obsessive regularity. (HT116)

Like Sylvie, Eva is in love with Nicolas, but unlike her she refuses to be complicitous in his games of domination. As she becomes fully aware of the violence in his film scenario and his life, she kisses her own image in the mirror (as Florentine Lacasse had done at an equally significant moment of her narrative journey). By this gesture she signifies her refusal of the role of reflector of the male gaze that Sylvie has played out to its logical conclusion:

EVA

Sylvie will die the way she did die; change nothing, modify nothing. The acts must be carried out slowly and to the very end, including ...

Closeup of Eva: she looks up from the text and sees herself in the mirror. Eva places her trembling mouth against the mirror, her lips meet her lips, her eyes, her eyes.

EVA

Poor Sylvie, poor Sylvie.

Eva takes her lips from the mirror as though tearing herself away from a kiss. (HT186)

Irigaray's 'object' has begun to speak, and to recognize her solidarity with her tragic sister; and it is perhaps not purely by chance that Aquin makes this emergence of woman as subject coincide with the end of the male narrative. The disappearance of Nicolas from the story is not, however, portrayed as the 'fault' of Eva; for this new

Eve carries none of the symbolic associations with evil attached to her biblical counterpart. Rather, the fall of this post-modern Adam follows from the impasse of his own narrative as it unfolds to its inevitable intersection with reality.

Aquin, Oedipus, and the power of the father

It has become almost a commonplace in modern critical discourse to refer to the Oedipal nature of narrative. From Barthes's intuition that 'every story ... is a return ... to Oedipus'[15] and that the pleasure of the text is 'an Oedipal pleasure – to denude, to know, to learn the origin and the end'[16] on through the proliferation of analogies between the text and the female body, the analysis of the psychoanalytic underpinnings of literary language has uncovered the same male story – the journey of Oedipus from the exile and anonymity of childhood through confrontation with the father to replacement of him as possessor of the forbidden site of *jouissance*: the mother's body.

More political and more despairing than the traditional Oedipus myth, Aquin's version is also consistent with the story of the male quest for identity as it has existed within Quebec culture. All his writing is traversed by the nostalgia for a mystical fusion with an unattainable other, a female presence from whom the narrator is separated by an all-powerful father figure. In his famous first novel, *Prochain Episode*, this structure of desire is inscribed in an eloquent allegory of Quebec's quest for independence, where the female object of desire is an image of the beloved woman-country, and the father figure has associations with the colonizer who blocks him in his quest. Aquin's later novels, in which he gradually abandons the theme of Quebec independence, become increasingly black and increasingly dominated by themes of male impotence and violence to women. It is only in *Hamlet's Twin* that the structure underlying this violence is revealed, and that Aquin sees to his dismay the power of the Father over all our narratives.

The destruction of the 'icon' Sylvie is consciously linked to dominant aesthetic and religious practices: the rites of introcision still practised in certain African cultures, the Christian Eucharist, and the 'pact' between reader and writer that is implicit in representation.

Nicolas begins his savage revenge against woman by an introcision of the clitoris, thus removing from Sylvie any capacity for experiencing her own pleasure or expressing her own desire: 'From now on your life is spoiled too' (HT194). Next he traces a line with his pocket-knife around each of her breasts, which he sucks in a devastating image of male impotence and rage: 'You've told me that I didn't know how to kiss your breasts. But your father knew how' (HT194). Finally he disfigures her face, the sign of Sylvie's identity, making a mask of it even as he weeps: 'Poor Sylvie, your tears are red' (HT196). Too violent to be depicted are the details contained in the pages that have been torn out of the film script and that apparently describe Nicolas drinking the blood flowing from Sylvie's vagina and consuming certain parts of her body before throwing the fragments of it into the precipice. As in Anne Hébert's *In the Shadow of the Wind*, the murder is made all the more intolerable by the fact that it is presented as the logical outcome of the story of the male subject and the female object, a 'love story' (HT151) pushed to its ultimate conclusion.

The major player in Aquin's version of *Hamlet* is not Hamlet, as one might think on a first reading, or even Fortinbras, the 'triumphant' prince Nicolas strives throughout the narrative to become. Nor is it Ophelia, although she is reflected both in Linda Noble, the character who plays her in the televised version, and in the tragic Sylvie. The villain of the piece and its principal actant is a Polonius to whom Aquin, in one of his inelegant jokes, gives the Polish name of Michel Lewandowski: a father-figure who remains off-stage and hidden throughout most of the story, but who manipulates the strings in which all the other characters will entangle themselves. The final *tour de force* in the novel's suspense, the point at which Nicolas's film scenario 'accidentally encompasses the truth' in 'a new combination of the truth-fiction motif' (HT180), is when, seeking some back-up Montreal footage for this film, he stumbles on Michel Lewandowski's house, the very 'Father's House' in which his own and Sylvie's fate has been sealed as if by an anterior decree. It is only at this point that the reader realizes the significance of Sylvie's utterances throughout the novel about the sacredness and the secrecy of names. For the character who was introduced to us as Sylvie Dubuque, and who changed her name to Sylvie Vanesse when she married Nicolas, is in reality Sylvie Lewandowski. Michel Lewandowski is of course her father, and he is also the unidentified man with whom the camera showed her in bed in several earlier scenes of the novel:

Until this moment, the viewer has decoded everything. Suddenly what he was keeping at a certain distance ... penetrates him violently; suddenly he understands ... that at the end of this enigma there is only one Sylvie ... lover and daughter of Michel Lewandowski ... The sudden revelation cannot allow the viewer to get back on his feet in a few seconds, or even to understand how this is really possible ... His brain has just been bombarded by solar particles charged with electricity and ... the walls of his skull are suddenly being swept by blank images. (HT175–6)

It is here, in the discovery that 'there is only one Sylvie ... lover and daughter of Michel Lewandowski,' that Aquin's own narrative and all his previous works 'encompass the truth' – not accidentally, like Nicolas's film scenario, but because of the unerring logic of their creator. Once the unitary Law of the Father that presides over its unfolding has been exposed to view, the infinite reflections and illusions of openness of the post-modern narrative reveal themselves as the escape tactics of an impotent son.

On the mythical level, the surprise to the reader lies in a sudden and unpredicted shift in emphasis. Aquin's exploration of 'the pornographic eye/I'[17] at the centre of Western culture's symbol systems and representational apparatus has led him back not only to Oedipus but to Electra, the daughter who continues to love her father, Agamemnon, and to believe in *his* love even after he has killed her sister, Iphigenia, and who conspires with her brother, Orestes, in the murder of their mother, Clytemnestra. It is the Law of the Father that holds both the sons and the daughters in thrall, producing the violence of the sons and the victimization of women. But without the complicity of the daughters in their own subjection the Law could not maintain its ascendancy. Sylvie adores her father, who appears in her memories of childhood imbued with the heroic grandeur of a Menaud: 'My childhood is filled with snow. It never stopped. And I thought it was so marvellous when you walked through the snow. The big snowflakes blinded me. And when it was too much for me you'd take me in your arms. Do you remember that, Papa?' (HT179). By consenting to her regressive desire for union with him, she has chosen to remain forever immobile – the ultimate incarnation of the woman-object: 'I can feel you inside me right up to my heart; you're touching everything that I am. You're everywhere, Papa, everywhere. Help, Papa! Kiss me. Life is disgusting' (HT179). In a similar fashion she will continue to express her love for her murderous husband right up to the final moment of her slow and sacrificial death: 'My love, I beg you. Stop while there's still time' (HT194). Another of Electra's daughters is of course Shakespeare's Ophelia, whose loyalty to her own father's manipulative charm is an essential element in the foundering of *her* love story.

'The time is out of joint. O cursèd spite / That ever I was born to set it right!' It is not Nicolas who could speak these words from *Hamlet*, for, like the post-modern artist always ready to try out a new version of his narrative without coming to terms with its impasse, he escapes unscathed to the appropriately named spot of Repulse Bay in the Canadian Arctic to search for a new group of actors to play in his film. As Eva says to Linda Noble, 'He *will* end up finishing his film. And because he's alive, he'll seem innocent' (HT202). It is Aquin himself who ceased writing after *Hamlet's Twin*, except for a few short essays like the mystical 'The text and the silence of the margins,'[18] which appeared a few months before his death. In it, the dissolving borders between the ego and the infinite are imaged by 'the text and the marginal silence which presses in on it, corners it and will soon devour it'; and Aquin adds: 'The price of individuation can never be sufficiently denounced.'[19] Less than three months later, he took a pistol inherited from his father, placed it to his brain, and ended his life. Like all the gestures in Aquin's life, this one was undoubtedly carefully chosen; and the analogy with Nicolas's head and the precipice seems not entirely fortuitous.

Epilogue: A different desire

If Aquin is about any one thing, however, it is contradiction; and *Hamlet's Twin* is not, finally, a tragedy. The novel ends with a strange epilogue, a mystical lesbian love scene between Eva Vos and Linda Noble, the sole protagonists who remain after Nicolas's departure and after Michel Lewandowski has hurled himself to his death from the window of his twelfth-floor office. Its inflated rhetoric makes no pretence at realism and is shot through with a Christian symbolism that builds on and attempts to transform the images of the Christian communion ritual present in the scene of Sylvie's murder. 'A particle of what has fled and what will follow,' Sylvie has become part of the embrace of Eva and Linda, a parthenogenesis in which body and spirit merge as the two lovers 'walk along the illuminating way' (HT205):

Eva: God is within me and I am entering God. I feel I am inhabiting him. When your tongue darts into me you lift the veil that separated me from the milky way, and now I am almost touching the great silence where life is born and dies and is born again on the cosmic scale, filling the void with a murmur of joy. (HT206)

A writer of transition, educated in the pre-Quiet Revolution period of the *collèges classiques*, religious absolutism, and federalist politics, Aquin expressed with passion and lucidity the necessity of a break with the past and the creation of a new cultural order; but was unable to make the break himself with the internalized values of the past.[20] *Hamlet's Twin* is finally a vision of a new fusion of the sacred and the temporal emerging as history moves towards what one of Aquin's favourite philosophers, Teilhard de Chardin, called the 'omega point'; but it is a vision still dominated by the all-powerful presence of God the Father, and one in which Aquin seems incapable of imagining a male presence, particularly his own. Although the juxtaposition of Christian imagery and lesbian eroticism as imagined by a male makes this epilogue a jarring read, it is meant, the author tells us, as a final 'kiss' for the reader.

Unlike a film, which as *Hamlet's Twin* demonstrated controls both the viewer's response and the reality it represents, this novel has been a journey in words and beyond them towards an exchange of infinite love, a 'mutually fertilizing pleasure whose course overlaps the eternal Communion' (HT207). The feminist writers who follow Aquin will go further than he in developing modes of representation that 'extend' into the real, 'approach' it without penetrating or capturing it, and allow the sacred to emerge in new non-patriarchal forms of fusion between self and other. But Aquin at least has rendered for his readers the full implications of what he has seen in our history. The final lines of his novel, in which he intervenes for the first time in the narrative in the first person singular, situate him without question within a history his writing desires, absolutely, to transform: 'Time devours me, but from its mouth I draw my stories, from its mysterious sedimentation I draw my seed of eternity' (HT208).

CHAPTER EIGHT

Reclaiming Electra:
The writing of France Théoret

I am the well-behaved little girl, the model daughter, and I have been imprisoned in my body. The good little girl has no space other than that of her body. It is her house. Trapped in her words, her whole relationship with knowledge defined by enclosure. O father who ravages the knowledge of your daughters, only a model daughter can reveal your name.
France Théoret, 'The Well-Behaved Little Girl'

EACH ONE CRIES OUT IN TURN: DOES AGAMEMNON LOVE ME? NO!
DOES AGAMEMNON LOVE ME? NO!
  THAT IS THE FATHER'S NO, SAID XANTHIPPE ... IT IS THE GOLDEN
MASK OF AGAMEMNON THAT SAYS NO. IT IS HIS MASK OF DEATH THAT
CONTINUES TO MAKE THE LAW. THE LAW WITHOUT LOVE ... THE LAW
THAT DICTATES THE MURDER OF DAUGHTERS, OF WOMEN, THE
MURDER OF MOTHERS. AND THE MURDER OF SONS IN WAR. IT IS A
DEADLY LAW.
Louky Bersianik, *Le Pique-nique sur l'Acropole*

The cover of the second edition of France Théoret's *Une Voix pour Odile*[1] (A voice for Odile) features a reproduction of the famous Manet painting *Bar at the Folies-Bergères*. In the centre of the painting stands the barmaid – simple and elegant in her low-cut black dress, small in the waist and large in the bust and hips, her enigmatic and somewhat melancholy gaze adding the final touch to the portrait

Edouard Manet, *A Bar at the Folies-Bergères*
Courtauld Institute Galleries, London (Courtauld Collection)

of the 'eternal feminine' she offers the viewer. Behind her, in a mirror, we see a gentleman in a top hat giving her his order at the bar. Serenity, light, and beauty emanate from this moment in a woman's life as seen by a male observer.

On the back of the book – and one wonders if it is simply a coincidence – there is a photograph of the author, France Théoret, also wearing a black dress and a simple necklace, and with her hair, like the barmaid's, cut in bangs. Behind her gaze also one senses an enigma, but it is a less resigned, more *tenacious* gaze than that of her nineteenth-century counterpart. Unlike the painting, the photograph does not contain a mirror. But in Théoret's work it is the text itself that is the mirror, one whose traversal will have shattering consequences for both author and reader.

Before the emergence of voice, representations – the images and models, language, knowledge, and transmitted cultural patterns that make up the symbolic order – enclose woman and paralyse her, defining her as an object and dividing her against herself. Internalized, the Father's gaze cuts her off from her own pleasure and censors her words before they can take shape:

She is ceaselessly haunted by her image in the mirror, looking for the signs of exhaustion around her eyes. The dark-rimmed eye is attached to its circle in an infinite reflection of its contours. From eye to eye. She accepts this as her fate and remains wary. Closed image. (vo30)

But what if, resisting this murder of her self, the bar girl were to begin to speak? To tell of the physical and mental fatigue hidden by her patient gaze? To reply to the succession of gentlemen who are constantly giving her orders? Or even better, what if she were to begin to *write*? For at this stage of women's history it is still true that 'certain sentences can be written that it would not be possible to speak' (vo31). Then, subverted from within, patriarchal representations would begin to wear thin. The entire project of France Théoret's writing is contained in the emergence of this voice that has never before spoken, that feels its way forward, constantly breaking and turning back on itself:

She is mute or stammering or crushed by the cry from within or delirious or saying the exact opposite of what she means. As far back as she can remember, she has experienced this difficulty in speaking – a problem in thinking, she has been told. A connection that doesn't take place, the terror, each time, that it will all come out wrong. A hesitation about what is to come. (vo30)

Like the other feminist writers of her generation – Nicole Brossard, Louky Bersianik, Madeleine Gagnon, and Denise Boucher, to name only the first who arrived on the Quebec literary scene – France Théoret differs from the woman writers of previous generations by her consciousness of the fact that she writes as a woman, in a relationship with other women and within a language and a symbolic order whose reduction of woman to the status of an object is now incontrovertible. In the centuries-long evolution of 'her story,' such a collective consciousness constitutes a key turning point. For in order for woman to cease being the immobile and silent object holding up a culture built on her absence, she must be able to recognize herself in the mirror of a gaze other than that of the Father – whose censorial presence in the works of Laure Conan, Germaine Guèvremont, Gabrielle Roy, and Anne Hébert blocked the possibility of relationship between the female characters, and therefore the ability of those characters to define themselves as subjects rather than objects. In a very real sense, these feminist texts are the works of 'sisters,' interchangeable despite their differences, and fully endowed with meaning only in the context and with the intertext of the other feminist writings: 'We will tell them about the resemblance that inhabits us ... and how our writing is becoming collective,' writes Madeleine Gagnon in her preface to one of Denise Boucher's works. 'How we will never again be *poètes maudites*, trapped in our individual alienations. Separated in their anthologies, their analyses, their libraries, their dissection tables, their literary awards, their contests which divide us from each other ... To all of these words we say: me too, me too, I could have written it; I will write it in your place; you will write it in mine. And others will emerge to write with us.'[2] The recovery of the figure of the mother, the patient archaeological search for traces of the feminine in the mythologies of the past, and finally the exploration of a new relationship between the dualities of body and spirit, emotion and thought, fiction and theory, are among the facets of the deconstruction of the patriarchal symbolic order undertaken as a shared task by these writings.

And yet, if only for the lucidity with which she confronts the situation of women within the Father's House, France Théoret's work is exemplary. From the monologue 'L'Echantillon' (The sample) presented as part of the collective feminist play *La Nef des sorcières* (The ship of witches) in 1976 on through four volumes of poetry – *Bloody Mary, Une Voix pour Odile, Vertiges*, and *Nécessairement putain* (Necessarily a prostitute) – to her novel *Nous parlerons comme on écrit*[3] (We shall speak like writing), and beyond, Théoret's traversal of language is undertaken as an opening of what is closed, an advance from the paralysis of the solitary woman-object created by culture to the relational space of a network of voices: the marginal, peripheral voices of the women of past and present, who, by speaking the pain, the silence, and the tenacious courage of their lives, make transformation possible. Assuming the nothingness of her situation as woman-object, the 'good little girl' explores the devastating consequences wrought by the Father's gaze and gradually opens her universe to other women, knowing that through her painful journey a radically different perspective is being written into history and discourse:

> Identity, knowledge, fiction and the political struggle as they grow out of our situation as women in the process of becoming subjects will explode the old structures ... Language says it in a huge surge forward. But in the minutes of each day it is lived in tiny steps.
> (VO52-3)

Thus Théoret's writing has its starting point precisely in that place from which women's lives have always held up the structure of the Father's House, whether through complicity or defeat: the position of Electra. In insisting that his daughter remain a child as long as possible, Charles de Montbrun clearly understood the nature of his own power and its necessary relation to the seduction of his daughter. Resisting this seduction, Théoret's writing at the same time reveals the enormity of its power – the Father's control over language and ideology, and therefore over the daily reality of women's lives.

From the father's gaze to the mothers' voice:
The poetic journey

To write the dark. To write women's suffering. To write this abjection. Not to summarize it by a cry, or limit it to the verb in the infinitive. It is understood that when confronted by the daughter's suffering the Good Father asks for a smile, frustrated by this wandering of hers which makes him feel powerless. Usually a daughter will acquiesce, not wanting to create further worries for a Father who, precisely because of his role, already has far too much to worry about. His daughter is a little joy. How dare she disappoint him by withholding her gaze? The daughter looks away, the Father loses his composure, this girl is a degenerate, a hysteric. Death has just swooped down on the house.[4]

Refusing the temptation to seek a feminist Utopia or a sense of illusory wholeness outside temporal reality, Théoret dares to say 'I am here,' 'I inhabit the Father's House and I am the product of its representations.' The voice that traverses her work is born not in the void, but rather from within the models and behaviours imposed on women by family and culture: hence the desolation of this writing that wanders through 'the desert of the Other' (BM24). Deprived of the structures that formerly gave them meaning, the patience and obedience inherited from female ancestors turn against the self, producing the obsessive figure of the 'ancient little girl with the tired smile' (*Néc. put.* 9). And, linked to the contemporary necessity of economic survival, the chain of submission perpetuates itself: 'I say yes and always and never rebel or hide or flee ... and it is an ancient tale, this story of the old child who has earned her living since the day she was born and not only that, who has taken pains to please you in all things' (*Néc. put.* 39). Born into the world and into language in the position of 'other,' woman experiences a need for relationship that in its negative form corresponds to patriarchal preconceptions of the feminine as hole, lack, passivity, masochism. It is this state of *openness* to the other that traps her and divides her against herself: 'Look at the landscape you have created, take the pulse of all my inhibitions and know that they come to me from you. I have allowed myself to be sculpted by you, I have let myself be dominated to the depths of my being and you follow me wherever I go' (*Néc. put.* 43).

The daughter's journey begins in immobility and gradually becomes movement, the slow advance of a body inscribing its traces on the stone walls of a Montreal neighbourhood, or a nearby village. It is the walk of someone who knows herself to be watched and who feels annihilated in her very substance, violently pushed back into the dead-end of a childhood street where red brick walls block all possibility of exit. In *Bloody Mary*, Théoret's first collection of poetry, this paralysis of the woman-object is broken out of by a language at times equal in violence and vulgarity to the one that victimizes her. Lacking a face and an identity, she feels herself devoured by the other, prisoner of a bloody and violated body:

Parcel of coagulated blood skin: envelope of what they called soul.
I screamed in the darkness of my stomach's walls when I asked for
you in vain. The imprisoned one the blood the stain.
(Everything is trembling here around me because I forgot: tell you
that I love you. You can put as much shit and as much laughter into
that word as you want ...) (BM9)

Unlike Anne Hébert, whose writing begins in a fairy-tale space peopled by passive Sleeping Beauty figures, Théoret insists on the absence of myths and legends centred on women and offering possible markers to guide her in her journey. While for the sons of Oedipus the legitimacy of a royal lineage is unquestioned, Electra's daughters awaken to themselves in an absolute non-space, with no certainty other than that of their alienated relationship to their bodies:

Once upon a time in the diarrhoea of a time that neither advances
nor goes backward, an infamous mass named Bloody Mary, scarcely
born, was abandoned in a square where no one ever ventured. Forest,
maze, labyrinth, windpipe. It is a mental space: with no Tom Thumb,

no Prince Charming. For the swollen-footed Oedipus a royal
shepherd. For Bloody Mary inside outside red on all surfaces. (BM9)

The hypocrisy of a code of honour that glorifies the father's values
while ignoring his reduction of his daughters to the status of sexual
objects had already been suggested by Laure Conan, in the Véronique Désileux section of *Angéline de Montbrun*. In Théoret's universe the reality is identical, but language, freed from censorship,
communicates all the violence and degradation of women's situation:

> – You gave me your word. – There are no words because there is my
> cunt. And since I've been old enough to think for myself you have
> only talked to me about my cunt. What use are words! – Where is
> your honour my daughter? – In my cunt, Papa. (*Vertiges* 18)

When dispossession is as all-embracing as this, when even the
metaphors associated with artistic production are founded in male
sexuality, writing can only be an act of war. The writing subject – 'a
pin-up girl,' 'on display,' 'locked up in appearances' – confronts a
blank page she perceives as 'carnivorous,' and takes hold of the pen
as if it were a dagger, a knife, or a penis offering the hope of escape:
'I hold the dagger I carry your revolver night is fatal for me I cannot
write' (BM8). Her writing emerges in chaos, missing its object,
remains blocked, delirious, repetitive, or in reverse order, translating
the effects of silence and the inadequacy of conventional discourse.
Turning in circles within the prison of representation, it has only
one *raison d'être* – to serve as a weapon against the images that
imprison the female self:

> The engorged one the possessed one the fucked one the painted one
> cunt odalisk slave tight-assed virgin succubus split his dick open split
> language open grit your teeth. Passes I make passes at myself I am
> my own brothel. (BM11)

And yet, from the opening lines of *Une Voix pour Odile* on, the
first steps in the quest of this woman seeking to transform herself
from object to subject become perceptible: 'I write from my place

of origin. I speak from where I am ... I, language, mother' (VO9, 13).
In this search for the source of her own voice in a return to the
maternal origins, one recognizes a path almost identical to that taken
by Anne Hébert and Gabrielle Roy, and perhaps the starting point
of all women's writing. Fusing her own search with that of the
collectivity of women, Théoret returns across the generations to the
bodies, warmth, and emotion too often cut off at their source in a
long line of silent and broken female ancestors:

> Waters of birth. I will go back to them, I will come to them by way
> of the hysterical mother, the aunt who worked outside the home and
> even the religious old maids ... I will go back to them blinded by
> emotion and by the strange divorce between the senses and thought.
> (VO25)

In these prose poems which also contain elements of fiction,
essay, manifesto, and autobiography, a voice emerges that carefully
maintains its closeness to the body and the unconscious, even as it
stubbornly seeks to deconstruct the rigidity of the representations
surrounding and enclosing it: 'A silence, I have it. I've caught up
with my body ... Not there, that's not quite it, I withdraw and
displace [the words] again and again' (VO12, 21). From the closed
circle of the censoring eye, from the gestures and cries of the 'unendingly identical' women (VO31), and the claustrophobic atmosphere
of the Father's House, these texts displace language towards the
margins, the periphery, allowing a multitude of voices to speak and
in so doing opening a gap in the unity of established knowledge: 'It
speaks from everywhere. That is the most precise point, the real
place from which it comes. There is no hierarchical order ... It is not
the unique that advances here. Here approaches, slides into view,
the block of history that has not always spoken the same way'
(VO21). From the 'enormous inherited patience of "there's no choice
but to keep on living" ' (VO20), Théoret fashions an aesthetic and
an existential stance: that of living and writing open to contradiction,
refusing all nostalgia for closure, being 'the theatre of all voices at
the same time' (VO55). Such a constant state of tension, in which
everything susceptible to being frozen into a representation is
opened and exploded, is not assumed without anguish: 'There are

some who say that I will never have an identity that I am both from here and from elsewhere. Always displaced' (VO21). 'Well, I live to move away from the centre and slowly I open wide the contradictions' (VO56).

The question of the representation of the real – and therefore of the novel – remains however an obsessive one, involving moral and political as well as aesthetic choices. For does not remaining open to all the marginal and dispossessed voices that traverse one without seeking to insert them into the fabric of history and culture mean to remain forever a 'little girl' in the house of the Father? 'When one speaks from everywhere, how are unity and responsibility possible?' (VO21). As Théoret's poetic work evolves, it becomes clear that it is preferable, and indeed necessary, for her to assume her status as a literary 'mother,' defining herself more explicitly in relation to the symbolic order, and taking on a position of responsibility within the house of language. Paradoxically, then, for this writer strongly influenced by the precepts of 'modernity,' it is the feeling of responsibility towards the voices of the dispossessed that leads her – as it had earlier led Gabrielle Roy – to enter the 'house' of literary realism and, having entered it, to open it wide to admit the real.

Realism in the modern style:
Nous parlerons comme on écrit

And yet I am haunted by one necessity, to give words their full measure so that, for one day at least, they will unfold as closely as possible the expression of daily existence. (NP107)

Is it possible to use the forms of realism not in order to 'capture' the real, but to approach it gently, noting precisely the subtlest of its nuances – that is, to remain constantly respectful of all the 'otherness' that is being brought into language through the gesture of writing? This recurrent question posed by women in face of male-dominated forms of realism is all the more acute for a woman writing in the era of 'modernity,' an avant-garde literary doctrine popular among many of Théoret's contemporaries that boasts of having relegated realism to the dusty shelves of literary history, along with all the other 'discourses of mastery.'[5]

In breaking with realism and mimetic representation, the Quebec writers of modernity argued that they were leaving behind the literary manifestation of traditional humanism, based on the opposition between a subject identified with unity (the author, the narrator, the literary character) and an 'objective' reality that was seen as equally unified and closed. In fact, since Joyce novelists have focused more specifically than in the past on the epistemological function of literature, breaking with established codes of knowledge to embrace openness, multiplicity, contradiction, and pleasure. And yet, in abandoning the possibility of a totalizing vision and a stable point of view, there is the accompanying risk of cutting the novel off from its ethical, moral, and political dimensions. For the modern novelist who seeks to speak with relevance to his or her society, the problem is how to suggest a *direction* through the infinite density of signs without falling into the dualisms that formerly offered the criteria for defining value. In the contemporary Quebec novel, the frenetic car chases of Aquin's work and the nervous laughter of Ducharme's characters as they contemplate the abyss are symptomatic of this dilemma of the impossibility of meaning.

In the context of Quebec history, the break with realism took place at the same time as the break with a past perceived as alienating, and there is little doubt that the lack of direction of the protagonists in the novels of the sixties corresponds to this rupture in the social fabric. Writing about the Quebec novel in 1976, Gilles Marcotte cannot allow himself to discuss the ethical exigencies formerly associated with the novel except in a tone of ironic nostalgia. Embroidering on the expectations of critics of a less 'sophisticated' age of Quebec literature, he imagines an impossible 'novel of maturity' that would have the 'amplitude' of *The Tin Flute*, the 'analytical subtlety' of the work of a Robert Elie or an André Langevin, where there would be a 'confrontation of reality,' and where the possibility of 'truly incarnate love relationships' would exist. In sum, he writes, 'writing or reading this novel we would be adults, capable of living fully.'[6]

But Marcotte's terms of reference are clearly those of realism, and he is forced to admit that the Quebec novel entered its period of flowering precisely at the moment when such a vision had become impossible. Rather than displaying a vision of 'maturity,' the novel of the 1960s is marked by a succession of childlike or emotionally disturbed narrators, an inability to live in the present, and novelistic structures in which the imaginary takes the place of the real or exists in a 'problematic relationship' with it.[7] Finally, says Marcotte, the loss of innocence that followed the era of realism has made it impossible to ask of the novel, as readers formerly did, that it provide some guidance for one's own life: 'It doesn't judge, it doesn't give lessons, that is no longer its business. It unveils and pushes to their limit the contradictions we are made of.'[8]

Could it be, however, that the subject-object split that contemporary literary theory has attempted to transcend by its rejection of realism is in fact the split between the *male* subject and the 'eternal feminine' he has projected onto the world? And that in their attempt to avoid this stance of 'mastery' the writers of modernity have simply thrown themselves into the other half of the binary hierarchy: the disorder of a universe still split because still fantasized by the male subject? The 'black anarchy' of the universe of Victor-Lévy Beaulieu, for example, is only the reverse image of the former domination of the world, rather than an attempt at its deconstruction. Never having shared in this dualistic world-view, women writers as they arrive at appropriation of their own subjectivity are also offering new formulations of the relationship between self and other, author and reader, the literary text and reality. According to France Théoret, 'subjectivity in the feminine is an appropriation in the sense of a conquest. Patriarchal reality demands of a woman that she pass through the zones of the unspeakable or the socially unacceptable in order to signify her reason ... To affirm reason in the feminine means to touch the cultural memory at the root of daily reality.'[9] Thus Théoret can state: 'I write the quest for mastery in a desire for decentring, that is, for relationship with an other ... The concentration of emotions can be a strength, a dynamic force, for it allows for inclusion of the other in communication.'[10]

Is it necessary to add that women have never seemed particularly interested in metaphysical balancing acts over the abyss? During the same period when Aquin, Ducharme, Beaulieu, and their male contemporaries were accumulating masks and manoeuvres to aid in their obsessive struggle with a void endowed with metaphorical overtones of both death and the womb, women writers were listening to the rhythms of the temporal realm and beginning to document women's daily existence. In the same year as Marcotte's essay diagnosed the rupture between the novel and reality, France Théoret and Nicole Brossard wrote in the introduction to *La Nef des sorcières*: 'Women are not in History, they only "have stories," or "make a fuss" [*font 'des histoires'*]. Their history will truly begin the day women tell, as in a thousand rumours, a thousand scandals, the small stories of their lives that have given strength to men and children ... Unease fabricates its own transformation. It turns into action.'[11]

With *Nous parlerons comme on écrit*, this fidelity to the historical experience of women is inscribed in the forms of modernity, producing a novel that is at once 'realist,' 'modern,' and astonishingly open to previously unexpressed dimensions of Quebec reality. Indeed, one cannot help thinking of the 'novel of maturity' imagined by Gilles Marcotte, for even as it participates in the wandering and openness of the novel of modernity Théoret's work poses the necessity and the possibility of ethical choices, proposes a political direction through the maze of contemporary ideologies, and invites the reader towards a difficult maturity.

APPROACHING THE REAL

It is by the voice that presents this tale – whether that of a narrator or of the author it is impossible to say, so close is *Nous parlerons comme on écrit* to autobiography – that an entire area of reality, previously unarticulated, enters language. There is something pressing, urgent, political about the tone of this voice, this need to make public certain private realities. First and foremost, the reality of the lives of a large number of women, and the situation of being *broken*, so familiar to women and yet so rarely admitted by them, which Théoret describes with extraordinary precision. Navigating through a whole series of defeats and attempts to escape from the real, the voice of the narrator insists on the fact that there is only one acceptable route, and that is the one that leads to full presence to reality; and only one absolutely unacceptable pain, 'the throbbing daily malaise of not being included in reality' (NP99). As well, Théoret allows the reality of the body to speak: the gestures, laughs and smiles, glances, or silences that so often escape expression emerge here like an energy and weave themselves into the meaning of the novel. But perhaps the most daring of the risks taken by the author in relation to language is the extraordinary series of musical sequences (music being the art that evokes facets of reality often designated as being 'beyond words'). For unlike previous writers who have imitated musical themes or structures in the form of the novel, Théoret goes further, actually communicating precisely in words what she *hears* in vocal musical works by Purcell, Liszt, Schoenberg, Mahler, Varèse, and others. Her tenacious woman's words seem intent on venturing into spaces traditionally forbidden to them – and always in order to infuse those spaces with life.

The insistence on the real and on realism extends as well to the literary echoes heard in the novel. First, a surprising echo in the context of the novel's modernism: that of *The Tin Flute*, Gabrielle Roy's triumph of realism, which Théoret, ignoring literary fashions, links up with across the ages. One closes Théoret's novel with the feeling of having met characters who are worthy descendants of Roy's Rose-Anna and Florentine Lacasse – strong, fragile, courageous women, all broken in some part of themselves, but survivors and positive models for the reader. Another echo is that of Brecht's ambition for a critical realism that would link the abstract and the concrete, ideologies and daily life – a realism that in Théoret's writing is displaced towards the margins and freed of all lingering traces of 'mastery' its discourse might contain.[12] Finally, in the search for a language endowed with enough subtlety and nuance to render the most secret dimensions of women's lives, there is a clear echo of Virginia Woolf, one of the writers most admired by Théoret. While the echo of Brecht is perhaps unconscious, the debt to Woolf is explicitly acknowledged: 'Over and over I tell the friend how Virginia, by putting doubt at the centre of her writing and transforming that doubt into its very substance, always at the risk of madness, established a few certainties for us' (NP21).

Never forgetting its aim of 'speaking close' to the real, of translating the imperceptible into words, France Théoret's writing is above all else a patient and unending attempt to approach reality and allow language to circulate within it as a life-giving force. To participate as a reader in this process of approaching the real involves deconstructing a whole series of dualities: life and writing, autobiography and fiction, art and political *engagement*, body and mind, realism and modernity. A recurrent theme in the novel is that of 'rupture' and 'continuity'; and yet even this dualism is deconstructed by Théoret's transformation of the French-Canadian past and the tradition of realism, both of which she integrates into modernity through her fidelity to women's reality.

RHYTHM AND VOICE:
MODES OF THE SUBJECT'S INSERTION IN THE REAL

At once autobiography, essay, and fiction, Théoret's novel is above all a rhythm and a voice: the most personal and the most situated of the elements of discourse. Like voice, rhythm can be a metaphor for the subject: when we say of someone that he has 'found his rhythm,' we mean that he has found *himself* within time, the material world, and human relationships. According to Henri Meschonnic, rhythm in language is 'the material aspect of meaning';[13] 'overflowing the realm of signs, it includes the most corporeal dimension of language.'[14] Preceding the division between the subject and 'objective' reality, rhythm is both subjective and 'trans-subjective': 'It is rhythm that produces and transforms the subject as much as it is the subject who emits a rhythm.'[15] Voice, too, resolves the dualistic separation of the individual from society and history, as suggested by the image of 'finding one's voice' (one's identity and function within a given group or society). For Meschonnic, 'voice, which seems the most personal and intimate aspect of the self, is in fact traversed by all that constitutes an era or a milieu.'[16] Finally, he argues, 'in the voice, the most physiological element is already social.'[17]

In contrast to the mad flights and pursuits that characterize the works of Aquin and Ducharme, the rhythm of *Nous parlerons comme on écrit* is slow, regular, deliberate, and calm even in moments of anguish. It is the rhythm of a walk: the itinerary of a woman-subject traversed by the voices and the silences of 'previous generations' (NP10) and seeking a path through the density of the signs of her world. Signs of the city, Montreal, joined to other great modern cities (Mexico, New York, Paris, Toronto), but also to the village and to the almost primitive space of the French-Canadian rural landscape of the past: 'I am a tenacious white memory, I carry previous generations in my veins and I participate in the obligatory task of living ... It is the silent voice that will speak, the one that puts its monsters to sleep every night' (NP10). It is the constant act of making death one's familiar that makes possible the patient and tenacious approach to life characteristic of Théoret's work, as the novel's opening sentence states with the utmost simplicity: 'When death goes by, I say "present." On my watch it is always time' (NP9). Before the spectacle of death presented in the paintings she sees on a trip to Mexico, the narrator experiences the desire to let herself sink into abandonment and total fusion, 'the desire more than ever not to feel the weight of earth' (NP114). But from this confrontation with death she learns 'to fully experience sensuality. Such a slow learner, knowledge only comes to me when all the senses are brought into play' (NP114).

Like the women's voices woven into the texture of the narrative, which tell of a strength that need not involve hardness or closing oneself off from others ('keep going and don't pay any attention, let them say and do what they like around you ... but walk, keep going ... it can be done' (NP67), this book accompanies the reader through everyday time, providing words to make visible and tangible the sensations that habitually escape representation, but that perhaps constitute the essential part of life. Although Théoret's voice sometimes seeks embodiment in a pact with representation and mimesis, she also adopts the modes of music, a more 'presentative' than representative art, in her attempt to give expression to the space *between* literary signs, where life emerges and meaning is elaborated. For the 'fragile one,' open and broken like so many other women, this traversal of language is undertaken at the risk of 'freezing into hardness,' for she must somehow open a path for herself between the equally imprisoning alternatives of silence or acquiescence to ideological codes that ignore women's reality. It is through the precise attention she pays to gesture, nuance, tone of voice, and the movements and hesitations of the body that Théoret succeeds in opening this prison of language and allowing the real to emerge.

HOW SHE IS SPLIT IN TWO

Like the journey of Angéline de Montbrun, that of Théoret's narrator begins with a fall, as arbitrary as it is necessary. A little girl falls on a sidewalk in east-end Montreal on a May morning while getting off a streetcar, hits her head, and loses consciousness. On the level of language, the split in her universe immediately becomes apparent in the narrator's hesitation between the 'correct' French term for 'streetcar' – 'tramway' – and the popular French-Canadian designation *'les petits chars.'* Already the rigidity of the language taught at school is infiltrating the little girl's consciousness and establishing a separation between her and her community of origin. The memories of the time before the fall are those of a period of freedom and light: the joy found in the precision of mathematics and the marvellous uselessness of Latin, and wild runs in the park traversed by a mad desire to reach the sun. After the fall, the young girl's experience of time becomes the hard necessity of inhabiting a body and a divided reality, of making choices; and it is this new relationship to the real that signals her entry into the time of writing: *'In illo tempore*, thus begins that which never ceases beginning again ... After that I never had the same relationship to writing' (NP13). The lost Paradise of this Eve of the 1950s, and the sun of this female Icarus, are associated less with a state of mystical fusion or emotional effusion ('I hate Quebec sentimentality,' [NP20]) than with the freedom of pure thought. Writing – precise, rhythmic, and pulsional – becomes a means of reinserting thought into the realm of matter: 'I think that thought operates in primitive sensuality' (NP14); 'Where is thought when nightmare takes over?' (NP15); 'Palpable thought. That's all that matters' (NP30).

THE EMERGENCE OF THE SUBJECT(S):
'I,' 'ONE,' 'SHE,' 'THEY,' 'WE'

If these dualities are to be woven together in a literary form that speaks to contemporary reality, it must be in a work that succeeds in integrating not only theory and fiction, but the individual and the collective, while at the same time avoiding traditional realism's no-longer-tenable pretence of representing a 'general truth' based on the 'typicality' of its characters. Through an ingenious utilization of narrative pronouns ('I,' 'one,' 'she,' 'they,' and 'we'), Théoret weaves a fabric that not only gives expression to her 'voices of difference' but also provides a movement and a direction for them. The two long sequences ('When death passes by' and 'It is irremediably broken') that together make up about two-thirds of the novel's length combine autobiographical fragments (narrated in the first or third person feminine singular), fragments that generalize on the basis of this experience (narrated by the pronouns 'one' (*on*) or 'they'), and fragments where women tell their stories ('she told me,' 'she recounts'). Thus there is complete interdependence on the formal level between the narrator's evolution towards the status of a subject, the emergence of the words of other women imprisoned in silence, and the elaboration of a political analysis based on these individual cases. Further, the title of the novel suggests, the power of these newly liberated women's words in turn opens onto a transformation represented by the future tense and a collective first-person plural: 'we shall speak like writing.'

Together, these fragments recount 'the apprenticeship of a woman born without language, destined to silence and obedience,' but who tells us from the outset that she has 'deflected the predestined course of existence. The point of living ... is to bring something to birth' (NP26). The statement is a significant one in the context of the reader-writer relationship, for, just as this woman's apprenticeship has been dependent on the support and inspiration provided by a network of women friends and mentors, she in turn offers herself as a model for her readers, thus moving the novel into the space of the real and enlarging the network of women in progress towards their own subjectivity.

TO BE BORN A GIRL

To be born a girl and to grow into womanhood in the crushing poverty of a pre-Quiet Revolution French-Canadian village is to be taught submission and silence in face of an intolerable reality: 'I watch, I observe the way my parents and the other adults live ... quickly I take it all in and say to myself in total despair, it's impossible, I must be mistaken. What I see can't be real' (NP15).

The little girl's relationship with the world and with language develops in the presence of a tradition of muteness as unyielding as 'patriarchal rock': the 'grumbling,' 'muttering,' and bursts of anger of the men, and the dispersion of women's words. Her inheritance is one of fear, hesitation, silence or stammering, and of a rigidity gradually acquired as a protection against the pain. When she expresses the desire to learn Latin, this gesture 'springing in full confidence from the unified space of my desire' awakens the fury of the domineering father: 'What's the point of it? What use will it be?' (NP18). As this super-ego is internalized, fear and self-censorship become her habitual modes of being: 'I must have been off track and out of touch with reality to have wanted to take Latin ... I give myself the whipping that I didn't get earlier' (NP18). As for the adults, trapped in the codes of behaviour that have assured French-Canadian survival for generations (duty, the family, the authority of the sacred Word), they have forgotten how to live and how to express themselves. The experience of rejection that destroys the little girl's sense of identity is simply a perpetuation of this generalized *mal de vivre*, as in the following scene of a family reunion where her grandfather has just offered her a glass of sweet wine: 'I like to be called Miss and I like his gesture, so I go closer in order to speak to him. He has nothing else to say. It seems as if I'm bothering him, he continues to move around the room. The family is so large' (NP39).

This little girl has learned very young that she has no right to be 'off track and out of touch with reality,' and the lesson will mark her for life. What is offered her as reality is, however, extraordinarily rigid and limited: the constant demands of economic necessity, the exhausting routine of her job as a waitress during adolescence ('I open my mouth to say good morning, the price, and thank you,' [NP25]), the shame associated with the body, the sentimental 'blackmail' surrounding the myth of the happiness of large families, and the obligatory submission to adults who 'mumble instead of speaking' (NP38). Reality is also the evident fact that when one is a woman one is an object of exchange: 'Meeting a woman who had once been exchanged for a cow, I seek out her gaze through the anguish I feel as I look at her' (NP50). It is a first experience of sex at the age of twenty-one with a brutal boy, mute and impassive, and in the depths of the act's sadness, a vision written in fiery letters: 'I will live in the novel' (NP52). And finally, reality is the experience of division among women created by the words of men: 'You're better than your sister. Your sister is better than you. Look at your cousin, she's far ahead of you' (NP50). Having left the village for the city and reached adulthood during the Quiet Revolution period, these same women find their professional milieux marked by an intellectualized and left-wing version of the same codes of domination: the division into rival groups, the imposition of the 'correct' political line, and the petty power struggles. From generation to generation the same practices are repeated, with the survival of the 'species' guaranteed by the silence of the broken ones.

RENEWING THE FACE OF REALISM

In face of such a reality, escape is not an acceptable option; the dilemma is how to find a form that will render its often unbearable presence. Traditional realism – as practised by a Zola, a Steinbeck, or a Roy – has a power of evocation that a committed writer like Théoret can not easily ignore. And yet, even when it exposes the brutality of situations similar to those described in *Nous parlerons comme on écrit*, it offers the reader relief from them by the clearly fictional nature of its traditional characterization and plot, and the distance provided by the vantage point of its omniscient narrator. While Théoret borrows some of the narrative strategies of traditional realism, she also deconstructs them, revealing their 'literarity' and drawing her reader even closer to the real.

In the section entitled 'Story in a Green Ball,' which contains a mirror reflection of the novel in its entirety, the author explores some of the possibilities offered by realism, appropriating for her novel the power of fictional characters and of plot. As the reader enters this 'story within the novel,' he or she notices a change of rhythm – the possibility of breathing more easily thanks to the escape offered by fiction. It is not entirely coincidental that this section of the novel is the only one that contains any references to nature: images of water, of a forest, and of green plant life that create a sense of displacement and refreshment after the hard realities of the preceding sections.

The echo of Roy's work, and particularly *The Tin Flute*, seems unmistakable in this section, marked by the contrast between city and country and centred on the engaging character of Louise Valois, a young girl vibrant with all the joy and the insecurities of adolescence despite the poverty and hardship of her family's situation. As in Conan's *Angéline de Montbrun*, it is through the epistolary form – the exchange of letters between two female characters – that the pleasure of friendship and the enjoyment of daily reality enter the text. A letter received from a school friend who is spending her summer by a lake awakens in Louise the possibility of transporting herself to another place through the power of her imagination. The unbearable heat of the city and the difficult reality of her own life are transformed by the images of a lake, a rowboat, a beach, a forest, and the thoughts of the letter she will write back to her friend. From the reader's angle of vision, the identification with Louise encouraged by the traditional fictional form makes all the more unbearable the brutal intrusion of reality into her imaginary world – her exhausted mother emerging from the bathroom with harsh words for her daughter: 'Do you want to see the foetus?' The image contains in miniature all the reality of aborted births and of lives prematurely cut off by various deaths that Théoret's novel places before the reader. In face of such a reality, fiction seems inadequate. And yet what remains in the reader's consciousness at the end of 'Story in a Green Ball' is the beauty of the life of a Louise Valois, who refuses to renounce the promise made by two young girls 'like a pact sealed in the schoolyard: we shall speak like writing' (NP92).[18]

While 'Story in a Green Ball' shows how the bubble of the imaginary can be burst by reality, it also shows how the prison of reality can be opened by the possibility of writing, the imaginary, and female friendship. 'Ariadne's Lament'[19] treats the other side of the tension between the real and the triad of writing/imagination/friendship. Placed near the end of a novel that brings us constantly into contact with the real, this story tells us that without the imagination and without rebellion, daily existence in such a reality can be a death in life.

Louise Valois is fourteen years old, and she has hope; Ariadne is scarcely four years older, and already she has learned to 'make do with reality,' paying for her compromise by an inner death that one suspects may be all too typical. Having passed through a period of psychological distress, she has found a formula to keep her suffering at bay: observe, stay in the background, don't bother anyone, watch what you say and do, for 'serenity is my most precious possession'

(NP154). She is 'the silent one who reasons' (NP155), who has learned to inhabit the image society has imposed on her by cutting herself off from all emotion: 'I neither laugh, nor cry, nor get excited, nor worry too much, I reason' (NP157). Having secured her peace of mind by eschewing such 'dangerous' activities as fantasy, reading, writing, and friendship, she gradually loses her ability to communicate: 'I speak less and less' (NP156).

An exceptional story? On the contrary, the details of the daily life of this young teacher – her perfect control of her class, the approval of her principal, her refusal to notice the various crises in the lives of her pupils because of her own fragility, her attendance at Mass three times a week, and her return to the family home on weekends so as not to be faced by the emptiness of her life in the city – all contribute to the portrait of a 'typical' member of her class, gender, and era (Montreal in the late 1950s), making her as 'representative' of her society as the characters in the traditional realist novel. But through a subtle shift in narrative point of view and verb tense at the end of the Ariadne section ('That year, if I committed the smallest infraction of the rules, I felt the full extent of it,' [NP159]), Théoret reveals the presence of an autobiographical dimension in this apparently fictional account. These things exist, she seems to be telling the reader, and like many, many others I have experienced them: this is not an 'exceptional case,' nor is it imaginary. And, as the quotation from Laure that closes 'Ariadne's Lament' states, 'The experience shared by many deserves something other than this conspiracy of silence, this secret complicity that veils it so thoroughly: the idea that certain subjects must not be discussed' (NP160).

TO DEFLECT THE COURSE OF HER DESTINY: AN ART OF NUANCE

'Before all the generations, and the cries of the night, may the clans awaken and turn in the direction of speech; may those who transmit the lineage through their protesting bodies cease to be skewered' (NP31). How can writing deflect the course of this self-perpetuating history of domination without itself taking on the rigidity of a polemic? Between the 'yes' of obedience and a 'no' that would be equally reductive, Théoret seeks a language capable of remaining faithful to the community even as it deconstructs the repetitive cycle of history: 'Look feverishly for the gap, slide into it, and deconstruct from within' (NP49).

Like Anne Hébert and Gabrielle Roy, Théoret is thus searching for a form of politically committed writing that will not fall into the formal trap of perpetuating the old codes of domination. In other words, the goal is not to *impose* a given set of ideas on the reality in question, but rather to allow that reality to 'speak,' to create a form that will allow the reader to hear the hitherto silent voices of those who have been crushed by culture. In *A Room of One's Own*,[20] Virginia Woolf alludes to the risk of what might be called 'aesthetic impurity' that threatens all committed writing, contrasting the 'incandescence' of Shakespeare with the anger that deforms much writing by women. Following Woolf's own example, Théoret navigates around this danger by bringing into literary language a women's way of speaking, always sensitive to nuance and contradiction: 'I am annihilated because I move in the realm of the approximate, I will not be admitted to circles where the goal is mastery' (NP71). The challenge, however, is to locate the elemental truth in those nuances, as do the extraordinary (and 'ordinary') women whose voices traverse the novel and guide the narrator on her journey: the fifty-five-year-old schoolteacher whose 'unified voice speaks of each thing in its entirety, one thing at a time' (NP101), and the woman of 'more than sixty' who 'in her long life ... has learned to be patient and passionate, generous and precise, becoming a woman who loves and who assumes the consequences of her words ... When she speaks, she no longer searches for her words and they come. She doesn't hesitate any more' (NP71). And finally the harmonious voice of the 'seventy-four-year-old woman' that recurs throughout the novel, telling the previously untold stories of women from the French-Canadian past: 'She tells, she insists, she presents. The only depth, passion. All nostalgia absent. Resentment unknown to her' (NP46).

This 'sonorous multiplicity' of voices emerging from silence and from the margins of culture is political, not only because of the content of the stories told, but because of its very corporality. What is speaking is the female body exploited for so long by ideologies and condemned to the reproduction not only of the species, but of society's codes of domination. When the narrator is alone, she often practises reading aloud for hours, seeking the warmth and energy of a true voice, projected from the centre of the body out to the world. In conversation with friends, she enjoys the moments when the body speaks, freed from the mechanics of reasoning: 'To forget oneself totally and project. That's all that matters' (NP30). Such words become 'gestures' (NP101), and the writing that corresponds to them will be productive of life: 'There are no words except for the one who opens herself, fully alive. An exact and truly connected word engenders new worlds' (NP95).

Such a writing of nuance succeeds in presenting a political analysis (rape and violence against women recur in almost every story, for example) while respecting what is unique in each woman's situation. Contrary to the commonly held male view that women are 'all the same' (NP112), each of these women is *different*, and the narrator recognizes the impossibility of generalizing on the basis of her own experience: 'I am much slower, I have many more fears than most women of my generation' (NP105). Alongside the 'broken ones,' there are women who seem to inhabit space without effort, and whose beauty and health are tokens of a new future: 'From the Maisonneuve district, passing through the Plateau Mont-Royal and Saint-Henri, now Saint-Colomban, she emerges and I am seized with emotion. To bring to birth, body and health, energy, all the senses in use. A vibrant desire for harmony' (NP51). But in the midst of difference there is a sharing of common experience, and there are gestures of solidarity that point to the possibility of change.

TELLING THE FAMILY SECRETS

The autobiographical 'I'

For Théoret, the act of making life flow in the rock of patriarchy begins with the telling of private truths about how one has oneself been broken, providing a record of the journey of the autobiographical 'I,' unprotected by the masks of fiction. After the incident of the forbidden Latin lessons, the narrator describes the entry into seven years of obedient silence, her loss of pleasure and of confidence, and the beginning of a rhythm of slowness that will last a lifetime: 'I have become soft. I say yes constantly. One day I admit to the fear of being beaten. Seven years later. I require the magic number of seven years before I can react. In seven years I will answer you, I will have figured out the right answer. Please grant me a seven-year extension. And I laugh now, I have figured out my rhythm.' (NP19)

The years at Normal School bring the realization that escape is impossible, and then rebellion of the body through illness: 'Two years in the grip of religion and I ask God not to let me see men's dicks. I stuff myself with food ... I become rigid and start to vomit constantly. They put me in the hospital' (NP25). After the period of hospitalization comes a long apprenticeship in the art of survival, marked by nights of insomnia during which old monsters awaken. During this period there is a discovery of prime importance, one that will give a sense of direction not only to the narrator's life, but to her writing: 'I have become she who does not want to die for the love of others exists ... My ears open to music' (NP32–3).

A direction: Towards reunion of the sisters

It is precisely this 'love of others' that is the generative force giving direction to Théoret's novel, creating a network of women's voices, which, as they emerge from the 'patriarchal rock,' state concisely the essential truth of *their* reality. It is surely not coincidental that the strongest of these voices, those that are closest to being 'centred' and to having a clear direction, are those of single or divorced women: the 'seventy-four-year-old woman,' the English-Canadian friend who 'loves Colette,' the woman who tells of the green ball, and others. Women have always taken pleasure in words, but too often they have exhausted themselves in an attempt to communicate with 'those who have hardened themselves into a shell of rock, by day and by night' (NP38). Lili, a friend from the narrator's childhood, 'speaks endlessly of her lover' and attempts suicide when he leaves her (NP52).[21] The 'aged single woman full of love and laughter' (NP35) has kept secret all her life the story of a terrible rape, and breaks her silence only when the narrator questions her about her first experience of love. These stories, 'not even important enough to be news filler' (NP35), spill out like family secrets, each one revealing another facet of the process by which women have been broken and reduced to silence.

Over and over in these stories recur the *leitmotivs* of passivity, the desire to please, the sense of duty, and the inability to define oneself as a subject – traditional 'feminine' traits that overflow into depression or madness. Having worked as a nurse all her life, the seventy-four-year-old woman extricates from silence and anonymity the stories of the women whose path she has crossed: the 'perfect mother' who took to sleeping day and night when her youngest child was eight years old ('She was rarely heard to complain,' [NP123]); the country woman who married at the age of thirty-five and was interned in Saint-Michel-Archange after the birth of her sixth child ('No one speaks of her in the family. She died quietly in the hospital,' [NP137]); the woman who stopped speaking after being chased from her home in punishment for having protested against her husband's abuse of their eighteen-year-old daughter ('She dies with her skin bloated by unspoken words and unshed tears, on a freezing day in February. Who remembers her? So proper, she who doesn't speak,' [NP102]). Each of the stories contains some variation on the drama of Sylvia Plath, the impeccable daughter who seeks to please everyone: 'She presents a perfect and unified face, cracks, and kills herself' (NP111).

In response to these stories, the strength and energy of shared women's words are Eros opposed to Thanatos, a sign of the emerging feminine. To find a language capable of reuniting the divided 'sisters' – Antigone, the 'well-behaved daughter,' and Electra, the daughter who dares to hate and whose desire for revenge drives her into depression and madness – is already a considerable step forward. But Théoret suggests that in order for their stories to become more than anecdotal evidence of an age-old adoration of the father and rejection of the mother, the sisters must cease waiting for their brother and take action into their own hands: 'And if Electra had been able to act in concert with her sister, she would have been healed of her hatred. But always the sister argues for moderation and reason, and women's incessant chorus of "being torn between" goes on ... Chained forever in indecisiveness, they continue to wait for the brother' (NP113).

ELECTRA: A SISTER TO BE RECLAIMED

Thus Théoret's novel, like Aquin's *Hamlet's Twin*, finds its conclusion in the myth of Electra, the symbol of the father-daughter link
that has upheld the structures of patriarchal culture. At first glance,
this daughter whose devotion to her father's memory leads her to
plot the murder of her mother seems an unlikely feminist heroine.
The opening scene of Sophocles' play shows her in a state of depression bordering on madness, as she awaits the arrival of her brother,
Orestes, and plans how she will convince him to avenge the death
of their father, Agamemnon, by killing their mother. Choosing to
place her loyalties in the 'men's camp' and stubbornly refusing any
sense of identification with her mother and sisters, she offers a
striking image of the patriarchal complicity between Father and
daughter. If we look at the Electra myth more closely, however, we
begin to see that the binary world-view that places sisters and brothers in enemy camps may be yet another of the patriarchal divisions
feminism must seek to deconstruct.

And indeed, Théoret's novel demonstrates that, when seen
through a feminist lens, Electra is in fact a sister to be reclaimed.
Women have spoken and written a great deal about love, she tells
us, but in order to understand fully the implications of love we must
be willing to look at its opposite: 'Hatred frightens us, but we must
be precise. Having heard the word "love" so often, how can we put
off looking at the reverse side of the coin? Electra in particular, but
Antigone as well, use this word "hate" that most of their sisters are
afraid to pronounce' (NP113).

Electra's hatred, according to Théoret, is the product of a block-
age, a defeat, a failure to resist: 'Where there is no resistance, no
struggle even with unequal weapons and at the price of the greatest
risks, hatred sees the light of day' (NP112–13). Further, this hatred
that brings Electra to the edge of madness is but the other face of
the obedience of the 'good little girl' – she who like Ariadne and all
her silent sisters agrees to live according to the dictates of masculine
'reason.' In the final analysis, both the hatred and the obedience are
symptoms of an inability to act that has imprisoned women in the
realm of words, waiting, and emotion: 'In a hollow within her Electra
carries the love and the hatred of many generations, for she cannot

carry true and effective vengeance. Alone with her sister, she spends her time thinking about how to be well-behaved, to have a reasonable opinion and good judgment. It's as if being with her sister brings words into play, while being with her brother makes action possible' (NP113).

And Théoret asks: 'Why is it Electra and not her brother who carries the burden of all this hatred?' (NP113). Why has patriarchal reason required of women that they live in the realm of emotion, at the price of their own lives? The deconstruction of these patriarchal dualities leads, finally, beyond the confines of the literary text to historical reality, as the love and hatred carried by women throughout the ages open onto the necessity for justice in the world: 'No more hate and no more love and no more words and no more feelings and may reason be toppled and judgment be questioned when the real possibility of action is lacking or denied ... When will the mirror reflection of our words become a reality?' (NP113).

CONCLUSION: AN IMPOSSIBLE REALISM?

Let us return in conclusion to the Quebec literary context, to the 'impossibility of realism' Gilles Marcotte illustrates so convincingly from a masculine perspective, and to the opposition between the concepts of 'realism' and 'the real' that was our own starting point. That that opposition is a false one when viewed from a women's perspective was made clear by the novels of Germaine Guèvremont and Gabrielle Roy, in which the forms of realism open and expand to embrace all the teeming multiplicity of the real. In turn, through a complex interweaving of 'realist' and 'modernist' techniques, France Théoret adapts the tradition of realism for her own age, inscribing the forward movement of the new woman-subject onto the field where the body, ideology, and contemporary history intersect. Emerging from the margins, her network of women's voices reclaims for the novel its ethical and political dimensions and suggests a direction through the complexity of the modern real.

And yet, in order for an authentic and critical realism to exist, there must be a dialectical interaction between the novel and the society it represents. In other words, there must be a possibility of *movement* or change in society in order for the novel to fulfil its function; and what Théoret's novel confronts, finally, is the immobility of history. It is for this reason that, despite its courageous facing down of death and of all the forces of diminishment, this novel does not in the final analysis succeed in becoming the important 'novel of maturity' dreamed of by Marcotte. In order for such a novel to be produced, Quebec society as well would have to have achieved a state of maturity, of which Marcotte's 'truly incarnate love relationships'²² would be a sign on the level of private life.²³ And what cries out by its absence in Théoret's work is precisely the existence of love relationships between women and men. The sexual act is present only as rape, and the only 'incarnate love relationships' are those that take place in the laughter and words shared among women.

In a novel so explicitly defined as an attempt at embodiment, such an extraordinary limitation of the *sexual* body cannot be without significance. One suspects it is a sign that the real has not changed, and is not changing, despite the succession of ideologies. For unlike music – which, as Théoret's novel demonstrates, permits the fusion of the voices of women and men – the novel is inscribed within the 'body of language' and carries in its very structure the blockages or limitations that exist within the real. It is for this reason that the narrator's walk falls back 'again and again' into a state of brokenness, and that, unlike the lyrical voices in the novel's song sequences, her voice has the urgency of a cry: 'Things around me are so broken, so broken, and they continue to fall apart, still in crumbs while the rock remains entire' (NP140). It is true that the night-time strollers on rue Saint-Denis have a more relaxed look about them than in the Quebec of the past, and that there is a feeling of freedom in the air, but there are still the suicides of such major writers as Claude Gauvreau and Hubert Aquin, and the late-night calls from women friends who have lost their desire to go on living: 'What is it that makes them speak of death so often?' (NP173). Like the narrator of Aquin's *Prochain Épisode*, who can add the word 'end' to his novel only in the context of a yet-to-be-created future, Théoret's narrator ends her walk in a gesture of resistance and openness: 'Even if I am alone, they will not get me. My hands are held out and empty'

(NP174). And like Aquin's title, which indicates the necessity of a 'next episode' in history, Théoret's enigmatic title *Nous parlerons comme on écrit* calls out for a future that will come into being only through the *action* engendered by writing.

Conclusion

The triangle of the patriarchal family explodes when the fourth person singular refuses to be rendered hysterical by the Name of the Father and the Son. The violet curtain of the great tradition of classical theatre bursts into flame when the daughter, burning up her contract, takes possession of her body in order to inhabit it for herself before welcoming a man and a child into it.

> Claire Lejeune, *Age poétique, âge politique*

When looked at as a whole, what is perhaps most striking about these works spanning more than a century of Quebec literature is the static, repetitive nature of the world-view they represent. While the 'dream of enduring forever' that shapes the novel of the land was never realized in the desired form of national invincibility, it would seem that it penetrated the structures of the imaginary and left an indelible mark on collective reality as experienced by women and men. As early as 1912, the voices heard by Maria Chapdelaine at the end of Louis Hémon's famous novel ('In the land of Quebec nothing must die and nothing must change') had indicated the power of the Father's Law over the collective unconscious. The contemporary echo of these lines in France Théoret's 'things ... are broken, so broken ... while the rock remains whole' is a sobering reminder of the extent to which the Québécois cultural text repeats itself from generation to generation.

Avatars of Angéline de Montbrun and Maurice Darville, the characters in this cultural text – motherless daughters, sensitive sons filled with rage, and couples wounded in their attempts at love – are clearly offshoots of the same large family. All seem to have grown up in the shadow of a severe paternal gaze, the sons sacrificing themselves and hardening in turn into the paternal mould, while the daughters resist, sensing instinctively that it is their own imprison-ment in the mother-image that guarantees the perpetuation of the system. And if the role (or the myth) of the perfect wife and mother is omnipresent in this text, the *real* mother – embodied, human, and loving – is absent, killed by 'the decree of [some] previous will'¹ that clearly seems a manifestation of the Father's Law. The only exception to this recurrent pattern, Gabrielle Roy's Rose-Anna Lacasse, exem-plifies this destruction of the mother by the maternal role even as she resists it with all the strength of her love.

Have 'his story' and 'her story' not evolved at all since their rural origins, then? Alas, if one judges by his Québécois descendants, Oedipus has become blinder than ever, deluded by the impression that the more his narrative increases in violence and rage, the more chance he will have of possessing the object that still eludes his grasp. As for Electra, exhausted from loving too much, she has finally decided almost in spite of herself to abandon her dream of a loving father and take control of her own story. And it is this reclaiming of her body, her desire, and her relation to the real that offers a possibility of salvation, not only for herself but for her brothers. The following reflection by Denise Boucher, inspired by the death of poet Patrick Straram in the spring of 1988, stresses the interdepen-dence of the fates of the sons sacrificed by culture and the daughters called by that same culture to serve as mothers to them:

Why does society require saints and scapegoats to ensure its survival? Why did Patrick offer himself up as critical fodder for the salvation of this world?

For two thousand years sons have been sacrificing themselves, each on his own cross. And for all these sons who offer themselves there must be mothers. How many *pietàs* were there in Patrick's life? You were lucky to find a few, Patrick, because we're not interested in playing that game any more. Or most of us aren't.²

This age-old gender struggle, in which men's fear of woman's power to give birth has paradoxically led them to seek to imprison her in her reproductive role, extends of course far beyond the borders of Quebec. And yet the violence done to women haunts the Québécois collective unconscious in a particularly dramatic way – perhaps because of the precise and visible fashion in which the edifice of traditional Quebec culture was built on women's reproductive capacity. If the works of writers like Anne Hébert, Victor-Lévy Beaulieu, Hubert Aquin, Nicole Brossard, France Théoret, and their contemporaries speak with particular relevance to the cultural transition being lived through in all present-day Western societies, it may be because of the inability or refusal of these writers to 'sublimate': that is, to ignore the voices of the demons we have banished to the cellar of the ancestral house.

In recent years, works by a relatively small number of male writers influenced by feminism have begun to appear, signalling a significant modification in the Québécois literary landscape, in that they break for the first time with the tradition of the male writer as 'tragic son.' In the prose poetry of Philippe Haeck,[3] words are primarily a means by which the poet 'listens' to daily reality in all its 'ordinariness' and celebrates the imperfection of the moment. This poetry explicitly acknowledges its debt to feminism and its desire to respond to the presence of women as subjects, as does Yvon Rivard's novel *Les Silences du corbeau* (The crow's silences). Situated in an ashram in India, Rivard's novel demystifies the figure of the mother and reveals it to be a male-created construction to which the 'sons' of culture cling even as they exploit the real women around them. In both Haeck's and Rivard's work, there is an authentic self-confidence that allows for the expression of vulnerability reminiscent of Roy's portrait of Emmanuel Létourneau. Like the French and Québécois feminisms of difference that have obviously inspired it, the following passage from *Les Silences du corbeau* may seem uncomfortably close to 'biological determinism'; but the respect for women's difference it expresses is part of a new and significant direction in Quebec men's writing:

Why are men incapable of silence like this? Sometimes I think that only women have succeeded in being born without tearing apart the night that envelops us, and that death, which we think we are distancing ourselves from at the speed of our words, will be more natural for them than it is for us. A sexist thought? Perhaps. Which doesn't change the fact that I'd like to be a woman in order to have access to the texture of what is before me and behind me, in order to finally be able to be and not be in some other mode than that of thought.[4]

This re-examination of the Quebec literary canon has been an attempt to show that, long before the arrival of feminism on the literary scene, there were women writers who refused the roles of Sorrowful Mother or woman-object assigned them by patriarchal culture, inscribing the traces of their subjectivity into literary language. On the level of literary form, it may be that it is their instinctive understanding of the murder of woman implicit in the traditional maternal role that has led women writers to deconstruct realism, a literary convention that seeks universal truth within the confines of the restrictive roles assigned by culture, eschews multiplicity and contradiction, and attempts to arrest the movement of the real in order better to 'capture' its meaning. In the writing of these women, as if solicited by an ancient memory, the texture of words and silences renews its ties with the maternal origin, transmitting its song of life to an exhausted culture.

Despite the gender differences that divide the authors examined here into two groups with contrasting reactions to their shared imprisonment in the Father's House, there is a network of voices (of women and of a small number of men) that transcend those differences, coming together in a common denunciation of the Law of the Father and the restrictive roles it assigns to all human beings. Among the male writers it is the most 'sensitive' – Saint-Denys Garneau, Hubert Aquin, Réjean Ducharme, and the non-Québécois Louis Hémon – who document the claustrophobic effects of the 'dream of enduring forever' and the tragedy it represents for the sons. This tragic tradition of male writers includes as well authors not examined in these pages – poets Octave Crémazie and Emile Nelligan, novelist Gilbert La Rocque, playwright Claude Gauvreau – and even as misogynist a writer as Victor-Lévy Beaulieu. Examined from a gender as well as a national perspective, these writers appear as a dynastic line of impotent sons, excluded from power and identity by the fact that the father is paradoxically both all-powerful and absent – symbolically identified with another culture like the H. de

Heutz figure in Aquin's *Prochain Episode,* or concealed at the summit of a religious or socio-economic hierarchy that masks the true nature of its power relationships behind a rhetoric of love and equality. Pushing to its limits the experience of intellectualism, sacrifice, and disembodied mysticism that is implicit in the dualistic world-view of Catholicism, these sensitive sons demonstrate the impossibility of 'living in the head,' the position traditionally assigned to men by patriarchy.

And yet this obvious victimization of the sons of Quebec culture neither excuses nor fully explains their inability to conceive of ways of seeing, knowing, and representing the real that would challenge the pornographic relation between subject and object. What their works make clear is that the reification of women is the essential component, and not just a coincidental side-effect, of the construction of male identity. The truth that the son is unable to face, the illusion he refuses to abandon in spite of the fact that he himself is dying of asphyxiation in the Father's House, is that of his power to reduce women and the world to the status of objects. The rigidity of this stance – which in broad ideological terms corresponds to the competitive individualism underlying capitalism and the technological imperative – is doubly ironic in the context of a culture itself dominated from without, and one that has taken pride in its collective resistance to that domination. Like Conan's Maurice Darville, the Québécois Oedipus allows himself to be deluded by the hope that, if he waits long enough, he in turn will accede to the Father's power. And as he sees this power repeatedly escape his grasp, it is the accumulated violence of more than two hundred years of frustration that he unleashes against his mother, his wife, his lover, or his sister.

Unlike their literary brothers, women writers since Laure Conan have inscribed in the cultural text the traces of their resistance to this reification of women and of the multiple elements or groups (nature, Native peoples, foreigners, the economically dispossessed) relegated to the status of 'other' by the Father's gaze. Implicit in the diachronic structure of the preceding chapters was the hope that as we moved from each of these works to the next we would see a new structure emerging, a cumulative movement of emerging women's subjectivities that would eventually shake the Father's House to its very foundations. In hindsight such an expectation seems naïve, given the solidity of the house and the degree of complicity or defeat manifested by its sons and daughters.

To a certain extent, however, these women's writings when taken as a whole *are* the site of a transformation. In each, at the point where the female characters – mothers, daughters, sisters, friends, or lovers – come together in spite of the obstacles separating them, there is a fleeting vision of a new mode of intersubjectivity, whose revolutionary implications should not be minimized. To say 'yes' to one's own body and to one's own image in the mirror as do Florentine Lacasse and Eva Vos is the first step towards the establishment of a network of reflections *other* than that of the Father's censoring gaze: a network that originates, to quote France Théoret once again, in the place where 'I,' 'language,' and 'mother' become one. To know, to represent, and to imagine the construction of identity in continuity with the feminine-maternal is the subversive activity begun in the words of Quebec women. If one judges by the works examined here, however, these words are still in large part unheard of unheeded by the male writers of the culture.

The radical revision of culture proposed by women is perhaps most succinctly suggested by the new dimensions attached to the concept of 'exchange' in their writing. Since the functioning of the patriarchal triangle depends on the exchange of an 'object' (a woman, a text, money, or a territory) meant to assure the power of the 'subject', it follows that a concept of exchange involving pleasure, giving, spending, and sharing represents a significant shift in the shape of the culture. Despite the alienation, madness, and silence that threaten female subjectivity in the women's writings we have examined, each of the works espouses such a vision; and it is this that constitutes their 'subversion' in a culture still founded on the need for domination and mastery.

Despite certain changes in the cultural landscape, the writings of the newest generation of women writers – Louise Bouchard, Nicole Houde, Carole Massé, and others[5] – are a sign of all the distance still separating women from a sense of 'belonging' in a culture they tend to depict as heading towards destruction. The tensions that structure Nicole Brossard's recent novel *Le Désert mauve*[6] (The mauve desert) reflect the still unresolved struggle between the cultural transformation sought by feminism and the threat of nuclear disaster. The murder of Angela Parkins by the 'long/oblong man' that marks the climax of the novel continues the tradition of the murder of women that has marked Quebec literature since the nineteenth century; and yet it is more terrifying than the earlier murders, because more anonymous, more abstract – the symptom of a civilization that has become pure technology. Echoing Saint-Denys Garneau's despairing questioning of *his* historical moment ('When did we devour our joy? ...'), Brossard's narrator reflects on the enormity of the disaster: 'The eye great work of desire fades ... The ravage is great. The oblong man stares straight ahead, completely detached from the scene. Angela Parkins lies on the blond wood of the dance floor, her body for all eternity become inflexible, exposed, a target. Melanie, daughter of the night, what can possibly have happened?'[7]

To this murder are opposed – as in earlier women's writings – the love, energy, gestures, and words that circulate among the female characters in the novel, 'women together for whom living seems truly a commitment,'[8] writes Brossard. And once again it is the image of a dance, a shared rhythm uniting human beings in body and spirit, reason and emotion, that carries this energy forward, as if seeking to bring new meanings into existence. The image of Melanie and Angela dancing together, united for a short instant before Angela's death, echoes and clarifies the meaning of earlier images of the emergence of the feminine – the dance of Florentine and Emmanuel, the walk of Marie-Amanda and Angélina, the songs of Maurice Darville and the Outlander, the love of Eva Vos and Linda Noble, and the shared women's words of France Théoret's novel:

I don't really know Angela Parkins, and yet here are our two bodies, together for a moment and then distant, slow and long in the distance of America. We are inseparable and apart for all eternity. We are the desert and the evidence that comes when the shadow sets. And perhaps the night and the colour of the dawn. The women have come closer to us ... Angela speaks, speaks, departs for some unknown destination, she says that everything begins again, words, paths, butterflies ... she says that we mustn't give up, that nothing is impossible if memory accomplishes in the improbable the certainty that keeps an eye open within us for the horizon and for beauty ... [9]

In her imposing history of patriarchal culture, *Beyond Power*, Marilyn French proposes pleasure as feminism's alternative to patriarchy, the only value that it is impossible to contain or dominate. 'But it is possible to live with an eye to delight rather than to domination,' she writes. 'And this is the feminist morality.'[10] Women's writing in Quebec has always known this, and in the energy that circulates in it between mothers and daughters, sisters and friends – and extends as well to the brothers, suitors, and fathers in the house – there is a potential for transformation worth paying attention to in the present period of cultural transition. In the final scene of Louky Bersianik's *Le Pique-nique sur l'Acropole*,[11] one of the female characters – a daughter in search of her mother – reaches out to one of the caryatids, the female statues that hold up the Erechthion, a section of the Acropolis. She begs her to escape from the marble pose in which she has been frozen and come to life, for women need the mothers they have been deprived of throughout history. As the novel ends, the caryatid is reaching out to her daughter, freeing herself at last of the burden of Western civilization that she has held up for centuries. It is for us, the readers, to imagine – and to create – the enormous crash that will ensue.

Postscript

As the reader will doubtless have gathered, the passages cited at the beginning of each chapter of this book are the links in a network of women whose thoughts and writings have been my guides on this journey through Quebec literature. One of the most inspiring of them has been Claire Lejeune, a Belgian feminist poet, philosopher, and friend whose metaphorical reflections on the personal and the political have a habit of cutting through to the essential meanings of contemporary culture. As has happened so frequently throughout the course of the book's composition, I find a passage copied from one of her works waiting for me and confirming my own intuitions as I reach its end. In order that the network may grow larger, I offer this passage to the reader in lieu of a conclusion:

Only love can bring about the revolution. The future can draw substance only from the complicity of the daughter's words and the son's ability to listen. It is in this incestuous passion of language and hearing that difference will be saved from the massacre, and will find the original daring to burn the Inquisitor.[12]

Notes

Preface

1 Irigaray, *Parler n'est jamais neutre*, 11, trans. mine

Introduction: Traces of a murder

1 Aquin, *Trou de mémoire*, 143, trans. mine (*Blackout*, trans. Alan Brown, 116)
2 Hébert, *Kamouraska*, trans. N. Shapiro, 249
3 Brossard, *The Aerial Letter*, trans. Marlene Wildeman, 79
4 Grignon, *Un Homme et son péché*, 100, trans. mine (*The Woman and the Miser*, trans. Yves Brunelle, 49)
5 Hébert, *Poems*, trans. Alan Brown, 29 (*Poèmes*, 48)
6 Bersianik, *Le Pique-nique sur l'Acropole*, 75, trans. mine
7 Cixous and Clément, *La Jeune Née*, 118–19, trans. mine (*The Newly-Born Woman*, trans. Betsy Wing)
8 See Gilbert and Gubar, *The Madwoman in the Attic.*
9 Hermann, *Les Voleuses de langue*
10 Françoise Collin, 'Il n'y a pas de cogito-femme,' 108–9, trans. mine
11 Teresa De Lauretis, *Alice Doesn't*, 186
12 Conan, *Angéline de Montbrun*, 42, trans. mine (*Angéline de Montbrun*, trans. Yves Brunelle)
13 Lamy, *D'Elles*, 15–35
14 I owe this example to some experiments by Normand de Bellefeuille and Hugues Corriveau described in *A double sens*, 40–50.
15 Barthes, *The Pleasure of the Text*, trans. Richard Miller, 47
16 Ibid., 37

17 The word 'co-naître' is from Belgian feminist Claire Lejeune, who read an early version of the manuscript.

18 Le Moyne, *Convergence*, trans. Philip Stratford, 61

19 A world-view perfectly illustrated by Roch Carrier's *Il n'y a pas de pays sans grand-père* (No country without grandfathers), see ch. 2, n.18.

20 Bourassa, *Femmes-hommes ou hommes et femmes?*, 69–70, trans. mine

21 Paquet, 'Le Féminisme (second article),' 8, trans. mine

22 Paquet, 'Le Féminisme (premier article),' 241, trans. mine

23 Jean Aicard, 'Le Poème de la mère,' 56, trans. mine

24 As in Anne Hébert's *Le Torrent* (1950) and Françoise Loranger's *Mathieu* (1949)

25 Lévi-Strauss, *The Elementary Structures of Kinship*, trans. J.H. Bell, J.R. von Sturmer, R. Needham, 62–3

26 See Rubin, 'The Traffic in Women,' 155–71.

27 The statue of the Virgin Mary in Denise Boucher's *Les Fées ont soif* (The fairies are thirsty) and those of the caryatids in Louky Bersianik's *Le Pique-nique sur l'Acropole* are concrete images of this imprisonment of the women of the past within the patriarchal symbolic order.

1 *Angéline de Montbrun* or the fall into writing

1 Roger Lemoine, introduction to *Oeuvres romanesques de Laure Conan*, vol. 1, reproduction not paginated, trans. mine

2 A highly speculative rejection, however, since it is deduced by Lemoine from a sentence written by Conan concerning her 'guilt' and from gossip by the descendants of her fiancé, Pierre-Alexis Tremblay. But even reconstituted in this way, the story of the vow of chastity taken by Tremblay and of his rejection of Conan because of an 'adventure' she might have had suggests to the modern reader that there might have been very concrete reasons for the anger that simmers beneath the surface of Conan's writing.

3 Irma Garcia, *Promenade femmilière*, vol. 1, 25, trans. mine

4 Casgrain, preface to *Angéline de Montbrun*, 9

5 Conan, *Angéline de Montbrun*, trans. Yves Brunelle (Toronto: University of Toronto Press 1974). Page references in the text are to this edition.

6 Casgrain, preface to *Angéline de Montbrun* 11, trans. mine

7 Casgrain, correspondence with Laure Conan, no. 61, letter of 9 Dec. 1882

8 Ibid., no. 97, letter of 1 Oct. 1883

9 Renée Des Ormes, 'Glanures dans les papiers pâlis de Laure Conan,' 125

10 It has taken a century for woman-centred analyses of Conan's work to begin to appear. See especially Verthuy, 'Femmes et patrie dans l'oeuvre romanesque de Laure Conan,' 396–40, trans. mine; and Green, 'Laure Conan and Mme de Lafayette,' 50–63.

11 Either by 'glorifying' it, as did Abbé Casgrain, for whom it was 'a book from which one emerges as if from a church, eyes turned towards heaven,

a prayer on the lips, the soul enlightened and clothes perfumed with incense' (preface to *Angéline de Montbrun*, 8, trans. mine), and Charles ab der Halden, for whom 'Angéline's psychology is singularly reassuring ... She loved her father as one loves one's master and one's God' (*Nouvelles études de littérature canadienne-française*, 199, trans. mine). Or, alternatively, by condemning it as dangerous or 'unhealthy.' For Jean Le Moyne, for example, Laure Conan 'writes under the sign of Electra, and that is all that is worth remembering about her work. In this regard it would be difficult to discover an unhealthier work in our literature than *Angéline de Montbrun*' (*Convergence*, trans. Philip Stratford, 79). And for Jean Ethier-Blais, she is 'a dangerous writer ... it is a good thing that she no longer has any influence' ('Laure Conan,' 11, trans. mine). For a more complete study of its critical reception, see Gabrielle Poulin, '*Angéline de Montbrun* ou les abîmes de la critique.'

12 Except for Gilles Marcotte who notes that in Conan's novels, 'Father equals nation ... the fathers form a screen before life itself, before the present. They are the embodiment of all that is forbidden ... ' *Une Littérature qui se fait*, 18–19, trans. mine.

13 See, for example, Bakhtin, *The Dialogic Imagination.*

14 See Belle-Isle, 'La Voix-séduction.'

15 Garcia, *Promenade femmilière*, 69–70

16 See, for example, Brossard, *The Aerial Letter*, trans. Marlene Wildeman; and Théoret, *Nous parlerons comme on écrit.*

17 See Green, 'Laure Conan and Mme de Lafayette.'

18 Hémon, *Maria Chapdelaine*, trans. W.H. Blake, 103

19 Nelligan, 'Le Vaisseau d'or' (The golden ship), in *Poésies complètes*, 44, trans. mine

20 Hébert, *Les Songes en équilibre*

21 See especially Cotnam, '*Angéline de Montbrun*: un cas patent de masochisme moral.'

22 Conan, *Si les Canadiennes le voulaient*

23 Conan, *Aux Canadiennes*, 11

24 Dionne, 'Entre terre et ciel,' 19–21, trans. mine

25 Quoted in Dionne, ibid., 20

26 Ibid.

27 Verthuy, 'Femmes et patrie,' 404

28 Conan, *L'Obscure Souffrance*, 42–3, trans. mine

29 Des Ormes, *Célébrités*, 52, trans. mine

2 Alphonsine Moisan's subversion

1 Ringuet, *Thirty Acres*, trans. Felix and Dorothea Walter

2 Hémon, *Maria Chapdelaine*, trans. W.H. Blake

3 Savard, *Master of the River*, trans. Richard Howard

4 Guèvremont, *The Outlander*, trans. Eric Sutton

5 The only other example of a female protagonist before Guèvremont is Albert Laberge's Paulima, called 'la Scouine,' who is presented explicitly in the text as representing masculine subjectivity: 'At sixteen, la Scouine was a big girl, or rather a big boy. In reality she had the squareness, the size, the shape, the expression, the movements, the mannerisms and the voice of a man.' *La Scouine*, 30, trans. mine (*Bitter Bread*, trans. Conrad Dion)

6 Grignon, *The Woman and the Miser*, trans. Yves Brunelle

7 Janine Boynard-Frot, *Un Matriarcat en procès*

8 Ibid., 215

9 Ibid.

10 Gérin-Lajoie, *Jean Rivard*, trans. Vida Bruce

11 See Brochu, 'Menaud ou l'impossible fête,' for an excellent analysis of these dualisms.

12 Grignon, *The Woman and the Miser*, preface, np

13 Ibid.

14 Eleuthère, *La Mère dans le roman canadien-français*, 47–52

15 Bessette, *Une Littérature en ébullition*, 91–107

16 de Gaspé, *Le Chercheur de trésors*, 96, trans. mine

17 Janine Boynard-Frot notes that in a survey of twenty-five female characters married at the beginning of their respective novels, 45 per cent disappear before the novel's end: 'Their final act is procreation. Once this role is fulfilled they are free to leave the story.' *Un Matriarcat en procès* 106–7, trans. mine

18 In Roch Carrier's *Il n'y a pas de pays sans grand-père*, the protagonist cannot remember his deceased wife's name: 'He searched in his memory as if in a pile of old papers ... After that Old Thomas was less and less preoccupied with the name of his dead wife, as if he had forgotten what he had forgotten ... It was with his Defunct that he lived; it was not with her name,' 18–19, trans. mine (*No Country without Grandfathers*, trans. Sheila Fischman). Carrier's novel, a continuation of the tradition of *Maria Chapdelaine* and *Master of the River*, makes explicit the misogyny that forms the basis for the 'dream of eternity.' The 'chaos' of the contemporary world that torments the old man is perceived as a loss of virility and control, related to an increase in the power of women, symbolized by the queen of England. The whole novel is drenched with nostalgia for the 'good old days,' structured according to a hierarchy that privileges God the Father/the king of France/the father of the family.

19 Bourassa, *Jacques et Marie*, 177, trans. mine

20 See Boynard-Frot, *Un Matriarcat en procès*, 175.

21 Ibid., 146. All quotations from *Jean Rivard* in this paragraph are from Boynard-Frot's book.

22 Ibid.

23 This does not mean that she has fulfilled her *own* dreams of happiness.

Samuel realizes this after her death: 'Here is she dead in this half-savage spot, leagues from other houses and churches ... And it is my fault that she has died so ... my fault ... my fault' (MC152).

24 Deschamps, 'Lecture de *Maria Chapdelaine*,' 151–67, trans. mine

25 Ibid., 161

26 Irigaray, *Ethique de la différence sexuelle*, 18, trans. mine. See the quotation at the beginning of the chapter. Into the fabrics she weaves and crochets, Marie, 'the beautiful weaver,' put 'all the warmth that was in her, for her father and for Joson, whom she would shield from the chill' (MR13).

27 See Brochu, 'Menaud ou l'impossible fête.'

28 Ibid., 278, trans. mine

29 Ibid., 266–7, 290–1. Writing in a context in which he had to take into account those who 'still doubt the existence or the value of the Québécois novel' (290), Brochu interprets the novel's dualisms in light of the national thematic. His final remarks seem however to point in the direction of feminist deconstruction: 'It is important to be conscious of and to analyse in greater depth this dualism of Quebec society ... in this way we will perhaps succeed in healing the wounds of our literature, by healing what Jacques Brault has called Quebec's "sickness" ' (291), trans. mine

30 'It was for him she had kept the house in order and light, for him she had ruined her youth to the rhythms of age; for him she had tried to soften the impact of the things that might clash with that free, fierce nature, and for him that she had shut herself up in that solitary life as in a convent' (MR57).

31 The nationalism of 'Speak White' (Montreal: L'Hexagone 1974) differs in its themes and its political vision from most of the nationalist texts produced by men in the same period. Instead of focusing on the recurring themes in the writing of men – the 'founding of a territory,' the nuptials with 'woman-nation,' and the quest for identity – Lalonde's poem is an anti-imperialist manifesto that oversteps all boundaries to include all oppressed peoples: 'We are not alone.'

32 The text contains revealing details about what constitutes a 'good relation-ship' within marriage. Euchariste at first resists the idea of marrying Alphonsine: 'He felt a great urge bubbling up inside himself and longed to take her, right there, without saying a word, under the canopy of branches, just as he had once taken the Fancine girl on the spur of a chance encounter ... Perhaps if she had been willing to yield he might never have married her. It would have meant a few more years of liberty for him' (TA22). After they are married, he habitually leaves Alphonsine alone while he goes drinking with his friends: 'Alphonsine made no complaints when he came home a little tipsy. He was never violent if he had too much to drink and, in any case, she was used to that sort of thing and it seemed quite natural in a man' (TA56). Euchariste's insensitivity to his wife's exhaustion ('Alphonsine would have to bear her appointed number,'

[TA68]) is most blatantly expressed after her death, when he passes her wake snoring on the second floor of the house (TA107).

33 For the narrator of *Thirty Acres*, Alphonsine's inability to cry is simply a sign of the harmony between her and the natural landscape: 'tears were futile by comparison with the magnitude of the forces surrounding her: the immeasurable indifference of the elements' (TA82).

34 Houde, *La Maison du remous*

35 Réage, *The Story of O*

3 Opening the house to the Other

1 Guèvremont, *The Outlander*, trans. Eric Sutton, 3

2 See in particular Duquette, *Germaine Guèvremont*; Major, 'Le Survenant et la figure d'Eros'; Vanasse, 'Le Survenant.'

3 Guèvremont, *The Outlander*, 143–290

4 A third novel, never completed, would have described the adventures of Marie-Didace as a young woman who leaves for the city.

5 Quoted in Leclerc, *Germaine Guèvremont*, 82

6 Ibid., 27

7 See Iqbal, 'Survenant le rédempteur.'

8 See Major, '*Le Survenant* et la figure d'Eros.'

9 See Eleuthère, *La Mère dans le roman canadien-français*, 37

10 In Bersianik's *Maternative*, 123–9, this realm is evoked by the image of Ortygie, a submerged island where the author imagines women living in freedom, awaiting the emergence of the feminine in culture.

11 'You laugh at me because I've got some flesh on my bones?' she asks the other women. 'Well, yes I have, and it isn't tallow either!' (O193). And regarding her life on a fishing boat in the company of twenty or thirty men at a time when she was a widow with a small son to support: 'So laugh I did, and kept my sorrows to myself. When the men heard me laugh, they were always after me one by one, each with a good excuse ... well, I was never afraid of them because I knew I could trust myself' (O195).

12 Lejeune, *L'Oeil de la lettre*, 73, trans. mine

13 According to Leclerc, Guèvremont's original title for the novel was *Phonsine. Germaine Guèvremont*, 62

14 Lejeune, *L'Oeil de la lettre*, 152, trans. mine

15 This love of flowers recalls Félicité Anger's magnificent garden at La Malbaie and looks forward to Marta Yaremko's garden in Gabrielle Roy's *Garden in the Wind* (*Un Jardin au bout du monde*).

4 The defeated son and the rebellious daughter

1 Hector de Saint-Denys Garneau's *Regards et Jeux dans l'espace* (Looks and games in space), the only volume of his poetry published during his

lifetime, appeared in 1937, and the negative critical response to this first incursion of 'modernism' into Quebec poetry was certainly a factor in the poet's increasing isolation and neurosis. A selection of poems written after this, and up until Garneau's death of a heart attack at the age of thirty-one in 1943, makes up the second section of the posthumously published *Poésies complètes*, translated by John Glassco as *Complete Poems of Saint-Denys Garneau*.

2 Anne Hébert's *Les Songes en équilibre* (Dreams in equilibrium) is untranslated. *Le Tombeau des rois* has been published as *The Tomb of the Kings* in a translation by Peter Miller, and a number of her subsequent poems are included in *Poèmes*, translated by Alan Brown as *Poems by Anne Hébert*.

3 Although there have been persistent rumours of suicide associated with his death, it is almost certain that Garneau, who had been diagnosed as suffering from a heart lesion in early adolescence, did in fact die of a heart attack.

4 Lapointe, 'Le Meurtre des femmes chez le théologien et chez le pornographe,' 213, trans. mine

5 *The Journal of Saint-Denys Garneau*, trans. John Glassco. 111

6 Beaulieu, *Manuel de la petite littérature du Québec*, 198, trans. mine

7 Hébert's first novel, *Les Chambres de bois* (The silent rooms, 1958), published during the period of composition of these poems, describes the awakening of Catherine, a young woman imprisoned in the closed rooms of the apartment of her impotent and cruel husband, Michel: an awakening made possible by the strange complicity that links Catherine to her suggestively named sister-in-law, Lia (*lier*, to link or to join).

8 Denise Boucher later used precisely the same image in her feminist play *Les Fées ont soif* (The fairies are thirsty, 1978), and aroused the wrath of the Archdiocese of Montreal, which obtained a temporary injunction against the play's publication.

5 When the voices of resistance become political

1 Roy, *The Tin Flute*. trans. Alan Brown

2 The resemblance is striking, for example, between *The Tin Flute* and feminist films from Studio D of the National Film Board (especially 'Speaking Our Peace,' 1985). In a conversation with Paula Gilbert Lewis, Gabrielle Roy insisted on the fact 'that she was not only in favour of women's liberation, but that she had been one of the first to support the movement.' See Lewis, 'La Dernière des grandes conteuses,' 567, trans. mine

3 'This ordinary little woman,' said the author, 'gentle and imaginative, I can admit today, almost forced herself into my story, completely changed its structure and managed to dominate it solely by the very unliterary quality of her tenderness. And I am extremely grateful today to Rose-Anna for having forced my hand, because without her humility and the strength of

her affection, I feel my story would not have been able to move you, which only goes to show that it is in offering ourselves to someone or to some higher purpose that we really deserve attention and that we accomplish our highest human destiny.' Roy, 'Retour à Saint-Henri,' 163, trans. mine ('Return to Saint-Henri,' in *The Fragile Lights of Earth*, trans. Alan Brown)

4 According to Gérard Bessette's psychoanalytical approach to Roy's work, the 'fixation' on the mother is also a product of the author's 'guilt' at having 'abandoned' her mother. *Une Littérature en ébullition*, 285–93

5 Roy, *The Cashier*, trans. Harry Binsse

6 Like Roy, Margaret Laurence was attracted by the freedom of the 'linked short story' form after writing an impressive first novel. According to Kent Thompson, she 'escaped the imposed sequence which is the psychological failing of the novel form. (That is, the novel – by its very adherence to chronology – is as false to the ways in which human beings develop as the short story form – by its dependence upon the implication of the whole from the part – is to human-time.)' Woodcock and Laurence, eds., *A Place to Stand On*, 233

7 Ricard, 'La Métamorphose d'un écrivain'

8 Roy, *Where Nests the Water Hen*, trans. Harry Binsse

9 Ricard, 'La Métamorphose d'un écrivain,' 441, trans. mine

10 Preface to *La Petite Poule d'eau*, quoted in Ricard, 'La Métamorphose d'un écrivain,' 449, trans. mine

11 Ricard, ibid., 449, trans. mine

12 Laflèche, 'Les Bonheurs d'occasion du roman québécois,' 107, trans. mine

13 Ibid., 109

14 Ibid., 110

15 Ibid., 109

16 Ibid., 109–10

17 For Pierre Vallières, writing in the early seventies, 'if Gabrielle Roy had continued in the line of *The Tin Flute*, she would have been heading the separatist movement today.' For André Brochu, in contrast, the novel speaks 'the language of the humanist, the internationalist, no doubt the only viable one at the time.' 'Thèmes et structures de *Bonheur d'occasion*,' 243

18 Ouellette-Michalska, *L'Amour de la carte postale*, 254, trans. mine

19 Laflèche, 'Les Bonheurs d'occasion,' 107

20 Alain, 'Bonheur d'occasion,' quoted in *Bonheur d'occasion* (1977), 390

21 See Brochu, 'Thèmes et structures,' n. 20, for an analysis of the 'linearity' of male space, the 'circularity' of female space.

22 Not only are the characters of Florentine's two suitors, Jean Lévesque and Emmanuel Létourneau, doubles and opposites, but the structure of the novel is carefully constructed to correspond to the symmetry between them. See Blais, 'L'Unité organique de *Bonheur d'occasion*.'

23 Except for little Marie-Didace Beauchemin who, even before the age of six, displays similar opposition to her mother.

24 Florentine's isolation and vulnerability are well captured in the recurring image of her as a snowflake tossed by the wind.

25 Bessette, *Une Littérature en ebullition*, 272–3

26 Causse, 'Le Monde comme volonté et comme représentation,' 152. See the quotation at the beginning of the chapter.

27 Emmanuel's search for a meaning for the war leads him from the individual to the collective ('It was no longer enough for him to know his own motive. He had to know the truth that was guiding them all' [TF376]), and from the collective to a recognition of difference ('He tried to reject the monstrous, paradoxical idea that came to him, but it was irresistible: none of them was going to war with the same goal as the others' [TF377]).

6 The corpse under the foundations of the house

1 Godbout, *Knife on the Table*, trans. Penny Williams

2 Chamberland, *L'Afficheur hurle*, 58–9, trans. mine

3 Jasmin, *La Corde au cou*

4 Aquin, *Blackout*, trans. Alan Brown

5 Renaud, *Broke City*, trans. David Homel

6 Aquin, *Prochain Épisode*, trans. Penny Williams

7 Aquin, *The Antiphonary*, trans. Alan Brown

8 Aquin, *Hamlet's Twin*, trans. Sheila Fischman

9 Beaulieu, *A Québécois Dream*, trans. Ray Chamberlain

10 For Bataille, Sade's works contain 'the clear and distinct consciousness, constantly renewed and reiterated, of what forms the basis of the erotic impulse ... His obsession is the soul of philosophy, the unity of subject and object; in this case, the achieving of identity through surpassing one's limits and attaining the fusion of the desiring subject and the desired object.' *La Littérature et le mal*, 146–7, trans. mine

11 In retrospect, the lack of interest in the nationalist project on the part of the women writers of the Quiet Revolution period is striking. Apart from Michèle Lalonde, whose celebrated poster-poem 'Speak White' proposes an anti-colonialist nationalism that overflows political boundaries and affirms the solidarity of all oppressed peoples and classes, women writers (Marie-Claire Blais, Anne Hébert, Gabrielle Roy, Louise Maheux-Forcier) seem to inhabit a literary universe distant from men's, more intimate, more sensuous, and apparently less political. It is only since the emergence of feminism that we can begin to identify a political dimension in these works – a much more radical subversion of the symbolic order than one finds in the work of their male contemporaries, for in them the body and the murdered subjectivities of the marginal are given voice, posing an uncooptable challenge to the Father's Law.

12 Hébert, *The Torrent*, trans. Gwendolyn Moore

13 Maheu, 'L'Oedipe colonial,' trans. mine

14   Ibid., 33–4
15   Ibid., 37
16   Ibid., 39
17   Ibid., 39
18   Aquin, *Prochain Episode*, 54
19   Godbout, *Hail Galarneau*, trans. Alan Brown, 45
20   Therrien looks at his photographs of the beautiful Emerence in precisely
     the same way as the male protagonist of the novel of the land looks at
     women, and as the omniscient narrator of traditional narrative surveys the
     world – by fragmenting the observed object in order to guarantee his
     possession of it: 'He ... played again with the photographs arranged on his
     outstretched legs. Each time he was stirred by the startling whiteness of
     Emerence's body which he now possessed after a fashion – no matter what
     she did to regain possession of herself – ever since she'd delivered herself up
     to him, more or less voluntarily; his camera had caught her and locked her
     away in a minute roll of film upon which a simple chemical operation had
     magically conferred all the appearances of a living presence. So successful
     had the process been that from now on he could do with her what he wanted:
     surprise her rolled over on her side, her long legs somewhat heavy but not
     overly so and pleated around the buttocks which were split in their dark
     centre, or bend over her outstretched body, his hands sliding towards the
     black tuft under which, because of him, a maddening desire for love eternally
     lingered.' Major, *Inspector Therrien*, trans. Mark Czarnecki, 21–2. One
     cannot help noticing, from Grignon's Séraphin to the heroes of Major
     and Victor-Lévy Beaulieu, the pornographic obsession with women's but-
     tocks – the most 'degraded' part of her body?
21   Beaulieu, *A Québécois Dream*, 53
22   Ducharme, *The Swallower Swallowed*, trans. Barbara Bray, 5
23   Aquin, *Blackout*, 90
24   Beaulieu, *Grandfathers*, trans. Marc Plourde
25   Aquin, *The Antiphonary*, 17
26   Whose name recalls that of John Ruskin, one of the aesthetes of patriarchal
     culture at its height.
27   'We've entered an infinite mutual creation through love and we're penetrat-
     ing each other with female seed.' Aquin's *Hamlet's Twin*, 204
28   Ducharme, *Le Nez qui voque*, 131, trans. mine
29   Aquin, 'Tout est miroir,' in *Blocs erratiques*, 31, trans. mine
30   Ducharme, *Le Nez qui voque*, 127, trans. mine
31   Ibid., 133
32   Aquin, *Hamlet's Twin*, 129
33   Hébert, *In the Shadow of the Wind*, trans. Sheila Fischman
34   'The noisy farts explode in the pot and the strong spurt of piss lasts forever,
     but the odors that come from all that resemble nothing he'd smelled

before. It's warm and sinks into his stomach, exciting him, like when he sees dogs fucking in the snow ... ' Beaulieu, *Grandfathers*, 65

35 'He had fallen forward on top of Renata, exhausted, emptied, almost unconscious. Renata, for her part, was out of breath, caught in the disorder of her opened skirts, covered with sperm, astonished, weeping like a poor creature who has just discovered a mystery the world had taken great pains to hide from her.' Aquin *The Antiphonary*, 71–2

36 Poulin, 'L'Ecriture enchantée,' 17, trans. mine

37 Two excellent articles discuss the role of voice and its relation to the novel's feminist content: Bishop, 'Distance, point de vue, voix et idéologie dans *Les Fous de bassan* d'Anne Hébert'; and Gould, 'Absence and Meaning in Anne Hébert's *Les Fous de bassan.*'

38 As Janet M. Paterson demonstrates in 'L'Envolée de l'écriture.'

39 See Bersianik, 'Noli Mi Tangere,' trans. Barbara Godard.

40 In Aquin's *Blackout*, Pierre X. Magnant admits to an identical motivation when speaking of his murder of Joan: 'No caress was ever gentler or less insistent. And never was suffocation closer to being a gesture of veneration ... That certainty which the strongest *quoad vitam* cannot give, I found in this final embrace; and, touching the oral zone, I also found my desires aroused by the very gesture that made its object unable to respond.' *Blackout*, 74

41 'Remember ... when the two of us would follow the girls ... reveling in their swaying thighs, to the point of disgust. Approach them, finally, to laugh in their faces,' he writes to Hotchkiss. Hébert, *In the Shadow of the Wind*, 176

42 Hébert, *Kamouraska*, trans. Norman Shapiro, 249

7 What Oedipus sees

1 Aquin, *Hamlet's Twin*, trans. Sheila Fischman

2 Bonenfant, 'Hubert Aquin, *Neige noire*,' 22

3 'While writing *Neige noire*, I had the feeling of being close to the end. I recognize that I really don't know whether I will continue to write.' Lachance, 'Hubert Aquin,' 23, trans. mine

4 That is, the person who controls the text in a system where the written is privileged over the real. According to Artaud, 'the author in classical theatre is the one who has language at his disposal, and ... the director is his slave.' Quoted in Derrida, *L'Ecriture et la différence*, 346, trans. mine

5 Irigaray, *Speculum of the Other Woman*, trans. Gillian C. Gill, 133–4

6 Ibid., 135

7 'Eva and Linda are approaching the illuminated theatre where the play which is being performed is a parable where all human works are enshrined.' Aquin, *Hamlet's Twin*, 208

8 See Brossard, *These Our Mothers*, trans. Barbara Godard.

9 The centrifugal shape of the pendant is reflected in the image of the 'illuminated theatre' that obsesses Nicolas, and in which 'the avenues come out of the centre like radii, the streets are circular and cut across the avenues and the central square is a masterpiece.' Aquin, *Hamlet's Twin*, 117

10 See Merivale, 'Chiaroscuro.'

11 Written in 1952 and published in *Les Ecrits du Canada français* in 1959. In 1952, Aquin wrote to his friend Louis-Georges Carrier: 'I'm afraid I will never write anything that doesn't reproduce the pattern of *Les Rédempteurs*. I am a prisoner of my own story and it seems to me inevitable; what I invent holds me captive.' Aquin, *Point de fuite*, 125, trans. mine

12 Aquin, *Prochain Episode*, trans. Penny Williams, 44

13 In a conversation with the author in 1974 Aquin claimed to have read and enjoyed Ernest Jones's *Hamlet and Oedipus* (New York: Norton 1949).

14 For example, René Lapierre, whose analysis of Aquin's novels centres on their lack of openness: 'His work refuses the practice of language that is leading contemporary literature towards the possible, the unpredictable, and towards that which is other than itself.' *L'Imaginaire captif*, 16, trans. mine

15 Barthes, *The Pleasure of the Text*, trans. Richard Miller, 10

16 Ibid.

17 See Finn, 'Patriarchy and Pleasure'

18 Aquin, 'Le Texte ou le silence marginal?' (The text and the silence of the margins). *Blocs erratiques*, 269–72

19 Ibid., 269, trans. mine

20 See my 'Hubert Aquin essayiste.'

8 Reclaiming Electra

1 See the list of works cited. Translations of all passages quoted from Théoret's work in this chapter are mine.

2 Madeleine Gagnon, preface to Denise Boucher, *Cyprine*, 9–10, trans. mine

3 Bibliographical details of the Théoret works named here are given in the list of works cited.

4 Théoret, *Entre raison et déraison* (Between reason and madness), 14

5 See Bayard, *The New Poetics in Canada and Quebec*, for a discussion of modernity (*la modernité*) in Quebec literature and its refusal of 'the trap of representation.' A paradox in the chronological 'labelling' of literary movements in Quebec is that 'post-modernism,' as exemplified by Aquin's self-reflexive narratives, arrives earlier than *la modernité*, with its emphasis on 'writing as production, as material output, fabricated, created, not derived or inherited' (187).

6 Marcotte, *Le Roman à l'imparfait*, 8, trans. mine

7 Ibid., 177
8 Ibid., 189
9 Théoret, *Entre raison et déraison*, 7
10 Gaudet, 'Une Ecriture responsable,' 115
11 Théoret, *La Nef des sorcières*, 8
12 For Brecht, 'Realism means: to unveil the complex causality of social
    relationships, to denounce the dominant ideas of the ruling class, to write
    from the point of view of the class that potentially holds the most effective
    solutions to the pressing problems facing the society of men, to emphasize
    the moment of evolution in each phenomenon, to be concrete even while
    facilitating the work of abstraction.' 'On realism,' quoted in Haeck, *L'Action
    restreinte*' 62, trans. mine
13 Henri Meschonnic, *Critique du rythme*, 83, trans. mine
14 Ibid., 73
15 Ibid., 83
16 Ibid., 284
17 Ibid., 293
18 In the interview with Gaudet, Théoret reveals the autobiographical origin
    of this scene, which gives the novel its title: 'The little girl in the schoolyard
    is not alone. There are two little girls, and they know quite clearly that
    they're little savages ... The sentence wasn't said by me, but by the other
    little girl, though I completely agreed with what she said. We were aware
    that we didn't know how to speak, that we spoke badly and we wanted to
    learn how to speak, even to give speeches. We wanted to change things in
    that area, and we knew it; for us, to speak like writing was to speak
    correctly. We were fascinated by language, by the dictations the nuns gave
    us. We wanted to speak that way, we thought it was very beautiful. We
    liked written language, even if we didn't like doing the dictations.' Gaudet,
    'Une Ecriture responsable,' 115, trans. mine
19 The title is inspired by Monteverdi's aria of the same name.
20 Woolf, *A Room of One's Own* (1929)
21 A scene that recalls the night the pregnant and abandoned Florentine
    Lacasse spends with her friend Marguerite in *The Tin Flute*.
22 Marcotte, *Le Roman à l'imparfait*, 8, trans. mine
23 See Van Schendel, 'L'Amour dans la littérature canadienne-française,' for
    an excellent and still pertinent analysis of how the absence or imbalance
    of the couple in Quebec literature reflects the larger cultural context: '...
    the elements that make or unmake the couple bring together in a striking
    synthesis the biological, emotional, or social conflicts that determine the
    play of relationships in society as a whole ... The physical dialectic of the
    love act reproduces the overall movement of social events even as it trans-
    forms it' (153, trans. mine). In Théoret's novel, the dialectic of the couple
    seems to be suspended until change takes place among men.

Conclusion

1   Hébert, *Le Torrent*, 9, trans. mine
2   Boucher, 'Journal intime,' 9, trans. mine
3   See Haeck, *The Clarity of Voices*, trans. Antonio D'Alfonso.
4   Rivard, *Les Silences du corbeau*, 218, trans. mine
5   See Bouchard, *Les Images*; Houde, *La Maison du remous*; Massé, *Nobody*.
6   Brossard, *Le Désert mauve*
7   Ibid., 220, trans. mine
8   Ibid., 27, trans. mine
9   Ibid., 49–50, trans. mine
10 French, *Beyond Power*, 542
11 Bersianik, *Le Pique-nique sur l'Acropole*
12 Lejeune, *L'Issue*, 37, trans. mine

Works cited

A. Quebec literary works

Aicard, Jean. 'Le Poème de la mère.' *La Revue moderne* (July 1924)

Aquin, Hubert. *The Antiphonary*, trans. Alan Brown. Toronto: House of Anansi
Press 1973. Trans. of *L'Antiphonaire*. Montreal: Le Cercle du Livre de France
1969

– *Blackout*, trans. Alan Brown. Toronto: House of Anansi Press 1974. Trans. of
Trou de mémoire. Montreal: Le Cercle du Livre de France 1968

– *Blocs erratiques* (Erratic blocks). Ed. by René Lapierre; Montreal: Quinze 1977

– *Hamlet's Twin*, trans. Sheila Fischman. Toronto: McClelland and Stewart 1979.
Trans. of *Neige noire*. Montreal: Editions La Presse 1974

– *Point de fuite* (Vanishing point). Ottawa: Le Cercle du Livre de France 1971

– *Prochain Episode*, trans. Penny Williams. Toronto: McClelland and Stewart,
New Canadian Library Series 1972. Trans. of *Prochain Episode*. Montreal: Le
Cercle du Livre de France 1965

– 'Les Rédempteurs' (The Redeemers). *Ecrits du Canada français* 5 (1959),
45–114

Beaulieu, Victor-Lévy. *Grandfathers*, trans. Marc Plourde. Montreal: Harvest
House 1974. Trans. of *Les Grands-pères*. Montreal: Editions du Jour 1971

– *Manuel de la petite littérature du Quebec* (Manual of Quebec popular literature).
Montreal: Editions de l'Aurore 1974

– *A Québécois Dream*, trans. Ray Chamberlain. Toronto: Exile Editions 1978.
Trans. of *Un Rêve québécois*. Montreal: Editions du Jour 1972

Bersianik, Louky, *Maternative*. Montreal: VLB Editeur 1980

– 'Noli Mi Tangere,' trans. Barbara Godard. *Room of One's Own* 4: 1–2 (Fall,
1978), 98–110

– *Le Pique-nique sur l'Acropole* (Picnic on the Acropolis). Montreal: VLB Editeur
1978

Bouchard, Louise. *Les Images*. Montreal: Les Herbes rouges 1985

Boucher, Denise. *Cyprine: Essai-collage pour être une femme* (Essay-collage on being a woman). Preface by Madeleine Gagnon. Montreal: Editions de l'Aurore 1978

– *The Fairies Are Thirsty*, trans. Alan Brown. Vancouver: Talonbooks 1982. Trans. of *Les Fées ont soif*. Quebec: Les Editions Intermède 1978

– 'Journal intime.' *La Parole métèque* 6 (Summer 1988), 9

Bourassa, Henri. *Femmes-hommes ou hommes et femmes? Études a bâtons rompus sur le féminisme* (Manly women or men and women? Random thoughts on feminism). Montreal: Imprimerie du Devoir 1925

Bourassa, Napoleon. *Jacques et Marie, souvenir d'un peuple dispersé* (Jacques and Marie: memories of a dispersed people). Montreal: Eusèbe Sénécal 1866. Reprint Montreal: Fides (Collection du Nénuphar) 1976

Brossard, Nicole. *The Aerial Letter*, trans. Marlene Wildeman. Toronto: Women's Press 1988. Trans. of *La Lettre aérienne*. Montreal: Les Editions du Remue-Menage 1985

– *Le Désert mauve* (The mauve desert). Montreal: L'Hexagone 1987

– *These Our Mothers or: The Disintegrating Chapter*, trans. Barbara Godard. Toronto: Coach House 1983. Trans. of *L'Amèr ou le chapitre effrité*. Montreal: Quinze 1977

Carrier, Roch. *No Country without Grandfathers*, trans. Sheila Fischman. Toronto: House of Anansi Press 1981. Trans. of *Il n'y a pas de pays sans grand-père*. Montreal: Stanké 1977. Reprint Montreal: Stanké (Collection Québec 10/10) 1979

Casgrain, H.-R. Correspondence with Laure Conan. Fonds Casgrain, Vol. 10, Archives du Séminaire de Québec

– Preface to *Angéline de Montbrun*. Quebec: Imprimerie Léger Brousseau 1884

Chamberland, Paul. *L'Afficheur hurle* (The signpainter shouts). Montreal: Parti pris 1964

Conan, Laure. *Angéline de Montbrun*, trans. Yves Brunelle. Toronto: University of Toronto Press 1974. Trans. of *Angéline de Montbrun*. Quebec: Imprimerie Léger Brousseau 1884. Reprint Montreal: Fides (Bibliothèque québécoise) 1980

– *Aux Canadiennes: le peuple canadien sera sobre si vous le voulez* (To Canadian women: the Canadian people will be sober if you so desire). Quebec: Cie. d'imprimerie commerciale 1913

– *L'Obscure Souffrance* (Hidden suffering). Quebec: L'Action sociale 1919

– *Si les Canadiennes le voulaient* (If Canadian women wanted). Quebec: Imprimerie Darveau 1886

de Bellefeuille, Normand, and Hugues Corriveau. *A double sens: échanges sur quelques pratiques modernes* (With a double meaning: exchanges on some practices of modernity). Montreal: Les Herbes rouges 1986

de Gaspé, P.A., fils. *Le Chercheur de trésors (ou l'influence d'un livre)* (The treasure seeker or the influence of a book). Quebec: William Cowan and Son 1837. Reprint Montreal: Réédition Québec 1968

Ducharme, Réjean. *Le Nez qui voque* (The equivocal nose). Paris: Gallimard 1967
- *The Swallower Swallowed*, trans. Barbara Bray. London: Hamish Hamilton 1968. Trans. of *L'Avalée des avalés*. Paris: Gallimard 1966. Reprint Montreal: Editions du Bélier (Coll. Aries) 1967

Gagnon, Madeleine. *Les Fleurs du catalpa* (Catalpa flowers). Montreal: VLB Editeur 1986

Garneau, Hector de Saint-Denys. *The Journal of Saint-Denys Garneau*, trans. John Glassco. Toronto: McClelland and Stewart 1962. Trans. of *Journal*. Montreal: Beauchemin 1954
- *Complete Poems of Saint-Denys Garneau*, trans. John Glassco. Ottawa: Oberon Press 1975. Trans. of *Poésies complètes*. Montreal: Fides 1949

Gérin-Lajoie, Antoine. *Jean Rivard*, trans. Vida Bruce. Toronto: McClelland and Stewart, New Canadian Library Series 1977. Trans. of *Jean Rivard le défricheur*, Montreal: Les Soirées canadiennes 1862; and *Jean Rivard économiste*, Montreal: Le Foyer canadien 1864. Reprint Montreal: Cahiers du Québec/Hurtubise HMH 1977

Godbout, Jacques. 'Écrire.' in *Le Réformiste: textes tranquilles* (The reformist: quiet texts), Montreal: Quinze 1975, 153–7
- *Hail Galarneau!*, trans. Alan Brown. Toronto: Longman Canada 1970. Trans. of *Salut Galarneau*. Paris: Seuil 1967
- *Knife on the Table*, trans. Penny Williams. Toronto: McClelland and Stewart 1976. Trans. of *Le Couteau sur la table*. Paris: Seuil 1965

Grignon, Claude-Henri. *The Woman and the Miser*, trans. Yves Brunelle. Montreal: Harvest House 1978. Trans. of *Un Homme et son péché*. Montreal: Les Editions du Vieux Chêne 1933. Reprint Montreal: Stanké (Collection Québec 10/10) 1977

Guèvremont, Germaine. *The Outlander*, trans. Eric Sutton. Toronto: McClelland and Stewart 1978. Trans. of *Le Survenant*, Montreal: Beauchemin 1945, and *Marie-Didace*, Montreal: Fides 1947

Haeck, Philippe. *L'Action restreinte/De la littérature* (Limited action/of literature). Montreal: L'Aurore 1975
- *The Clarity of Voices (Selected Poems 1974–1981)*, trans. Antonio D'Alfonso. Montreal: Guernica Editions 1985

Hébert, Anne. *In the Shadow of the Wind*, trans. Sheila Fischman. Toronto: Stoddart 1983. Trans. of *Les Fous de bassan*. Paris: Seuil 1982
- *Kamouraska*, trans. Norman Shapiro. New York: Contact Press 1967. Trans. of *Kamouraska*. Paris: Seuil 1970
- *Poems*. trans. Alan Brown. Don Mills: Musson 1975. Trans. of *Poèmes*. Paris: Seuil 1960
- *The Silent Rooms*, trans. Kathy Mezei. Don Mills: Musson 1974. Trans. of *Les Chambres de bois*. Paris: Seuil 1958

– *Les Songes en équilibre* (Dreams in equilibrium). Montreal: Les Editions de l'Arbre 1944
– *The Tomb of the Kings*, trans. Peter Miller. Toronto: Contact Press 1967. Trans. of *Le Tombeau des rois*. Paris: Seuil 1953
– *The Torrent*, trans. Gwendolyn Moore. Montreal: Harvest House 1973. Trans. of *Le Torrent*. Montreal: Beauchemin, 1950. Reprint Montreal: HMH (Collection l'Arbre) 1972
Hémon, Louis. *Maria Chapdelaine*, trans. W.H. Blake. Toronto: Macmillan 1940. Trans. of *Maria Chapdelaine* (1912). Reprint Montreal: Fides (Bibliothèque canadienne-française) 1975
Houde, Nicole. *La Maison du remous* (The house by the whirlpool). Montreal: Editions de la Pleine Lune 1986
Jasmin, Claude. *La Corde au cou* (The noose tightens). Ottawa: Le Cercle du Livre de France 1960
Laberge, Albert. *Bitter Bread*, trans. Conrad Dion. Toronto: Harvest House 1977. Trans. of *La Scouine* (1918). Reprint Montreal: L'Actuelle 1972
Loranger, Françoise. *Mathieu*. Montreal: Le Cercle du Livre de France 1949. Reprint Montreal: CLF Poche 1967
Maheu, Pierre. 'L'Oedipe colonial' (The colonial Oedipus). *Parti pris* 1:9–11 (Summer 1964), 19–29. Reprinted in Pierre Maheu, *Un Parti pris révolutionnaire* (The choice of revolution). Montreal: Parti pris 1983, 27–38
Major, André. *Inspector Therrien*, trans. Mark Czarnecki. Toronto: Porcépic 1980. Trans. of *L'Épidémie*, Montreal: Editions du Jour 1975
Massé, Carole. *Nobody*. Montreal: Les Herbes rouges 1985
Nelligan, Emile. *Poésies complètes*, comp. Luc Lacoursière. Montreal: Fides 1952
Renaud, Jacques. *Broke City*, trans. David Homel. Montreal: Guernica Editions 1984. Trans. of *Le Cassé*. Montreal: Parti pris 1964
Ringuet (Phillippe Panneton). *Thirty Acres*, trans. Felix and Dorothea Walter. Toronto: Macmillan 1940. Trans. of *Trente arpents*. Paris: Flammarion 1938. Reprint Paris: Flammarion (Collection 'J'ai lu') 1980
Rivard, Yvon. *Les Silences du corbeau* (The crow's silences). Montreal: Editions du Boréal-Express 1986
Roy, Gabrielle. *The Cashier*, trans. Harry Binsse. Toronto: McClelland and Stewart 1955. Trans. of *Alexandre Chenevert*. Montreal: Beauchemin 1954
– *Garden in the Wind*, trans. Alan Brown. Toronto: McClelland and Stewart 1977. Trans. of *Un Jardin au bout du monde et autres nouvelles*. Montreal: Beauchemin 1975
– 'Return to Saint-Henri' (reception speech to the Royal Society of Canada). In *The Fragile Lights of Earth*, trans. Alan Brown. Toronto: McClelland and Stewart 1982. 157–71. Trans of *Fragiles lumières de la terre*. Montreal: Quinze 1978
– *The Tin Flute*, trans. Alan Brown. Toronto: McClelland and Stewart 1955.

Trans. of *Bonheur d'occasion*. Montreal: Beauchemin 1945. Reprint Montreal: Stanké (Collection Québec 10/10) 1977
- *Where Nests the Water Hen*, trans. Harry Binsse. Toronto: McClelland and Stewart, New Canadian Library Series 1980. Trans. of *La Petite Poule d'eau*. Montreal: Beauchemin 1950
Savard, Félix-Antoine. *Master of the River*, trans. Richard Howard. Montreal: Harvest House 1976. Trans. of *Menaud maître-draveur*. Quebec: Librairie Garneau 1937. Reprint Montreal: Fides (Bibliothèque canadienne-française) 1973
Théoret, France. *Bloody Mary*. Montreal: Les Herbes rouges 1977
- *Entre raison et déraison* (Between reason and madness). Montreal: Les Herbes rouges 1987
- *Nécessairement putain* (Necessarily a prostitute). Montreal: Les Herbes rouges 1980
- *Nous parlerons comme on écrit* (We shall speak like writing). Montreal: Les Herbes rouges 1982
- 'La Petite Fille sage' (The well-behaved little girl). *Les Têtes de pioche* 4 (June 1976), 39
- *Vertiges*. Montreal: Les Herbes rouges 1979
- *Une Voix pour Odile*. Montreal: Les Herbes rouges 1978
- (with Nicole Brossard). Preface, *La Nef des sorcières* (The ship of witches). Montreal: Quinze 1976

B. Quebec literary criticism

ab der Halden, Charles. *Nouvelles études de littérature canadienne-française*. Paris: Rudeval Editeur 1907
Alain, Albert. 'Bonheur d'occasion.' *Le Devoir*, 15 Sept. 1945
Belle-Isle, Francine. 'La Voix-séduction: à propos de Laure Conan.' *Etudes littéraires* 2 (1978), 459–72
Bessette, Gérard. *Une Littérature en ébullition* (A literature at the boiling point). Montreal: Editions du Jour 1968
Bishop, Neil. 'Distance, point de vue, voix et idéologie dans *Les Fous de bassan* d'Anne Hébert.' *Voix et images* 9: 2 (Winter 1984), 113–30
Blais, Jacques, 'L'Unité organique de *Bonheur d'occasion*,' *Etudes françaises* 6: 1 (Feb. 1970), 25–50
Bonenfant, Joseph. 'Hubert Aquin, *Neige noire*.' *Livres et auteurs québécois 1974*. Quebec: Les Presses de l'Université Laval 1975, 20–3
Boynard-Frot, Janine. *Un Matriarcat en procès: analyse systématique de romans canadiens-français 1860–1960*. Montreal: Les Presses de l'Université de Montreal. Collection 'Lignes québécoises' 1982
Brochu, André. 'Menaud ou l'impossible fête.' *L'Action nationale* 56: 3 (Nov. 1966), 266–91. Reprinted in A. Brochu, *L'Instance critique*. Montreal: Leméac 1974, 247–74

– 'Thèmes et structures de *Bonheur d'occasion*.' *L'Instance critique*. Montreal: Leméac 1974, 206–46

Cotnam, Jacques. '*Angéline de Montbrun*: un cas patent de masochisme moral.' *Journal of Canadian Fiction* 2: 3 (Summer 1973), 152–60

Deschamps, Nicole. 'Lecture de Maria Chapdelaine.' *Etudes françaises* 6: 2 (May 1968), 151–67

Des Ormes, Renée. *Célébrités*. Quebec: Privately printed 1927

– 'Glanures dans les papiers pâlis de Laure Conan.' *Revue de l'Université Laval* 9:2 (Oct. 1954), 120–35

Dionne, René. 'Entre terre et ciel: pour une lecture littéraire de l'oeuvre de Laure Conan.' *Lettres québécoises* 1:1 (Mar. 1976), 19–21

Duquette, Jean-Pierre. *Germaine Guèvremont, une route, une maison*. Montreal: Les Presses de l'Université de Montreal. Collection 'Lignes québécoises' 1973

Eleuthère, Sr Sainte-Marie. *La Mère dans le roman canadien-français*. Quebec: Les Presses de l'Université Laval, Collection 'Vie des lettres canadiennes' 1964

Ethier-Blais, Jean. 'Laure Conan.' *Le Devoir*, 14 Oct. 1961, 11

Gaudet, Gérald. 'Une Ecriture responsable' (interview with France Théoret). *Estuaire* 38 (1985), 103–17

Gould, Karen. 'Absence and Meaning in Anne Hébert's *Les Fous de bassan*.' *The French Review* 59:6 (May 1986), 921–30

Green, Mary Jean. 'Laure Conan and Mme de Lafayette: Rewriting the Female Plot.' *Essays on Canadian Writing* 34 (Spring 1987), 50–63

Iqbal, Françoise Maccabée. 'Survenant le rédempteur.' In *Solitude rompue*, ed. Cécile Cloutier-Wojciechowska and Réjean Robidoux, Ottawa: Editions de l'Université d'Ottawa 1986, 248–56

Lachance, Micheline. 'Hubert Aquin: le sentiment d'être près de la fin' (The feeling of being close to the end) (interview with Aquin). *Québec-Presse*, 3 Nov. 1974, 23

Laflèche, Guy. 'Les Bonheurs d'occasion du roman québécois.' *Voix et images* 3:1 (Sept. 1977), 96–115

Lapierre, René. *L'Imaginaire captif: Hubert Aquin*. Montreal: Quinze 1981

Leclerc, Rita. *Germaine Guèvremont*. Montreal: Fides (Collection 'Ecrivains canadiens d'aujourd'hui') 1963

Lemoine, Roger. Introduction to *Oeuvres romanesques de Laure Conan*, vol. 1, Montreal: Fides 1974

Le Moyne, Jean. *Convergence: Essays from Quebec*, trans. Philip Stratford. Toronto: Ryerson Press, 1966. Trans. of *Convergences*. Montreal: HMH 1961

Lewis, Paula Gilbert. 'La Dernière des grandes conteuses: une conversation avec Gabrielle Roy.' *Etudes littéraires* 17:3 (Winter 1984), 563–76

Major, Robert. '*Le Survenant* et la figure d'Eros dans l'oeuvre de G. Guèvremont.' *Voix et images* 2:2 (Dec. 1976), 195–208

Marcotte, Gilles. *Une Littérature qui se fait*. Montreal: Editions la Presse 1962

– *Le Roman à l'imparfait* (The novel in the imperfect). Montreal: Editions la Presse 1976

Merivale, Patricia. 'Chiaroscuro: *Neige noire/Hamlet's Twin*,' *Dalhousie Review* 60:2 (Summer 1980), 318–33

Paterson, Janet M. 'L'Envolée de l'écriture: *Les Fous de bassan* d'Anne Hébert' (Writing in flight: Anne Hébert's *Les Fous de bassan*). *Voix et images* 9:3 (Spring 1984), 143–51

Poulin, Gabrielle. '*Angéline de Montbrun* ou les abîmes de la critique' (*Angéline de Montbrun* or the abysses of criticism). *Revue d'histoire littéraire du Québec et du Canada français* 5 (1983), 125–32

– 'L'Ecriture enchantée: *Les Fous de bassan* d'Anne Hébert.' *Lettres québécoises* 28 (Winter 1982–3), 17–18

Ricard, François. 'La Métamorphose d'un écrivain. Essai biographique.' *Etudes littéraires* 17:3 (Winter 1984), 441–55

Smart, Patricia. 'Hubert Aquin essayiste.' In *L'Essai et la prose d'idées au Québec: archives des lettres canadiennes*, vol. 6, ed. F. Gallays, S. Simard, P. Wyczynski, Montreal: Fides, 1985, 513–25

Vanasse, André. 'Le Survenant.' *Dictionnaire des oeuvres littéraires du Québec*, vol. 3, Montreal: Fides 1982, 953–9

Van Schendel, Michel. 'L'Amour dans la littérature canadienne-française.' *Littérature et société canadiennes-françaises*, deuxième colloque de la revue *Recherches sociographiques*, Quebec, Presses de l'Université Laval 1964, 153–65

Verthuy, Maïr. 'Femmes et patrie dans l'oeuvre romanesque de Laure Conan.' In *Solitude rompue*, ed. Cécile Cloutier-Wojciechowska and Réjean Robidoux, Ottawa: Editions de l'Université d'Ottawa 1986, 396–404

C. Other works

Bakhtin, M.M. *The Dialogic Imagination: Four Essays*, trans. J. Michael Holquist. Austin: University of Texas Press 1981

Barthes, Roland. *The Pleasure of the Text*, trans. Richard Miller. New York: Hill and Wang 1975. Trans. of *Le Plaisir du texte*. Paris: Seuil 1973

Bataille, Georges, *Le Littérature et le mal*. Paris: Gallimard (Collection NRF) 1957

Bayard, Caroline. *The New Poetics in Canada and Quebec: From Concretism to Post-Modernism*. Toronto: University of Toronto Press 1989

Causse, Michele. 'Le Monde comme volonté et comme représentation' (The world as will and as representation). In *L'Emergence d'une culture au féminin*, ed. M. Zavalloni, Montreal: Editions Saint-Martin 1987, 147–61

Cixous, Hélène, and Catherine Clément. *The Newly-born woman*, trans. Betsy Wing. Minneapolis: University of Minnesota Press 1985. Trans. of *La Jeune Née*. Paris: 10/18 (Série Féminin Futur) 1975

Collin, Françoise. 'Il n'y a pas de cogito-femme' (There is no female cogito). In *L'Emergence d'une culture au féminin*, ed. M. Zavalloni, Montreal: Les Editions Saint-Martin 1987, 107–16

De Lauretis, Teresa. *Alice Doesn't: Feminism, Semiotics, Cinema*. Bloomington: Indiana University Press 1982

Derrida, Jacques. *L'Ecriture et la différence* (Writing and difference). Paris: Seuil 1967

Finn, Geraldine. 'Patriarchy and Pleasure: The Pornographic Eye/I.' *Canadian Journal of Political and Social Theory* 9: 1–2 (Winter 1985), 81–95

French, Marilyn. *Beyond Power: Of Women, Men, and Morals*. New York: Ballantine Books 1986

Garcia, Irma. *Promenade femmilière: recherches sur l'écriture féminine* (Womanly wanderings: a study of women's writing). 2 vols. Paris: Editions des Femmes 1981

Gilbert, Sandra M., and Susan Gubar. *The Madwoman in the Attic: The Woman Writer and the Nineteenth-Century Literary Imagination*. New Haven: Yale University Press 1979

Griffin, Susan. *Pornography and Silence*. New York: Harper and Row 1981

Hermann, Claudine. *Les Voleuses de langue*. Paris: Editions des Femmes 1976

Irigaray, Luce. *Ethique de la différence sexuelle* (The ethics of sexual difference). Paris: Minuit 1984

– *Parler n'est jamais neutre* (Speaking is never neuter). Paris: Minuit 1985

– *Speculum of the Other Woman*, trans. Gillian C. Gill. Ithaca, NY: Cornell University Press 1985. Trans. of *Spéculum de l'autre femme*. Paris: Minuit 1974

Kappeler, Susanne. *The Pornography of Representation*. Minneapolis: University of Minnesota Press 1986

Lamy, Suzanne. *D'Elles*. Montreal: L'Hexagone 1979

Lapointe, Jeanne. 'Le Meurtre des femmes chez le théologien et chez le pornographe.' In *Féminité, subversion, écriture*, ed. S. Lamy et I. Pagès, Montreal: Editions du Remue-Ménage 1983, 209–21

Lejeune, Claire. *Age poétique, âge politique*. Montreal: L'Hexagone 1987

– *L'Atelier* (The workshop). Brussels: Le Cormier 1979

– *L'Issue* (The way out). Brussels: Le Cormier 1980

– *L'Oeil de la lettre* (The eye of the letter). Brussels: Le Cormier 1984

Lévi-Strauss, Claude. *The Elementary Structures of Kinship*, trans. J.H. Bell, J.R. von Sturmer, R. Needham. Boston: Beacon Press 1969. Trans. of *Les Structures élémentaires de la parenté*. Paris: Presses Universitaires de France 1949

Meschonnic, Henri. *Critique du rythme: anthropologie historique du langage*. Paris: Verdier 1982

Ouellette-Michalska, Madeleine. *L'Amour de la carte postale*. Montreal: Québec/Amérique (Collection 'Littérature d'Amérique') 1987

Paquet, Mgr. L.-A. 'Le Féminisme (premier article).' *Le Canada français* 1:4 (Dec. 1918), 233–46

– 'Le Féminisme (second article).' *Le Canada français* 2:1 (Feb. 1919). 5–21

Réage, Pauline. *The Story of O*. New York: Ballantine Books, 1981. Trans. of *L'Histoire d'O*. Paris: Jean-Jacques Panvert 1954

Rubin, Gayle. 'The Traffic in Women: Notes on the Political Economy of Sex.' In *Feminist Frameworks: Theoretical Accounts of the Relations between Women and Men*, ed. Alison M. Jagger and Paula R. Strahl, New York: McGraw-Hill 1978

Wolf, Christa. *Cassandra: A Novel and Four Essays*, trans. Jan. van Heurck. New York: Farrar, Straus and Giroux 1984. Trans. of *Kassandra*. Darmstadt: Herman Luchterhand 1983

Woodcock, George, and Margaret Laurence. *A Place to Stand On: Essays by and about Margaret Laurence*. Edmonton: NeWest Press 1983

Woolf, Virginia. *A Room of One's Own*. New York: Harcourt, Brace and Co. 1929

Index